Managing Business
Microcomputer Systems

Judith M. Frank

A Brady Book
Published by Prentice Hall Press
New York, New York 10023

A Brady Book
Published by Prentice Hall Press
A Division of Simon & Schuster, Inc.
Gulf + Western Building
One Gulf + Western Plaza
New York, New York 10023

PRENTICE HALL PRESS is a trademark of Simon & Schuster, Inc.

Manufactured in the United States of America

1 2 3 4 5 6 7 8 9 10

Library of Congress Cataloging-in-Publication Data

Frank, Judith M.
  Managing business microcomputer systems.

  Includes index.
  1. Business—Data processing—Management.
2. Microcomputers. I. Title.
HF5548.2.F7196 1987   004.16   86-20495
ISBN 0-13-548447-2 (pbk.)

To the memory of my parents,
Nickolas Frank and Yvonne Belanger Frank

Acknowledgments

Writing a book is a unique experience. I would like to thank the people who helped me during the process of writing this one:

Anita Glass, for her early invaluable criticism.

The individuals whom the publisher selected to review the manuscript, for their criticism, suggestions, and support.

Constance Barr of Intel Corporation, Kathleen Doler of Borland International, Inc., Johanna Fiore of Ashton-Tate, and Katherine Reardon of MicroPro International Corporation for providing access to their companies' products.

Rosemary Morrissey of IBM, for her unfailing ability to have information at my door within 24 hours of each request.

The articulate and intelligent staff members of ComputerLand of Albany, California.

Terry Anderson, my editor, Milissa Koloski, Gene Bicknell, the illustrator, and others at Brady, especially Carol Crowell, the copy editor and designer, for shepherding the book.

My friends and my family, especially Frances Waner, Brent Green, and Suzanne Frank for their boundless understanding.

Special thanks to Bob. Without his encouragement, this book would not exist.

Limits of Liability and Disclaimer of Warranty

The author and publisher of this book have used their best efforts in preparing this book and the programs contained in it. These efforts include the development, research, and testing of the theories and programs to determine their effectiveness. The author and publisher make no warranty of any kind, expressed or implied, with regard to these programs or the documentation contained in this book. The author and publisher shall not be liable in any event for incidental or consequential damages in connection with, or arising out of, the furnishing, performance, or use of these programs.

Registered Trademarks

Above Board is a trademark of Intel Corporation.

Epson FX-80 printer is a trademark of Epson America, Inc.

Framework is a trademark of Ashton-Tate.

Hayes modem is a trademark of Hayes Computer Products, Inc.

IBM, IBM PC, PC-AT, PC-XT, PC Network, Displaywriter, PC DOS, and Translator Unit are trademarks of International Business Machines Corporation.

MS DOS and XENIX are trademarks of Microsoft Corporation.

NEC 7710 is a trademark of NEC Information Systems, Inc.

Norton Utilities is a trademark of Peter Norton Computing.

Sidekick and SuperKey are trademarks of Borland International, Inc.

UNIX is a trademark of AT&T Bell Laboratories.

Wordstar is a trademark of MicroPro International.

Contents

Preface

Every microcomputer system needs a manager, and every system manager needs a system management plan. It's true no matter what the size or complexity of the microcomputer system.

Over the years, I have learned the ingredients of a successful plan. I decided to write this book because I want to save you, another microcomputer system manager, unnecessary work and needless frustration.

The information in this book comes from my experience both as a system manager and as a systems consultant in a variety of business environments. You will find detailed, practical advice distilled from countless meetings, testing, and heart-stopping moments with systems on the blink.

I have seen many businesses manage with a mixture of guesswork and good luck . . . until trouble intrudes. It can be different for you. With the help of this book you can learn to eliminate the guesswork and take control of your system before trouble begins.

Conduct the system evaluation in Chapter One to find out how healthy your system is, whether it is operating at its potential or is on the edge of disaster. Ensuing chapters describe how to design your own custom-made system management plan. Through step-by-step instruction you will learn how to develop tools and techniques to help you manage your computer system effectively. You will learn how to optimize system performance, how to manage system resources, and how to cope with the inevitable trouble that strikes every system.

This book has a practical orientation and combines the "how to" with the "what to do." So, in addition to step-by-step instructions, you will find sample forms and procedures to use as they are or to adapt to your particular needs. Special tips and warnings are sprinkled throughout the book to alert you to key concerns and how to handle them.

Most likely, you will use these pages as you would a workbook, from start to finish. But information is presented in modules so that you can zero in on the selections immediately useful to you should you choose to do so.

You need this book whether you are a new manager or a seasoned one who wants to ensure that you have a stable and effective system management plan. With its help, you will better serve the needs of your firm and the people it employs.

How to Use the Forms in This Book

This book contains twenty-five forms and checklists for your use, most of them to help you build your system library. Before you use any one of them, decide how you want to use it. These two ways are available:

1. Duplicate the forms with a copy machine, enlarging them as you wish. This method has the advantages of being relatively simple and quick. Although you can use it with virtually all of the forms, it lends itself best to the checklists and to forms that contain graphic representations, such as the switch settings map (Figure 2.3).
2. Create the forms using your system's software, the best being your database management program. This method offers several advantages. First, it allows you to make any changes to the forms that you wish. Second, because some information— such as a unique identifier for equipment—appears on multiple forms, this method eliminates the need to insert repetitious information. Third, when calculations must be done, your software can perform them for you. Fourth, you will have the flexibility to print sections or composites of information from a single database to fill your various needs. Finally, with this method you can make updates without difficulty.

Recommended Method to Use Each Form

For most forms, there is one best method for use. Refer to the the following list for recommendations. The list also identifies each form by table or figure number, if any, and indicates the page on which it appears.

Conventions Used in This Book

Material applies to most microcomputer systems. You will find examples for the UNIX, XENIX, MS-DOS, and PC-DOS operating systems. For conciseness, I have elected to use simply UNIX

when information pertains to both UNIX and XENIX and simply
DOS when information pertains to both MS-DOS and PC-DOS.

Throughout the book, UNIX and XENIX commands and file
names appear in boldfaced lower case; MS-DOS and PC-DOS commands and file names appear in upper case.

Forms and Their Recommended Methods for Use

Forms and Their Recommended Methods for Use
(Continued)

List of Figures

List of Tables

Part I

Take Charge of the System

1

Overview

Introduction

Suppose you walk into your office tomorrow to find everyone complaining that the computer's speed suddenly had slowed to a crawl. Or imagine your vendor calls to say that the trouble with one of your personal computer's hard disks has been repaired, but everything stored on it had to be erased in the process.

Hopefully, you would not panic.

You should have little trouble finding the solution to the first problem and no trouble at all handling the second. But, if either scene strikes fear in your heart, you have much to do to develop your system management plan.

Microcomputer managers must handle system slowdowns with dispatch and keep backup copies of everything stored on hard disks as insurance against a possible loss of data and software.

System managers also do a lot more.

This chapter defines your role and responsibilities and describes why your job is so important to your company. To know how you and your system measure up, complete the system evaluation at the end of this chapter. If the foregoing scenes do not give you pause, you might find others in the evaluation that do. But, more important, the evaluation will show you how healthy your system is now and what you can do to keep it that way or to nurse it back to health.

What *you* should do now probably differs from what another manager should do. Maybe you need a procedure for emergency equipment replacement while another system manager desperately needs a means to secure information transmitted over telephone lines. So, use the evaluation to identify both where your system needs immediate attention and which sections in this book you should turn to first. Whatever your system's condition, this chapter can put you well on your way in deciding how to tailor-make your own system management plan.

1.1. The System Manager's Job

Five years ago I was told "We're buying a computer and you'll be in charge of it." When I heard those words, I did not know what managing a microcomputer system would entail. I hastily read the manuals to learn system administration tasks. But, even then, I knew reading manuals was not enough, that managing a computer system was both more interesting and more demanding than merely backing up files or establishing logons.

At the time, there was little help for a microcomputer system manager. Many firms did not even recognize the need for the job, much less understand what it involves. Since then, I have met many people in the same predicament. Microcomputer system management remains a young profession, so the situation is relatively unchanged. As with any young profession, micro management is still fairly wide-open, drawing people from diverse backgrounds.

In this section we will briefly touch on the experience and qualities system managers should have, define three categories of business computer systems, and finally, take a close look at your responsibilities and the implications for your firm.

Who Manages Micros?

Most likely you did something other than manage a computer before you assumed your present position. You might be among those who had extensive hands-on computer experience, both inside and outside of the machine. Or maybe you previously used computers only for word processing or data analysis. It is even possible that you are one of those with no prior familiarity with computers who recently was selected to manage a sophisticated microcomputer system.

Whatever your previous experience, it is likely that you were chosen as much and maybe even more for your personal qualities as for your knowledge of computers. Honesty, intelligence, a good sense of humor, and first-rate communication skills are high on the list of requirements. The ideal system manager also has the curiosity of a research scientist, the persistence of a cat, and the energy of an Olympic athlete.

Regardless of your work setting, you need all of these qualities to keep your system running smoothly. You need the same communication skills to train a new employee and the same tenacity to track down the cause of a printer problem, whether you work for a small firm or a national company. Arguably, you need a better sense of humor the more complicated your system.

The Type of System You Manage

The type of system that you manage generally will fall into one of three categories:

1. **Stand-alone personal computer.** The simplest micro system is a stand-alone personal computer (PC) with one keyboard, one monitor, and one enclosure (called a *system unit*) that houses a power supply, disk drives, the central processing unit (CPU), which controls and manipulates data, and other electronic circuit boards that allow the computer to work for you. Most stand-alone PC's have at least one printer attached. Some have other peripheral equipment, such as a modem, to transmit data over telephone lines.

2. **Local area network.** Personal computers can be linked to form the second type of system, a local area network (LAN). These systems allow people to share software programs, information, and peripheral equipment, such as printers and modems.

    You can designate one or more personal computers as network servers to provide processing power and storage space for other PC's on the system. On some systems, servers are never used as workstations, but instead are devoted entirely to serving the network. In that case, every bit of processing power goes to manage the network and handle its resources, including the server's hard disk, other shared hard disks, and printers.

3. **Multi-user system.** The third type of system, a multi-user system, is one in which multiple users share one CPU. Terminals or PC's masquerading as terminals in what is called *terminal emulation mode* depend on the central host to meet their processing needs. In addition to processing power, multi-user computers share software programs, information, and peripherals with each terminal attached to the system.

    These categories of systems are not rigid. The lines between networks and multi-user systems grow blurrier by the month. For example, you might have a terminal with no local processing power that relies completely on an IBM PC-AT in a system that otherwise is a PC local area network. Or two PC's linked in a LAN also can be attached as terminals to a multi-user microcomputer.

Even the idea of a shared CPU signifying a multi-user system does not hold all of the time. You can have terminals attached to a multi-user system that houses in one enclosure a series of CPU's, with each CPU exclusively used by only one terminal.

Semantics aside, you will have no trouble understanding how your system and situation fit with the particulars in this book.

Scope of the System Manager's Job

Whatever type of system you manage, you share a lot with managers of other systems. What are the roles that you fill? You're a planner, a technician, and a troubleshooter. Sometimes you're a teacher, a librarian, a diplomat, and even a therapist. But, managing virtually any system comes down to juggling your time to coordinate three responsibilities:

1. Know your system.
2. Use the system to its limit.
3. Avoid trouble and solve problems.

A system manager satisfies the three areas of responsibility in specific ways, which are summarized in Table 1.1. In the rest of this section, we will look one level closer at each item to see more of what your position requires of you. Considerably more detail about each area is provided throughout this book.

1. **Know your system.** It is vital that you understand your system. This is a two-pronged matter. First, you should establish a broad knowledge of your system as it is currently. Second, you should cultivate a deep and ongoing understanding because your system will change as people discover new ways to use the existing system, and as you add new software and hardware. Because knowing your system requires continued learning, you will never reach a day when you can say "Ah, I finally know it all!"

Here is what it means to fully understand your system:
   a. *Understand the functional capabilities of each system component.* Know what the system's equipment is capable of doing. Sometimes that is a matter of being familiar with

the manuals. For example, the one that came with your monitor should advise you of whether or not you can view color graphics on the screen. Other times, knowing system capability is a matter of common sense. For instance, if you have a letter-quality printer with only one print wheel, most likely you are unable to use it to print a page with differing fonts and type sizes, even if your software allows it.

b. *Be familiar with the system's software.* It is a rare person who fully understands everything that even one software package offers, partly because complete understanding involves more than reading manuals. You will discover a lot when you and other staff members experiment with a program. Ultimately, however, you personally should be as knowledgeable as you can be about all of your system's software.

Most important, you must understand how to use your operating system from the system management perspective. For example, an intimate knowledge of your operating system could enable you to advise the personnel manager how best to protect sensitive employee records.

c. *Know your way around your vendor-provided documentation.* Even if we cared to, few of us could memorize everything that there is to know about our computer equipment and software. Your vendor-provided manuals are excellent for reference if you acquire two skills:

First, you have to know what the documentation contains, no matter how voluminous it is. Usually, it is insufficient to rely solely on an index or a table of contents. Spend time to acquire the special familiarity that can direct you immediately to a passage that you need.

Second, you must know what the documentation omits. You are completely on your own when it comes to learning how to recognize when information that you need does not appear anywhere in your manuals!

Sometimes locating the answers to even simple questions can be frustrating. For example, one day you might find yourself shocked at how long it takes to determine whether you can control where to place legends on a graph. Or you might have a terrible time trying to find the meaning of a particular message that appears on the display screen. I once was unable to find any explanation for a message in my system's word processing program documentation. I had to comb more than eight hundred pages before concluding that it had been omitted. The deeper your acquaintance with your manuals, the more efficient you can be.

d. *Stay informed about the computer industry in general and about advances for your system in particular.* Things change quickly in the world of computers. It is too much to expect vendors to keep every client informed about software revisions, about new enhancements or products that are available, or about new and improved ways to use existing products.

As a result, you have to be on the lookout in order not to miss things of potential importance to you and your system. One good way to stay informed is to read the computer press and publications specifically directed to people in your industry. Another is to stay in touch with your vendor and convey that you want to maintain and build upon the high-quality system your company purchased.

e. *Keep a complete, organized, and up-to-date system library.* It takes time and patience to organize and maintain a system library, but it is worth the investment. Without a system library, you are severely handicapped in managing your system.

Your library should document every facet of your system, and thus should contain more than most people probably expect. For instance, many new system managers doubt the importance of documenting how those little switches on the backs of printers are set because they find it unthinkable that anyone would want to fiddle with them. As you will see in Chapter Two, documenting switch settings is only one example of documentation that you must create yourself if you intend to have a complete system library.

You need a means to organize your library to fend off mysterious piles of paper and missing documents.

And, to keep your library current, you need to build in procedures to update it with each addition or alteration to your system.

f. *Stay aware of how you and the system are doing.* Stay alert to how well you are managing the system and to its condition. Otherwise you might run into trouble.

For example, one system manager lost the trust of several people when a remote terminal functioned unreliably for two weeks. These people had demanding responsibilities of their own, and it mattered little to them that no one had told the system manager that there was a problem with the terminal.

It is important that you know at all times how the system behaves and how people use it. Regularly visit or speak with people who use your system at each of its locations. Be observant. That way you will always know the "state of the system."

2. **Use the system to its limit.** Performance is a major reason that your company has a computer, and you can do a lot to promote its top performance. For instance, you can establish a procedure for people to keep the deadwood off a hard disk for better system performance, quicker disk backup, and shorter directory listings. Or you might buy additional random access memory (RAM) so that the system has enough room to accommodate new productivity software packages, such as a pop-up notepad or an on-line thesaurus.

Here are several ways you should use your system to its limit:

a. *Set up software to meet the needs of staff members and the firm.* Every company has special needs of its computer system. Even though your system may have been custom-configured when it arrived, it is likely that you will find ways to build upon that configuration. For example, for new and untrained employees, you might devise a special version of your word processing program that automatically offers the maximum on-screen help available with the program. More experienced employees using the program probably would prefer a version that offers little or no automatic on-screen help.

Because people's needs change, stay in touch with

people so you can continue to be responsive. For example, you might find the accountant planning to use the system for a new application that would run more efficiently if you set up a larger RAM disk (see Section 5.2) than the accounting office's computers currently have established.

b. *Coordinate the use of system resources so they are available when needed.* See that people have access to the equipment that they need. When resources are unavailable, people are hampered in doing their work. Consequently, idle equipment often is preferable to making people wait until a terminal or a printer is free. Sometimes, availablity depends only on how well-stocked your supply room is with paper, printer ribbon, or diskettes. When you run out of ribbons, your printer might just as well be broken.

In addition to equipment, you also want to see that people fairly and efficiently use RAM, processing time (CPU time), and disk storage space. Chances are that there will be times when one of these resources is in short supply. Often, merely implementing a procedure can resolve a problem. For example, you and others can keep disk storage space available if you perform regular disk housekeeping (details in Section 4.2).

c. *Evaluate the system to identify ways to improve it.* Conduct periodic evaluations to identify ways to make a changing system better serve a changing company. For example, through such an evaluation, you might learn that disk space has been tight since you introduced a spreadsheet program. Solutions you might consider include buying an additional hard disk or adjusting disk storage procedures.

Or, after consulting with various staff members, you might identify applications that could help your firm achieve business gains or meet other goals. For example, you might discover that managers want a software package to help them make strategic business decisions.

d. *Consider, evaluate, and install new equipment, software, and upgrades for your existing system.* Combat whatever might allow the system to stagnate or deteriorate. Better, take an active stance toward its development.

With each new advance in the computer field, you might consider a change to your system. Does the new version of your operating system offer features that you feel are worth the price? Is it cost-effective to buy the new turbo-speed modems? Earth-shattering industry breakthroughs are only one type of event that should prompt you to consider new products or upgrades. Mundane events, such as your printer being worn out, might have the same effect.

Whenever you decide to develop your system, you have to evaluate each potential product according to at least three criteria. You have to judge whether the product can meet your needs; you have to know whether it is compatible with your existing system; and you must understand how the product will affect the people who use your system.

Of course, once a product passes your evaluation and you have purchased it, you should install it according to the manufacturer's instructions and be sure to run tests before releasing it for company-wide use.

e. *Train people to use the system.* Make the system accessible to people at all levels of your firm, including top managers, middle managers, and so on. Whenever it will benefit the firm, you want people to take advantage of the system.

Studies show lack of training to be one of the most significant barriers to the successful use of business computers. I once visited the West Coast offices of a well-known national firm where I was shown a back room packed tightly with unopened personal computers. Inadequate training was blamed.

Little or no training also is one reason that people devise incredibly creative ways to make it seem they are using a computer system when actually they are avoiding it, sometimes entirely. One company manager was appalled to learn that inadequately trained staff members were preparing spreadsheets using calculators and type-writers. For four months, these frustrated people made it appear that they were using a computer!

Good training includes sensitivity to people's needs. People learn differently. Design your training program to accommodate how the individuals learn. Be sure your program teaches people not only how to use the equipment and software, but also how to follow established in-house procedures. Keep people on course; be sure they are not isolated or set adrift. Provide as much on-site support as you can to help them to use the system well.

3. **Avoid trouble and solve problems.** The third and final area of system management responsibility is coping with potential and actual trouble. Usually, when there is risk, there is also the opportunity for gain. For a microcomputer system manager, that frequently is not true. Here is where blame comes easily and thanks are sparse. For instance, people notice immediately if you fail in troubleshooting, while they sometimes barely acknowledge how much easier work has been since you installed a tape backup device on the system. But, if you handle this responsibility well, you know that you are serving your system and your company.

The following is an overview of what you need to do to avoid trouble and resolve problems:

a. *Keep staff members informed.* You *must* keep people informed. No other task is as easy or as important. What is needed is more than simple good public relations. Most people function poorly when kept in the dark. I once saw frenzied analysts dependent on a computer to meet a rigid deadline who were able to calm down *only* after they were told what to expect . . . which was that the system probably would be down until some hours after the deadline had passed. After an initial venting of frustration, these people accommodated themselves and their work.

When people understand what is happening and are told the truth, they usually can make necessary adjustments. Generally, people can cope as long as you communicate with them.

b. *Establish and guide the in-house users' group.* Many companies benefit from having a number of staff members who function as an in-house users' group. This task could just as easily fall under the first two system management responsibility areas because if you have an in-house users' group, it affects everything you do.

First, your users' group keeps you aware of how the system is doing, so your knowledge stays current. Second, you and group members will identify ways to manipulate the system into providing better service, so you all get the most you can from the system. Third, you will probably find out about trouble and potential trouble much earlier than you would without a group, so you can do a better job of avoiding crises and resolving problems.

c. *Protect your company by securing the system.* It is your responsibility to protect every part of the system: its equipment, its software, and the data that people store on it. You will find it invaluable to establish and implement security measures. For example, have you done your best to ensure that no one can copy or steal your most precious and sensitive data? Mistakes can be costly in both lost productivity and actual dollars, ranging from stolen (and therefore unavailable) equipment to an expensive lawsuit.

d. *Protect your company by maintaining the system.* System maintenance is another way you protect your firm and its system. A long-neglected floppy disk drive that slowly slips out of alignment may one day be your undoing when it expires and you discover that the disks it has written on are unreadable by other drives.

e. *Solve mysteries and resolve problems.* No matter what steps you take to avoid trouble, you will encounter problems with the system. (Just think about Murphy's Law—anything that *can* go wrong *will* go wrong—and you will understand why computers and trouble are old friends.) The key is to be prepared and to persist.

Persistence is most important when you are most puzzled. The proportion of recognizable problems to mysteries you encounter will depend on your experience. Some mysteries demand your attention. Others appear not to. Do not be fooled. You have to handle both kinds. Whenever trouble appears, whether it is familiar or puzzling, track down its source to eliminate it.

Help for the System Manager

At this point, you might be asking yourself, "Managing a computer system involves so much work, must I do it alone?" The answer depends on your system's size and complexity and on the number of people using it. Some micro managers supervise a staff of several people; others manage their systems alone.

Whether or not the job is more than an individual can handle at your firm, it is important that one person be responsible for overseeing the system, someone who coordinates everything listed on Table 1.1. Every system needs a person who understands how to keep it running smoothly, who tangles with trouble, and who can make decisions during a crisis.

Can and should you expect help? Yes and no, on both counts. Because you are ultimately responsible, you cannot expect someone else to volunteer to take your place; but, you need not be alone.

First, regardless of your system's size, it is generally a good idea to teach other people how to do some of the common tasks, both to give them greater control over their jobs and to remove some of the burden from your shoulders. Show people how to back up files, how to start and reboot the system safely, and how to cope with common problems. For their sakes and for everyone else's, be sure people know what they are doing before they assume responsiblity for any system management task.

Second, there will be times when you are unavailable. (Even system managers need vacations.) Fate tends to bring trouble to systems when the manager is absent. Cover yourself and the system. Designate a specific person as your backup and see that he or she is trained to take charge in your absence.

Ten Benefits for Your Company

The scope of your system management responsibility is staggering, but so are its benefits, which extend far beyond your own personal satisfaction. The more effectively you do your job, the more your company has to gain.

Table 1.1

SUMMARY OF SYSTEM MANAGEMENT FUNCTIONS

---

1. Know Your System

a. Understand the functional capabilities of each system component
b. Be familiar with the system's software
c. Know your way around your vendor-provided documentation
d. Stay informed about the computer industry in general and about advances for your system in particular
e. Keep a complete, organized, and up-to-date system library
f. Stay aware of how you and the system are doing

2. Use the System to Its Limit

a. Set up software to meet the needs of staff members and the firm
b. Coordinate the use of system resources so they are available when needed
c. Evaluate the system to identify ways to improve it
d. Consider, evaluate, and install new equipment, software, and upgrades for your existing system
e. Train people to use the system

3. Avoid Trouble and Solve Problems

a. Keep staff members informed
b. Establish and guide the in-house users' group
c. Protect your company by securing the system
d. Protect your company by maintaining the system
e. Solve mysteries and resolve problems

Before your next salary review, show your superior the list of benefits that you bring to your company (see Table 1.2). It may be sobering for you and your superior to realize how much your company depends on its computer system and its manager. In fact, your firm probably would go out of business if it had serious trouble with items one through four below.

1. **Trustworthy data.** Consider the impact that data integrity has on each staff member's work. Yet, how often can you fully trust the quality of information you use? Manage your computer system well, and you will improve the odds that its data is reliable. For example, if you install a simple procedure to check the integrity of data files on a regular basis, you can prevent or minimize the impact of accidental file damage.

2. **Data security.** You probably know how easy it can be for someone to steal or tamper with information stored electronically. Consider the possibility of an employee copying a diskette that contains your company's most secret documents. Violations are more difficult when you put well-conceived security measures in place.

3. **Protection against complete loss of data.** A shocking percentage of firms are vulnerable to a complete loss of their data. The main problem is a laxity about backing up files. A Northern California library stood to lose more than 250,000 books from its multiple-branch system when a hard disk failed, and people had not backed up the circulation records. With a regularly followed data file backup procedure, you avoid putting your company in jeopardy of losing all of its information when a hard disk fails.

4. **Reduced system downtime.** System downtime is expensive. You can keep downtime to a minimum with preventive maintenance and effective troubleshooting. As a result, people have the equipment and software they need in order to be productive and to meet their deadlines.

5. **Full use and optimal availability of system resources.** Systems can be used minimally or allocated foolishly. Through planning, coordination, and scheduling, you ensure that people use system resources properly. You see that people are trained to make the most of the system so that your company is not threatened with having a roomful of unpacked computers. You eliminate roadblocks people might encounter when trying to use the system. You see

that priority work makes it through when there is a conflict. While you are the system manager, no one will have to say, "I was unable to have the report printed in time for the meeting because someone else had the printer engaged."

6. **Natural, rational, and cost-effective system development.** Every system changes, whether or not someone guides it. Many firms have suffered from the chaos of disorganized development, such as owning several different software packages that accomplish the same task. Ask the manager of such a firm to describe the nightmare of seeing that every employee is trained or of figuring out how to share data created using various programs. You avoid these problems by making certain that your firm has a standard for every category of software it owns.

   You know how best to control the direction that your system's development takes, whether you are in the process of buying additional equipment and software or deciding a more efficient way to configure the existing system.

7. **Limited legal liability.** Liability is a potential menace for every system. Limit this liability—and its expense—by taking reasonable precautions and implementing a security plan. As a result, your company need not worry too much about software theft or information leaks.

8. **Staff member confidence in the system.** With the system under your care, people know exactly what to expect . . . not just of the system itself, but of themselves and of you. (This trust brings the added benefit of a potential reduction in staff turnover.)

9. **Increased staff productivity.** Increased productivity comes from each of the foregoing eight benefits. For instance, trustworthy data and reduced downtime are two ingredients that help people to accomplish first-rate work on a timely basis.

10. **Economic well-being.** Ultimately, the most important benefit to accrue from a well-managed system is greater economic well-being for your firm. The tools you provide others in your firm contribute directly to your firm's balance sheet. Profit-making concerns should enjoy a greater profit margin; non-profit concerns should be able to provide more or better service for each dollar spent.

```
┌─────────────────────────────────────────────────┐
│                   Table 1.2                       │
│  ───────────────────────────────────────────     │
│                                                   │
│     TEN BENEFITS OF SYSTEM MANAGEMENT             │
│  ───────────────────────────────────────────     │
│                                                   │
│    1. Trustworthy data                            │
│    2. Data security                               │
│    3. Protection against complete loss of data    │
│    4. Reduced system downtime                      │
│    5. Full use and optimal availability of system │
│       resources                                    │
│    6. Natural, rational, and cost-effective system│
│       development                                  │
│    7. Limited legal liability                      │
│    8. Staff member confidence in the system        │
│    9. Increased staff productivity                 │
│   10. Economic well-being                          │
└─────────────────────────────────────────────────┘
```

1.2 A System Evaluation: Find Out How Well-Managed Your System Is

Since you live with your system every day, chances are that you have an impression of how healthy it is. If you think it is doing all right, it probably is. But today's good impressions evaporate with tomorrow's trouble. Complete the evaluation in this section to identify your system's strengths and weaknesses.

The evaluation is in two parts. Part I will show you how effectively you can perform your responsibilities. Part II will tell you how well-prepared you are for trouble or crises. Virtually everything the evaluation addresses is covered in the rest of this book. If you are unfamiliar with some of the situations or terms introduced in the evaluation, refer to the glossary for help as you work through the questions.

When you complete Parts I and II, you will interpret your answers. Use the results to plan a strategy to improve your system management program.

Part I: How Effectively Can You Perform System Management Tasks?

Part I should help you gauge how well you are able to manage the system from day to day. This part asks three questions, each of which covers several topics, with each topic followed by a chapter reference to direct you to where in this book you will find help. For example, look at the first two topics under question number one:

1. DO YOU HAVE ESTABLISHED AND CONSISTENT PROCEDURES FOR:

Yes   No

_____   _____   1. Equipment replacement [Ch 8]

_____   _____   2. Eliminating nagging and ongoing system delays [Ch 4, 5]

If you need a procedure for equipment replacement, you can turn to Chapter 8 for assistance. Likewise, turn to Chapters 4 and 5 to learn how to eliminate system delays.

Part II: How Well-Prepared Are You for Trouble or Catastrophe?

Part II of the evaluation will tell you if you are ready for crises. Bear in mind that while the calamities mentioned here may be extreme, they are not exceptional.

Column A asks that you answer yes or no to the question. Columns B and C ask you to judge the potential risk and potential loss for the situation each question poses.

For example, suppose you are responding to item #1, "Do you know how to guard your data against a hard disk failure?":

1. Use Column A to indicate whether you know the precautions to take to protect your data. Answer yes or no.
2. Column B asks you to judge *for your system* whether the likelihood of a hard disk failure is high or low. (The probability is high if you have recently observed READ/WRITE or SEEK messages.) Mark the appropriate column.
3. Column C asks you to decide whether the potential loss from a hard disk failure would be great or small *for your system*. In the case of hard disk failure, if you have a complete backup of data and software on diskettes or tape, the potential loss probably is small. If you do not have these backups, you are risking catastrophe. Mark the appropriate column.

A System Evaluation

PART I: HOW EFFECTIVELY CAN YOU PERFORM SYSTEM MANAGEMENT TASKS?

Instructions: Answer yes or no to each question in Part I.

1. DO YOU HAVE ESTABLISHED AND CONSISTENT PROCEDURES FOR:

Yes	No	
____	____	1. Equipment replacement [Ch 8]
____	____	2. Eliminating nagging and ongoing system delays [Ch 4, 5]
____	____	3. Handling system failure [Ch 8]
____	____	4. Deleting unnecessary program and data files [Ch 4]
____	____	5. Problem diagnosis and solving [Ch 8]
____	____	6. Training people to use new equipment or software [Ch 7]
____	____	7. Making full and partial backups [Ch 7]
____	____	8. Adding new users and deleting old ones [Ch 6]
____	____	9. Avoiding trouble with equipment [Ch 7]
____	____	10. Securing the system [Ch 6]
____	____	11. Protecting your data [Ch 6, 7]
____	____	12. Managing a hard disk [Ch 4]
____	____	13. Documenting customized responses to software installation programs [Ch 3]
____	____	14. Protecting your firm against liability for software theft [Ch 6]
____	____	15. Protecting your firm against client information disclosure [Ch 6]
____	____	16. Managing processes for peak system performance [Ch 4, 5, 7]
____	____	17. Monitoring the system [Ch 6, 7]
____	____	18. Keeping necessary supplies on hand [Ch 7]
____	____	19. Evaluating, selecting, and installing equipment and software upgrades [Ch 5, 6, 7]
____	____	20. Protecting backups with off-site storage [Ch 3, 7]

2. IS THE FOLLOWING INFORMATION MAINTAINED IN CURRENT FORM IN YOUR SYSTEM LIBRARY?

Yes	No	
____	____	1. Every manual associated with each software package and piece of equipment available on your system [Ch 2, 3]
____	____	2. A map identifying the location and status of each piece of equipment on the system [Ch 2]
____	____	3. A map identifying contents and boundaries of hard disk partitions [Ch 4]
____	____	4. Both original and backup diskettes of each software package available for your system. (Skip this item if your software packages cannot be copied because of protection schemes.) [Ch 3]

A System Evaluation

PART I: HOW EFFECTIVELY CAN YOU PERFORM SYSTEM MANAGEMENT TASKS?

(continued)

Yes   No

_____ _____   5. Documentation of your custom installation of each version of each software package on your system [Ch 3]

_____ _____   6. Hard copies of system files [Ch 3]

_____ _____   7. Names and telephone numbers of others managing a system like yours [Ch 8]

_____ _____   8. A fully configured previous version of your operating system [Ch 3]

_____ _____   9. Data file archives [Ch 3]

_____ _____   10. A complete backup of current data files [Ch 3, 7]

3. DO YOU HAVE SCHEDULES FOR THE FOLLOWING ONGOING PROCEDURES?

Yes   No

_____ _____   1. Full and partial data file backup [Ch 7]

_____ _____   2. Retiring passwords [Ch 6]

_____ _____   3. Equipment inspection [Ch 7]

_____ _____   4. System evaluation [Ch 1]

_____ _____   5. Data integrity inspection [Ch 7]

END OF PART I
PLEASE CONTINUE WITH PART II

PART II: HOW WELL-PREPARED ARE YOU FOR TROUBLE OR CATASTROPHE?

Instructions: For each question, answer yes or no in Column A. In Column B, identify whether the potential risk is high or low. Use Column C to indicate if the potential loss is great or small.

Column A			Column B		Column C	
Yes	**No**		**Potential Risk** [High Low]		**Potential Loss** [Great Small]	
_____	_____	1. Do you know how to guard your data against a hard disk failure? [Ch 7, 8]	_____	_____	_____	_____
_____	_____	2. Can you identify signs of impending disk drive trouble? [Ch 7, 8]	_____	_____	_____	_____
_____	_____	3. Can you recognize and eliminate a sudden deterioration in system response? [Ch 8]	_____	_____	_____	_____
_____	_____	4. Do you and others know which operations are hazardous to you and to the system? [Ch 7, 8]	_____	_____	_____	_____
_____	_____	5. Are you aware of types of diskettes that pose danger to certain workstations? [Ch 3, 7]	_____	_____	_____	_____
_____	_____	6. Are all former employees prevented from logging on to your system? [Ch 6]	_____	_____	_____	_____
_____	_____	7. Is your firm protected against liability for software theft? [Ch 6]	_____	_____	_____	_____
_____	_____	8. Can you be sure your electronic mailboxes are private? [Ch 6]	_____	_____	_____	_____
_____	_____	9. Are you prepared if someone accidentally changes the switch settings on the back of a printer or terminal? [Ch 2]	_____	_____	_____	_____
_____	_____	10. Are you prepared if the modem fails while transmitting urgent information? [Ch 8]	_____	_____	_____	_____
_____	_____	11. Is the system protected against power line aberrations? [Ch 7]	_____	_____	_____	_____

A System Evaluation

PART II: HOW WELL-PREPARED ARE YOU FOR TROUBLE OR CATASTROPHE?

(continued)

Column A			Column B		Column C	
Yes	**No**		**Potential Risk**		**Potential Loss**	
			[High	Low]	[Great	Small]
____	____	12. Would you be able to replace your data and software if a fire consumed the computer room and everything in it? [Ch 3, 7]	____	____	____	____
____	____	13. Do you know what you will do when equipment fails or is accidentally damaged? [Ch 8]	____	____	____	____

Interpret the Evaluation to See How Healthy Your System Is

Because you had to scrutinize your system to answer the questions in the evaluation, even now you should have a better idea than before about how healthy your system is.

But, you need to take this exercise a few steps further. Let's interpret your responses so that you can identify what you have to do first to shape a system management plan that will work for you and your firm. We will begin with your responses to Part I.

Interpret Part I: How Effectively Can You Perform System Management Tasks?

Look at your responses to Part I. The issues are straightforward. You either have the various procedures, documentation, and schedules, or you do not have them.

To interpret your responses, consider the relative priority of procedures, documentation, and schedules. Although priorities differ for each system, if your system is typical, you probably have the following priorities. If need be, change the order to whatever priority makes sense for you.

Category

Top Priority: Having established procedures
Second Priority: Having current information in the system library
Third Priority: Having schedules to implement procedures

Tally the number of your negative responses. Assuming the priority order above, generally, you should not panic if you have three or fewer negative responses in each category. However, take immediate steps to turn each no into a yes. More than three negative responses in any one category can be serious.

Take time to look at your positive responses. Congratulate yourself for what you already have under control.

Turn now to your responses to the questions in Part II. ·

Interpret Part II:
How Well-Prepared Are You?

Part II of the evaluation asks you to establish the potential risk and financial loss associated with each of its thirteen items. You will interpret your responses to Part II in two steps, recording them on Table 1.3.

First, take a moment to review Table 1.3. Boxes A through D on the table each contain the numbers one through thirteen, representing each of the thirteen questions. See how the table helps you chart the relative risk and potential loss for each of the thirteen situations posed in Part II.

Here is what each box on Table 1.3 represents:

Box	Represents
A	low relative risk & small potential loss
B	low relative risk & great potential loss
C	high relative risk & small potential loss
D	high relative risk & great potential loss

Step One. Plot your responses. Note the relative risk and potential loss that you assigned to each situation in items one through thirteen. Record your negative and positive responses by circling the number of each situation in the appropriate box on Table 1.3. You will determine the appropriate box based on the combination of relative risk and potential loss. This means that each of your responses should fall in only one of the four boxes, A through D on the table.

For example, if you responded no to question #1, meaning you do not know how to guard your data against a hard disk crash, and you rated the situation as relatively high risk with potentially great loss, then circle the number one in box D. Had you rated this situation as one with relatively low risk and potentially small loss, you would circle the number one in box A instead.

Plot both negative responses and positive responses because they are equally important to your interpretation of this part of the evaluation. Be sure to distinguish yes and no responses. For instance, you can circle positive responses in green and negative responses in red.

Step Two. Interpret your responses. After you have plotted all thirteen of your responses, you are ready to see where you stand.

Box D is the critical box. It is a good indicator of your overall readiness, for better or worse. Negative responses in box D are red alert items that demand your immediate attention because both the potential risk and the potential loss are high.

Positive responses in box D indicate that you are well-prepared for the most risky and potentially expensive trouble likely to happen. Congratulate yourself for these!

Notice the pattern of your negative responses. No negative responses in box D is a very good sign. More than two negative responses in box D might forebode impending calamity. Negative responses plotted in boxes A through C will be most useful for you to establish priorities so that you can eliminate weaknesses in your management program.

Next look at the overall pattern of your positive responses. These indicate the areas you have under control.

Compare the patterns of negative and positive responses. Are there boxes in which positive responses are outnumbered by the negative? In which boxes are the negative responses outnumbered by the positive? Can you draw any conclusions from the balance between positive and negative responses in each box? How does your level of preparedness compare with the extent of risk and loss? Do you tend to be best prepared for situations of High Risk/Great Loss? Or have

Table 1.3

INTERPRET PART II: HOW WELL-PREPARED ARE YOU BASED ON THE LEVEL OF RELATIVE RISK AND POTENTIAL LOSS?

		POTENTIAL LOSS		
		SMALL LOSS		GREAT LOSS

RELATIVE RISK

LOW RISK	BOX A			BOX B		
	1	2	3	1	2	3
	4	5	6	4	5	6
	7	8	9	7	8	9
	10	11	12	10	11	12
		13			13	

HIGH RISK	BOX C			BOX D		
	1	2	3	1	2	3
	4	5	6	4	5	6
	7	8	9	7	8	9
	10	11	12	10	11	12
		13			13	

LEGEND

Box	Represents
A	low relative risk & small potential loss
B	low relative risk & great potential loss
C	high relative risk & small potential loss
D	high relative risk & great potential loss

TYPICAL INTERPRETATION

Box	Negative Response Means
A	= Important, not deadly
B & C	= Serious. You judge which to handle first
D	= Red Alert. Handle NOW

*Refer to instructions in text to complete Table 1.3.

you concentrated on Low Risk/Small Loss areas, possibly because they are easiest to handle?

Chart Your Course

By now you should have an accurate picture of how healthy your system is. You know which changes are needed urgently and which you might make with less haste.

Before you start, chart a plan for yourself. Decide what to do first. For each area, base your decision on how serious a threat you will expose the system to if you take no action.

These guidelines should be helpful:

1. *For Part I.* Remember the order of priority most systems have for issues raised in Part I: procedures first, an up-to-date library second, schedules third. Unless you have different priorities for your system, address these in 1-2-3 order.
2. *For Part II.* First, turn to your annotated Table 1.3. Remember, box D is the most critical box. Negative responses need immediate attention. If you neglect them, you are exposing your company to unacceptable and avoidable risk. Resolve these *now*.

    Next, remember that negative responses in boxes B and C are serious. Judge for yourself which ones you should handle first.

    Finally, box A negative responses are important, but not deadly. Handle these last.

Conclusion

As long as you are organized, system management does not require a herculean effort. Use the rest of this book to develop custom-made documents and procedures to give your company and its people the computer support they deserve.

If your evaluation spotlighted something urgent, work through the chapters out of sequence. Maybe it is imperative for you to establish a procedure to handle system failure before you do anything else. If so, zero in first on the appropriate section in Chapter 8. If you must work out of sequence, be sure to return to sections you omit the first time around. Cover each chapter. Do not neglect any aspect, because it all ties together!

You might prefer to continue with the book in chapter sequence. If so, Chapter 2 will set you underway in establishing your system library, a foundation of the organization every system manager needs.

Whatever section you turn to next, when you have completed the book, come back to the evaluation and take it again. You'll see how much you've gained!

2

Establish
A System Library:
The Hardware

Introduction

Now that you know how you and your system measure up, the next step is to organize. Good organization begins with a system library that will prepare you for most challenges.

What is in a system library? Manuals, of course, but there is more. Much of the information you need is not in the manuals that came with your system, and, no matter how good your memory is, it is unlikely that you can keep track unless you write things down. Even if you can, you still have to prepare for days when you are unavailable. You need detailed records that describe in specific terms your equipment and software in order to avoid the confusion that results from incomplete or inaccurate library information.

Building a system library is so big a job that it warrants two chapters to describe how to establish one. (You will find a complete list of recommended library contents in Section 3.4.)

This chapter deals with hardware documents. Whatever type of system you manage—stand-alone PC's, a local area network, or a multi-user system—you must know what equipment you have, where it is located, and how it is connected. You also need to know what each computer hides under its hood: How much disk storage space and how much RAM does each computer have? What internal circuit boards does each have? Is there room for expansion? This chapter will help you to organize all of that information on five documents: a system sketch, a system devices map, a peripheral devices map, a system boards map, and a switch settings map.

I urge you to use a database management program to develop each of these documents (with the obvious exception of the first, the system sketch). This way, you will take advantage of your computer's power to help you manage your system. Efficiency is one reason to do it. Some of the needed information repeats itself throughout the series of documents. Even more important, using a database management program will make updating your documents a simple task. Finally, with this method you have the flexibility to print specified sections of the database according to your needs. For example, you might isolate equipment information by department in order to plan overall system expansion. And, if you decide to add a hard disk to every computer on your system, you will be able to print a list of PC's that do not have hard disks.

If you decide to use a database management program to develop your hardware documentation, first read the sections in this chapter that describe every document in the set—beginning with the system devices map and ending with the switch settings map—so that you can design your database ahead of time.

Since each document that you will develop builds on the previous one, start at the beginning for best results. You might find elements that do not apply to your system, though it is unlikely. If you are unsure about the need for a particular document or its contents, refer to your system's manuals for help.

2.1 Sketch Your System

A system sketch is a visual representation of the entire system: the equipment and how it fits into the overall picture. A system sketch is not always mandatory, but it is worth having. Let's look at just one instance where a system sketch is valuable:

Suppose you have placed a service call for a troublesome workstation. Your vendor promised to send Gene, his service technician, between 9 a.m. and 4 p.m. today. You have to step away from your office for twenty minutes. Before you leave, you inform front office personnel about the expected service call. The moment you leave, Gene arrives. You are not there, so he has to rely on the information he receives from the front office. Unfortunately, they misdirect him, so he examines the wrong piece of equipment. Seasoned technicians have encountered many cases of equipment reported to be malfunctioning when the "problem" actually is an improper use of the equipment. Gene has no way of knowing that you have a real problem with a piece of equipment other than the one he examines.

When you return, Gene is gone. Now what? All you can do is place another service call. Your frustration is matched only by the frustration of the person who regularly uses the malfunctioning workstation.

Had Gene been armed with your annotated system sketch, he could have located the problem workstation on his own and the equipment would have been fixed on a timely basis.

Even when you *are* available, you can use the sketch to steer service personnel to the right place when you decide that you will not accompany them. You also can use it to coordinate temporary equipment replacements. And it will be a convenient reference for you when you plan system expansion. The first time you use the sketch might well be to create the other documents described in this chapter.

If your system consists of two or three stand-alone personal computers, you probably could get by without this document. But, the larger your system is, the more useful and important the sketch will be.

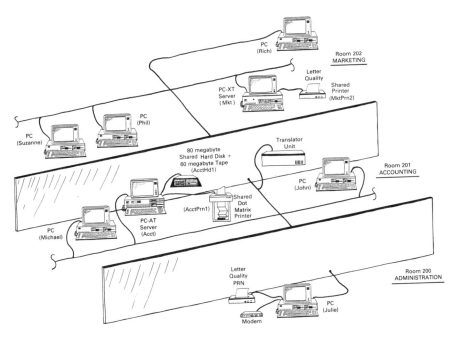

Figure 2.1. Sample Local Area Network.

You will find two sample systems to use to develop your system sketch. Figure 2.1 shows a LAN; Figure 2.2 shows a multi-user system. Whether or not you make a sketch, be sure to review the sketches for the sample systems because they are used as examples throughout this chapter.

1. **Local Area Network Sketch.** Figure 2.1 represents a LAN that is based on the IBM PC Network and that serves a company's administration, accounting, and marketing depart-

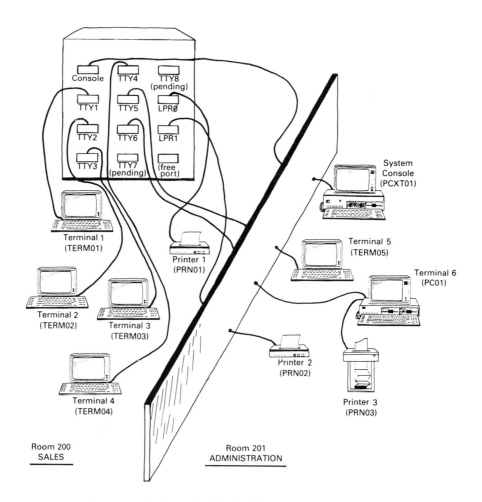

Figure 2.2. Sample Multi-User System.

ments. All three departments use the network's two dedicated servers: the IBM PC-AT, its dot-matrix printer, and its external hard disk and tape unit located in the accounting department; and the IBM PC-XT and its letter-quality printer, located in marketing. Individuals use the system's six PC's. A letter-quality printer and a modem are dedicated to Julie's PC in administration.

2. **Multi-User System Sketch.** Figure 2.2 represents a multi-user system that serves the administration and sales depart-

ments in a small firm. The sample system has twelve ports, points where a cable connects equipment to the central system enclosure. The sample multi-user system centrally can support two printers and up to nine terminals, including the system console. Two terminals, TTY7 and TTY8, are pending. The single free port could be used to add a modem. The IBM PC-XT and the IBM PC in administration both emulate terminals on the system; the PC has its own printer.

Tips to Develop a System Sketch

Refer to the sample systems to prepare a sketch of yours. The following tips should help.

Tip #1. Your sketch should show the physical space that your system occupies, including divisions between rooms, floors, and buildings. If they are available, use the architect's drawings of your facility as the basis for your sketch. Architect's drawings are particularly useful if your system is large and complex or if it occupies different floors.

Tip #2. Plan your sketch by comparing your system, your organization, and the layout of your facility with what is depicted in the sample you have chosen as your guide (Figure 2.1 or 2.2). Look for differences. How do the number and types of equipment on your system differ from those in your sample system? How do the departmental divisions in your organization compare? How does the physical layout of equipment in the sample system compare with yours?

Tip #3. Keep your goals in mind: You want your sketch to show the hardware your system has and where it is located. You want the sketch to reflect the function each piece of hardware serves in the context of the whole system. And you want to be able to identify specialized equipment at a glance, such as the two LAN servers (Figure 2.1) and the multi-user system console (Figure 2.2).

Tip #4. Each piece of hardware has a unique name on the sample sketch you are using: the LAN's PC in Room 200 is called Julie; the multi-user system's printer in Room 200 is called PRN01. Ignore these names for the time being. In the process of creating the next document, your system devices map, you will assign names to your hardware and add them to your sketch.

Tip #5 for LAN managers. If you manage a local area network, be sure to distinguish network servers, shared equipment, and dedicated devices. If you have critical nodes, PC's in the network that will bring down the network when they malfunction, identify them on the sketch.

2.2 Document System Components

You need detailed information about each piece of equipment depicted in your system sketch. Collect the necessary identifying information on a system devices map, the companion to your system sketch. The system devices map is a must for every system manager (unless you are in charge of only one personal computer). Here is one example to illustrate why you need a devices map.

Suppose you manage a multi-user system. A workstation stops functioning. You do not know whether the problem is with the workstation itself, with its cable, or with the port. You suspect the port, so you decide to test it by connecting the workstation and its cable to another port. A trial-and-error search to find which cable you want out of ten or twenty is both frustrating and time-consuming. With your system devices map, you will locate instantly the cable in question.

The system devices map is more than a simple equipment listing. You will use it to identify equipment from each of these angles:

1. serial number
2. location
3. how the system names it (for a LAN) or how it is attached to the system (for a multi-user system)
4. the type and capacity of its local storage
5. its function in relation to the overall system (for a LAN)

This and other information on your devices map should enable you to better use, manage, and control each piece of system hardware. Consolidating the information on a system devices map will be useful to you for a variety of purposes in addition to the troubleshooting situation posed above. You will know at a glance which PC has a 20 megabyte hard disk and which has only diskette drives. You will refer to this map when you conduct your regular equipment inventory and when you plan system growth.

Tables 2.1 and 2.2 represent system devices maps for the sample local area network (Figure 2.1) and the sample multi-user system (Figure 2.2). The nine categories of information on the tables are summarized on Table 2.3 and are explained in detail in the step-by-step instructions below.

Important Note to Managers of Stand-Alone PC's

Information for stand-alone PC's is consolidated with that for the other two types of systems. Thus, if you have stand-alone PC's *and a LAN*, you should follow the instructions for the local area network devices map. If you have stand-alone PC's *and a multi-user system*, follow the instructions for the multi-user system devices map. If you have *only* stand-alone personal computers, follow the instructions for either map. You will be alerted to special instructions that apply to you.

Tip for Managers of Multi-User Systems

The information in Columns 4, 6, and 7 on the sample system devices map (Table 2.2) is strikingly similar. Together, these columns identify the relationship between each device, its cable, and its port.

It is important that you understand and establish clear distinctions among the three. Each one refers to a unique and concrete item:

1. a piece of equipment (the device, Column 4)
2. the cable that connects the device to the computer (Column 6)
3. the place on the computer to connect a device's cable (the port, Column 7).

Device, cable, and port relationships do not last forever. Assigning them unique names is the easiest way to keep track of each one. That way, when and if you have to break a device/cable/port connection, each one retains its name, making it possible to manage all three.

Table 2.1

LOCAL AREA NETWORK SYSTEM DEVICES MAP

For Sample Local Area Network: Figure 2.1

Date _____   Prepared By _____

Device (1)	Serial Number (2)	Location (3)	Device Name (4)	Local Storage (5)	Network Name (6)	Function (7)	Staff Members (8)	Comment (9)
IBM PC-AT	507220	Rm 201	PCAT01	20 Meg hd 1.2Meg fld 360K fld 512K RAM	Acct	Server	n/a	
IBM PC-XT	304957	Rm 202	PCXT01	20 Meg hd 360K fld 640K RAM	Mkt	Server	n/a	
IBM PC	288649	Rm 201	PC01	2/360K fld 640K RAM	Michael	Wkstation	Michael	8087 Chip
IBM PC	300223	Rm 201	PC02	2/360K fld 640K RAM	John	Wkstation	John	8087 Chip
IBM PC	503444	Rm 202	PC03	2/360K fld 640K RAM	Rich	Wkstation	Rich	
IBM PC	220556	Rm 202	PC04	2/360K fld 640K RAM	Phil	Wkstation	Phil	
IBM PC	440333	Rm 202	PC05	2/360K fld 640K RAM	Suzanne	Wkstation	Suzanne Theresa Lydia	

Table 2.1

LOCAL AREA NETWORK SYSTEM DEVICES MAP

For Sample Local Area Network: Figure 2.1

Date _____   Prepared By _____

(continued)

Device (1)	Serial Number (2)	Location (3)	Device Name (4)	Local Storage (5)	Network Name (6)	Function (7)	Staff Members (8)	Comment (9)
IBM PC	304442	Rm 200	PC06	2/360K fld 640K RAM	Julie	Wkstation	Julie Gina	
Hard Disk & Tape Unit Tallgrass 6180	5044	Rm 201	HD01	80 Meg hd 60 Meg tape	AcctHd1	Shared	n/a	
Dot Matrix Printer Epson FX-80	300245	Rm 201	PRN01	2K buf	AcctPrn1	Shared	n/a	
Letter Quality Printers NEC 7710 NEC 7710	503281 33302	Rm 202 Rm 200	PRN02 PRN03	2K buf 2K buf	MktPrn2 n/a	Shared Dedi- cated to Julie	n/a Julie	
Hayes Modem	49555	Rm 200	MDM01		n/a	Dedi- cated to Julie	Julie	
Translator Unit	5033	Rm 201	TRS01		n/a		n/a	

Table 2.2

MULTI-USER SYSTEM DEVICES MAP

For Sample Multi-User System: Figure 2.2

Date _____   Prepared By _____

Device (1)	Serial Number (2)	Location (3)	Device Name (4)	Local Storage (5)	Cable Name (6)	Port Name (7)	User ID (8)	Comment (9)
IBM PC-XT	802932	Rm 201	PCXT01	20 Meg hd 360K fld 640K RAM	Console	Console	Theresa	System Manager
Televideo 925	419378	Rm 200	TERM01	1 pgs	TermA	TTY1	Louise	
Televideo 950	328341	Rm 200	TERM02	2 pgs	TermB	TTY2	Robert	
Televideo 950	400384	Rm 200	TERM03	4 pgs	TermC	TTY3	Iris	
Televideo 950	588290	Rm 200	TERM04	4 pgs	TermD	TTY4	Katie	
Televideo 950	388571	Rm 201	TERM05	2 pgs	TermE	TTY5	Suzie	
IBM PC	602844	Rm 201	PC01	2/360K fld 640K RAM	TermF	TTY6	Timmy	8087 Chip
Letter Quality Printers								
Nec 7710	59602	Rm 200	PRN01	2K buf	PrnA	LPR0	n/a	
Nec 7710	58038	Rm 201	PRN02	2K buf	PrnB	LPR1	n/a	
Dot Matrix Printer								
Epson FX-80	48817	Rm 201	PRN03	2K buf	n/a	n/a	n/a	Dedicated

Table 2.3

EXPLANATION OF CATEGORIES ON THE SYSTEM DEVICES MAPS
(in alphabetical order)

Category	Explanation	Example Local Area Network's IBM PC-AT (Figure 2.1)	Example Multi-User System's IBM PC (Figure 2.2)
Cable Name	Use this field to name each cable on the system. (Multi-user system map only. Disregard for stand-alone PC's.)	n/a	TermF
Comment	Use this field to specify important information about the device.	8087 math co-processor chip	8087 math co-processor chip
Device	Device type and model, manufacturer's name	IBM PC-AT	IBM PC
Device Name	A discrete, unchanging name the system manager assigns to each device.	PCAT01	PC01
Function	The device's role in the network. (LAN map only. Disregard for stand-alone PC's.)	Server	n/a
Local Storage	Type and capacity of local storage available on each device: hard disk, floppy disk drives, RAM, and buffers. (kilobytes or megabytes).	20 Meg hd 1.2 Meg fld 360K fld 512K RAM	2/360K fld 640K RAM
Location	Identifies where the device is located.	Room 201	Room 201

Table 2.3

EXPLANATION OF CATEGORIES
ON THE SYSTEM DEVICES MAPS
(in alphabetical order)

(continued)

Category	Explanation	Example Local Area Network's IBM PC-AT (Figure 2.1)	Example Multi-User System's IBM PC (Figure 2.2)
Network Name	The name by which the network knows the device. (LAN map only. Disregard for stand-alone PC's.)	Acct	n/a
Port Name	Use this field for the discrete name assigned to each port on each enclosure on the system. (Multi-user system map only. Disregard for stand-alone PC's.)	n/a	TTY6
Serial Number	Serial number assigned by the manufacturer	507220	602844
Staff Members	Names of staff members who use the device to send or receive messages. (LAN map only. For stand-alone PC's, see the step-by-step directions.)	Server: n/a	n/a
User ID	Use this column to identify the person associated with the terminal or personal computer. (Multi-user system map only. For stand-alone PC's, see the step-by-step directions.)	n/a	Timmy

Develop a System Devices Map

Prepare your system devices map with your system sketch nearby. For best results, read the entire series of steps before you start.

Once again, I urge you to use your database management program to create this map. Whether or not you use a database management program, collect information about your equipment using one of the blank system devices maps (Table 2.4 or 2.5).

Step One: Plan the map. The first step is to consider your requirements. Compare your system with the sample system you are using (Figure 2.1 or 2.2). Depending upon how your system differs from the sample, you might decide to change some of the column headings. For example, if your system is located in only one room, eliminate Column 3 for location. Determine the format you need before proceeding.

Step Two: Identify each device (Columns 1 & 2). Use Column 1 for the device type, model, and the manufacturer's name. Column 2 is for the serial number assigned to the device. Complete these columns for each device on the system.

Remember, the system devices map is a comprehensive listing of *all* devices, so be sure to include equipment not physically connected to your network or multi-user computer. (For equipment that is physically independent of your larger system, such as a lone PC and its printer, you will complete every column except Columns 6 and 7. You will leave these blank because they are for information that is either LAN-specific or multi-user-system-specific.)

Step Three: Identify the location (Column 3). Insert in Column 3 where each device is located.

Step Four: Name each device (Column 4). Serial numbers are not the most meaningful means of identification. Only when dealing with the vendor, the police, or an insurance company do serial numbers adequately help you keep track of equipment. Otherwise, serial numbers are cumbersome. For your system management purposes, a unique device name (Column 4) can be an efficient way to identify each device and also to keep track of how many similar pieces of equipment your system has.

To assign names to your devices, refer to your sample system and its devices map for guidance. Device names consecutively number each device according to its type. For example, the IBM PC on the sample multi-user system has the device name PC01, for

Table 2.4

LOCAL AREA NETWORK SYSTEM DEVICES MAP
Date _____   Prepared By _____

Device (1)	Serial Number (2)	Location (3)	Device Name (4)	Local Storage (5)	Network Name (6)	Function (7)	Staff Members (8)	Comment (9)

Table 2.5

MULTI-USER SYSTEM DEVICES MAP
Date _____   Prepared By _____

Device (1)	Serial Number (2)	Location (3)	Device Name (4)	Local Storage (5)	Cable Name (6)	Port Name (7)	User ID (8)	Comment (9)

PC number one. Should PC's be added to this system, they would be named PC02, PC03, and so on.

Equipment in the sample systems is coded with these abbreviations:

Device	Code
Personal Computer	PC
Terminal	TERM
Hard Disk/Tape Unit	HD
Printer	PRN
Modem	MDM
Translator Unit	TRS
System Unit	SU

You might use a different coding system. But, whatever codes you use, the device name should be as much a part of a device as its serial number, unchanging no matter where the equipment might travel in your company.

Step Five: Physically label each device. To each device, affix a label that bears the unique device name you assigned in step four. Place these labels where you can see them easily.

Step Six: List local storage for each device (Column 5). Various devices on your system have local storage capability. This storage can be mass storage (such as the 20 megabytes on a PC-AT's hard disk or the 60 megabytes on a tape backup unit), or it can be transient storage (such as the 2 kilobytes of space available in a printer's buffer, its holding platform for characters on their way to be printed). Terminals on your system also might have local storage for the video screen, called *pages* of memory.

List in Column 5 both the type and capacity of storage available locally on each device. For personal computers, indicate not only the amount of storage on each hard disk and floppy disk drive, but also the amount of RAM. For terminals, indicate the number of pages of memory; for printers, insert the size of internal buffers.

Use the following codes to identify storage types.

Storage Type	Code
Hard Disk	hd
Floppy Disk	fld
Pages of Memory	pgs
Tape	tape
Buffer	buf
Random Access Memory	RAM

Steps Seven, Eight, and Nine. Instructions for a local area network and a multi-user system diverge for steps seven, eight, and nine. Follow the instructions below for your system. If you manage only stand-alone PC's, go directly to step nine where you will find special instructions.

Local Area Network

Follow these steps if you manage a local area network.

Step Seven: Identify network names (Column 6). Insert in Column 6 your network's name for each device. The network name is the name that the network software uses to identify a device. For example, the IBM PC Network asks you to assign each computer a unique name.

In the sample LAN, network names are assigned according to who "owns" each device in the network. Each PC is assigned the name of the principle person operating it, Michael, for instance. The PC-AT, a server for the network, is assigned the name of its department, Acct.

Shared peripheral devices have compound names consisting of (1) the name of the computer that shares the device and (2) the name of the device itself. Therefore, the network name for the shared dot-matrix printer, AcctPrn1, is derived by combining the name of the IBM PC-AT which shares it, Acct, with the printer's unique name, Prn01, printer number 1

Multi-User System

Follow these steps if you manage a multi-user system.

Step Seven: Identify each cable on the system (Column 6). This step has two parts. You have to name each cable and physically label it:

(a) Use Column 6 to name each cable according to the type of device it connects to the system. Remember that a cable name should not be identical to specific device or port names because sometimes it is necessary to swap them. Refer to the sample multi-user system devices map as a guide to name system cables. For example, the cable attached to the first Televideo terminal listed (device TERM01), is named TermA.

(b) Attach to each cable a tag that indicates the name you assigned to it. To help yourself with troubleshooting, attach one of these tags to each end of the cable: at the computer end and at the device end.

Leave Column 6 blank for stand-alone PC's.

Step Eight: Identify each port on the system (Column 7). Earlier, a port was described as a place on the computer that on the system. (The zero is dropped in the network name to keep the number of characters to eight.)

Do not assign a network name to a device that is not functionally part of the network. This includes stand-alone PC's and dedicated equipment. For example, on the sample LAN, the printer and the modem attached to Julie's IBM PC do not have network names.

Step Eight: Identify each device's function (Column 7). Use this column to identify the function each device performs in the network. Indicate which computers are workstations and which are network servers. Also indicate whether a peripheral device is shared or dedicated.

Leave Column 7 blank for stand-alone PC's.

Step Nine: Staff members (Column 8). The IBM PC Network allows each computer to receive on-screen messages for more than one person. For networks like that, you need to keep track of who is receiving messages and at which computers. On the sample map, both Julie and Gina receive messages at PC06. If your system works this way, insert in Column 8 the names of people receiving messages at each computer.

allows you to connect devices to it, such as terminals and printers. Your vendor might have named your ports for you. You can find out by looking at the port locations on each enclosure to see if port names are marked. If they have been *and* if your system has only one enclosure, insert those names in Column 7 and skip to step nine. Otherwise, continue with this two-part step.

(a) Use Column 7 to name each port on the system. A port name is the name that the operating system uses to identify that port and the device connected to it. The operating system keeps track of these names in one of many system files. For example, UNIX identifies the ports terminals use in its **/etc/ttys** system file.

Identify every port, including any that are unassigned.

(b) Label each port on the system, whether you have one or multiple enclosures. If your system has multiple enclosures, include on the label a code to identify both the port and the enclosure. Thus, if you had two enclosures, each with nine ports, you could add a prefix to each port name that would identify which enclosure the port pertains to.

Leave Column 7 blank for stand-alone PC's.

Step Nine: User ID (Col-

For stand-alone PC's you can use this column to identify who uses each PC.

umn 8). Use this column to identify who uses each workstation or stand-alone PC.

Step Ten: Add comments (Column 9). Use Column 9 for comments. On the sample maps, this column notes which PC's have a math co-processor chip (8087), an optional chip that eases the load on the CPU by performing calculations with lightning speed. You might use this column to identify equipment specified as backups or equipment that you are planning to add, but have not installed yet.

Step Eleven: Date and distribute the map. Date and distribute copies of the system devices map. You will need a copy at your desk and at other strategic locations, such as in each room or on each floor that the system occupies. Be sure to keep a separate copy secure in the system library.

Step Twelve: Add names to the system sketch. With your completed system devices map in hand, add a name for each device to your system sketch. Refer to the sample sketches. The sample LAN (Figure 2.1) shows the network's name for the device: Suzanne, Rich, AcctPrn1, etc. The sample multi-user system (Figure 2.2) shows the device name, TERM01, PC01, and so on.

2.3 Identify Peripheral Equipment

If your system includes personal computers, you need a peripheral devices map. This map records the operating system name that each PC uses locally to identify the peripheral devices it uses, such as printers, plotters, and modems. For example, your PC's that run the DOS operating system probably use LPT1 and LPT2 to name the first and second printer attached to them.

These names are handy in a number of situations. First, suppose you are working on a PC that has both a letter-quality and a dot-matrix printer attached. When you want to switch printers, you will need to know how the PC names each one so that you can tell the computer to change between them.

The second example requires some explanation. Suppose you manage the sample LAN (Figure 2.1) and it is time to add the letter-quality printer to the PC–XT. You want every personal computer on the system to be able to use this printer. Now, each PC has a name for the printers it uses, such as LPT1 or LPT2 mentioned above. To set up the printer so that Suzanne, Phil, and others can print with it from their own workstations, you have to establish the name each PC will call the new printer. This is an easy task if you have a current peripheral devices map because you can see at a glance the names each PC already has assigned to existing printers and the names that remain available.

You might be asking why not have all PC's use the same name, say LPT1, for the new printer. If every PC were to use the same name for each peripheral, recordkeeping would be rather simple. But, real life systems usually do not work this way. It is possible and even likely that two PC's use different names for the same printer.

The sample (Figure 2.1) local area network's peripheral devices map (Table 2.6) illustrates that point. Michael's computer calls the shared Epson FX-80 printer LPT1, but Julie's calls it LPT2. The reason these two computers use different names is that Julie assigned LPT1 to her own Nec 7710 printer (PRN03), which she uses more frequently than the Epson. Michael, on the other hand, gave LPT1 to the FX-80 and LPT2 to the shared NEC (PRN02).

You may not be the one who actually assigns names to peripherals. Maybe you prefer people to handle this task for their own workstations. Regardless of who decides the names each PC uses for its peripherals, a peripheral devices map is an indispensable document because you need the information to manage system resources and to plan where additional equipment might be desirable or even allowed. For instance, the system manager of the sample LAN can see immediately that all three of the PC's listed could accept an LPT3 and that Julie's PC is the only one that has access to the modem.

An Important Note

The peripheral devices map and the system devices map share information. Yet, the peripheral devices map serves its special purpose, differing from the other map in the following three respects.

First, it takes the local PC perspective rather than that of the system as a whole. Second, that perspective means it records information only about peripheral devices each PC uses.

Obviously, if one of your personal computers does not address one of your printers, the PC will not have a name for it. So, for example, only Julie's PC has a name for the NEC printer (PRN03) because she never shares it. Likewise, if you have a printer on your multi-user system that is accessed only through terminals or PC's masquerading as terminals in terminal emulation mode, the printer would not be mentioned on the peripheral devices map because none of your PC's would have a name for it. The third difference is the *raison d'etre* for the peripheral devices map: it *alone* provides the local operating system name that your PC's use for their peripherals.

Develop a Peripheral Devices Map

The peripheral devices map for a local area network is slightly different from one for a multi-user system. Refer to the partially completed samples for each type of system on Tables 2.6 and 2.7. Each draws information from its respective system devices map. Use one of the blank peripheral devices maps (Table 2.8 or 2.9).

Step One: Identify system personal computers and the peripheral devices each uses. The sample peripheral devices map is divided into two parts: one for each personal computer and one for its peripheral devices. The goal is to record each personal computer's name for each device it uses, so be sure to include each PC in your company, even those that stand alone.

Step Two: Complete all columns except Column 3. Column 3 is the only column that asks for information not found on the system devices map. Hold off on this column until step three.

For the other columns, extract information from your system devices map. If you are adding to a database that you began with the system devices map, you already have this information.

Step Three: Indicate each PC's local name for each of the peripheral devices it has attached to it (Column 3). The local name is the operating system name that each computer uses to identify devices as if they were attached locally. (Managers of multi-user systems will recognize local names as similar to the port name on your system devices map.)

Step Four: Date and distribute the map. You need a copy of the peripheral devices map at your desk, at other strategic locations,

Table 2.6

LOCAL AREA NETWORK PERIPHERAL DEVICES MAP

For Sample Local Area Network: Figure 2.1

Date _____ Prepared By _____

PERSONAL COMPUTER			PERIPHERAL DEVICE		
Device Name (1)	Network Name (2)	Local Name For Peripheral Device (3)	Peripheral Device (4)	Device Name (5)	Device Network Name (6)
PC01	Michael	LPT1 LPT2 LPT3	Epson FX-80 NEC 7710 unassigned	PRN01 PRN02	AcctPrn1 MktPrn2
PC02	John	LPT1 LPT2 LPT3	NEC 7710 Epson FX-80 unassigned	PRN02 PRN01	MktPrn2 AcctPrn1
⋮	⋮	⋮	⋮	⋮	⋮
PC06	Julie	LPT1 LPT2 LPT3 COM1	NEC 7710 Epson FX-80 unassigned Hayes Modem	PRN03 PRN01 MDM01	n/a AcctPrn1 n/a

Table 2.7

MULTI-USER SYSTEM PERIPHERAL DEVICES MAP

For Sample Multi-User System: Figure 2.2

Date _____ Prepared By _____

PERSONAL COMPUTER			PERIPHERAL DEVICE	
Device Name (1)	User ID (2)	Local Name for Peripheral Device (3)	Peripheral Device (4)	Device Name (5)
PC01	Timmy	LPT1	Epson FX-80	PRN03
		LPT2	NEC 7710	PRN02
		LPT3	unassigned	

Table 2.8

LOCAL AREA NETWORK PERIPHERAL DEVICES MAP
Date _____   Prepared By _____

PERSONAL COMPUTER			PERIPHERAL DEVICE		
Device Name (1)	Network Name (2)	Local Name For Peripheral Device (3)	Peripheral Device (4)	Device Name (5)	Device Network Name (6)

Table 2.9

MULTI-USER SYSTEM PERIPHERAL DEVICES MAP
Date _____   Prepared By _____

PERSONAL COMPUTER			PERIPHERAL DEVICE	
Device Name (1)	User ID (2)	Local Name for Peripheral Device (3)	Peripheral Device (4)	Device Name (5)

and in the system library. Most managers find it helpful to keep a copy of this map at each PC listed on the map.

Congratulations. You are now more than halfway through the hardware documentation you need.

2.4 Document Switch Settings

A switch settings map documents the on/off status of those tiny switches located on various parts of the system. You have probably noticed switches on printers, on terminals, and maybe even on the internal circuit boards of personal computers.

These switch settings control how your system is set up, or configured. For example, one or more switches on a terminal might set the speed (baud rate) that data is transmitted between the terminal and the computer. Selected switches on an IBM PC-XT establish the number of disk drives and the amount of RAM the computer can use.

Most likely, you will need the switch settings map less often than the other maps we have looked at. But, when you need it, it is invaluable. In Chapter One, I mentioned that for some inexplicable reason, people often play with switches on equipment. I have yet to establish a motive, but it happens with such remarkable frequency that at the first sign of trouble with a system, I check to see that the switches are set correctly.

Suppose the switch settings on a printer or terminal are changed accidentally. An amateur mathematician can tell you the number of combinations you might try before you stumble on the right one. Deciphering vendor documentation can be little better. There is no need to stumble at all if you have documented the switch settings on your equipment as they were set when your system arrived.

Develop a Switch Settings Map

Use the blank switch settings map (Figure 2.3). To make sure you document switch settings for every device, keep your system sketch or system devices map nearby. (If you have not yet made them, refer to the appropriate sections earlier in this chapter.)

Step One: Power off as needed. Although some of your equipment has switches in an exterior location, it is likely you will have to open system enclosures to check the settings for some

---

Tip

There can be a disparity between the actual configuration and the way you have to set your system's switches. For example, if you are using part of RAM to simulate a disk drive you might have your switches set to reflect a number of drives that is different from the actual number of physical disk drives on your system.

switches. If so, be sure to turn off the power before you put your hands inside of equipment.

Step Two: Plan the maps. If you have standard configurations for specified equipment, such as for each IBM PC on the system, it makes sense to prepare only one standard switch settings map that you can duplicate as you need it. Make separate maps for equipment with switch settings that deviate from the standard.

Tip

Do not be alarmed if you cannot find switches where you expect them. Not all devices use switches. For example, some people expect to find switch blocks 1 and 2 on the main circuit board, called the motherboard, of an IBM PC-AT. There are none because the PC-AT's configuration is set with software instead of switches.

Step Three: Complete a map for each device. The switch settings map is organized by device. Complete a map (Figure 2.3) for each device that has switch blocks. In the space provided, insert each device's name, which you can take from your system devices map. Underneath each switch block in the figure, identify the location, for instance "Switch: #1 on the motherboard" for an IBM PC.

For each device, indicate the on/off setting of each switch on each switch block. (Simply look at each switch block to see which position each switch holds.) Figure 2.3 allows room for eight switches. Some switch blocks on your system may have fewer. For

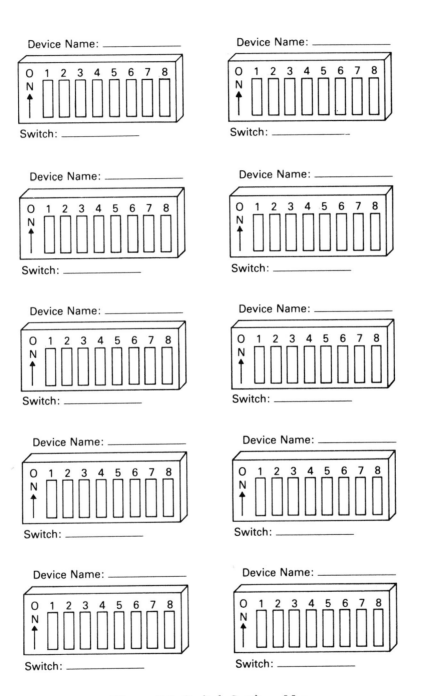

Figure 2.3. Switch Settings Map.

example, one of the switch blocks on an Epson FX-80 printer has only four switches to set. In this case, ignore the unneeded spaces when you fill in the map. For the time being also ignore switches located on the removable circuit boards installed inside of system enclosures. You will document those in the next section.

Step Four: Date and distribute. Date and distribute copies of the switch settings maps. Keep a complete set at your desk and in the system library. Nearby each device, keep a copy of the switch settings map that represents its settings.

2.5 Look Under the Hood

In this section, we will climb inside of your computer where we will find more essentials to document: your system's various circuit boards (also called boards, cards, adapters, or adapter cards) and the slots they occupy.

Typically, circuit boards provide one or more communication paths for the computer to send and sometimes receive data. For example, IBM's Monochrome Display and Printer Adapter card (Figure 2.4) allows the computer to send information to both a video display and a printer, two basic system needs. Some boards permit you to increase your system's capability or capacity, such as Intel's Above Board, which allows you to add RAM.

The principles apply to any system designed with removable circuit boards. For our example, let's peek inside of an IBM PC-AT. Figure 2.5 is the system unit of an IBM PC-AT which has a monochrome display (not shown), a hard disk, two diskette drives, and a printer (not shown). With eight slots available for circuit boards, the PC-AT in the figure has these boards installed:

1. A Monochrome Display and Printer Adapter card is installed in slot one. As we have seen, this card allows the computer to communicate with you on the video screen and it has a port to connect the AT with its printer.
2. A Fixed Disk and Diskette Drive Adapter card is installed in slot eight. This board allows the computer to save files to or retrieve them from the disk drives.

You can add capability to the PC-AT in Figure 2.5 because only two of its eight slots are filled. Like this system, most micro-

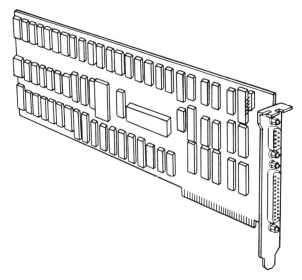

Figure 2.4. Monochrome Display and Printer Adapter Card.
(Courtesy of International Business Machines Corporation)

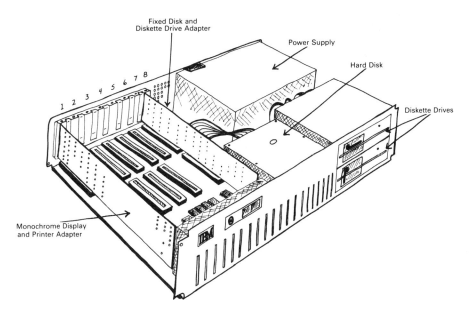

Figure 2.5. Inside an IBM PC-AT. The figure takes you under the hood of the system unit of an IBM PC-AT that supports a printer and a monochrome display.

computers designed with removable boards have more slots than are required to fill the basic functions.

System Boards Map

That brings us to the system boards map, which tracks all expansion slots and circuit boards installed in each one of your system's enclosures. Most people never see their system's expansion slots or boards because they are located out of sight. These slots and removable boards sit "backstage," so it is more difficult to keep track of them than of other equipment. Furthermore, if the IBM PC-AT in Figure 2.5 were closed, you would have insufficient information about the circuit boards it might contain, as we will see in a moment.

The need for a system boards map is less clear than for the system sketch, the system devices map, or the peripheral devices map. So, let's look at four examples to see when a boards map comes in handy.

First, your company has a chance to buy memory expansion boards at a fantastic savings. You must act quickly. Do you have to dash around with a screwdriver to physically check which PC's are able to accept more memory and also have an empty slot? (The two are not synonymous.) With a boards map in your library, you have this information without leaving your desk.

Second, you are adding a printer to the system and need a place to connect it. It is possible that one of your existing boards has a port available. Your boards map tells you immediately whether one is free and, if so, which computer has it.

Third, suppose a memory expansion card goes out on your boss's PC just when he or she has to complete a report by the end of the day. Scan your system boards map to find which PC's have a memory card you might "loan" your boss. (You still have to cope with the problem of who needs the memory more—your boss or the person operating the PC with the available memory.) Of course, with no boards map you eventually would find a memory board, but not without wasting your time and needlessly disrupting other people.

Fourth, imagine managing a multi-user system with a problem terminal. The vendor on the telephone suggests that you reseat the board that connects the problem terminal to the computer. With a system boards map, you can open the system enclosure and instantly know which board to test without having to shuffle around inside.

As you can see, the system boards map can be extremely useful. Follow these steps to complete one for your system. First, please take note of the warning.

| Warning |

Protect yourself and your system against incineration. When you look at the back of an enclosure, it is sometimes unclear phat occupies a slot or if the slot is filled at all. You probably will have to open one or more enclosures, maybe even demove a board or two, to complete the system boards map. It is dangerous to do this with the power on. Protect yourself and your system: disengage ALL power supplies BEFORE you put your hands inside of an enclosure.

Develop a System Boards Map

You will find it helpful to have your system sketch or system devices map nearby when you prepare the system boards map. This way, you can see easily that you have included every system enclosure which contains electronic circuit boards.

The system boards map for a LAN and a multi-user system have identical formats. The system boards map and the step-by-step instructions below assume that you have a system devices map.

Step One: Plan the map. Survey your system devices map to account for your system components. Consider the following six issues.

First, if your system's boards came from different vendors, consider adding a column to insert the name of each board's manufacturer.

Second, if you have a standard configuration for identical equipment, such as one for IBM PC's, you could prepare a section of a boards map for this purpose and identify it as the standard configuration. Then add specifics only for other enclosures and for PC's that deviate from the standard. The partially completed sample boards map (Table 2.10) follows this method. For instance, PC01 through PC05 on the sample local area network (Figure 2.1) are configured according to the standard, so their slots are not itemized. PC06, however, deviates from the standard configuration because it has a printer and a modem attached, so it is listed separately.

Third, remember that the system boards map documents all removable circuit boards located in every enclosure. This means that you should document (1) boards on enclosures that stand alone, including those in a PC that is independent of your LAN or multi-user system; and (2) boards that support devices sharing the same enclosure as the boards themselves, such as the disk drive adapter card that supports disk drives housed inside of the IBM PC-AT in Figure 2.5.

Fourth, remember that a single board sometimes serves more than one function. For instance, standard PC's in the sample local area network have a board in Slot #1 that not only supports a monochrome display, but also has a parallel port available to attach a printer.

Fifth, some boards have switches that must be set to on or off position as described earlier in this chapter. If that is the case with your system, you will need a column to document the switch settings for each board. (See the sample boards map, Table 2.10. The 384K RAM card for standard PC's has one switch block with switches 2, 3, 4, 5, and 8 set on.)

Sixth, if you have resisted the idea of using a database management program to develop your hardware configuration documents, please give very serious consideration to doing so now.

Step Two: Identify each enclosure and its slot numbers. (Columns 1 & 2). Use Column 1 on Table 2.11 to identify each enclosure with the device name you assigned to it when you developed your system devices map. Insert in Column 2 consecutive numbers for each expansion slot the enclosure has, regardless of whether the slot is filled or empty.

Step Three: Insert the serial number of each board (Column 3). Check purchasing/receiving documents or physically examine each circuit board (with the **POWER OFF**) to find the serial number for each board. Insert that number in Column 3.

Step Four: Identify each slot's status (Column 4). Identify the status of each expansion slot. Refer to the sample map (Table

2.10). Use Column 4 to specify which devices each board supports and which slots and ports are available.

Distinguish serial from parallel ports. Why? Serial ports and parallel ports transmit information differently, so you want to identify each type you have. The difference between them can be likened to how they each would send eight horses from point A to point B. Serial ports send one horse at a time; a parallel port would send all eight at once. A parallel port appears to have the advantage of sending data more efficiently, and it would have that advantage if sending eight horses all at once were always possible. But it is not. Sometimes you have to send your horses one at a time, such as when you send information over a telephone line. This means that you want to plan when to use your serial ports, for example when transmitting information over a modem, and when to use your parallel ports, for example when printing a file on the office printer.

Step Five: Document board switch settings (Column 5). Some of your boards might have switch blocks like those you documented in the previous section. If so, use Column 5 to record switch settings located on each board that has them. A simple way to do this is to insert only the number of each switch set to the on position. (Refer again to the sample map, Table 2.10.)

Step Six: Date and distribute. Date and distribute copies of the boards maps. You should have a copy at your desk and at other strategic locations, such as at each enclosure represented on the map. Keep a master copy in the system library.

Conclusion

The hardware documentation you have just created puts you in charge of your equipment and organizes much of the information you need in order to make quick decisions. With the system boards map behind you, you have established half of the foundation for your system library. With the next chapter, you will develop the other half.

Table 2.10

SYSTEM BOARDS MAP
Date _____   Prepared By _____
(sample)

ENCLOSURE		EXPANSION SLOT		
Device Name (1)	Slot # (2)	Serial # (3)	Status (4)	Board Switch Settings[1] (5)
Standard IBM PC	1	—	Monochrome Display	
			Parallel Port Available	
	2	—	Network Adapter Card	
	3	—	384K Random Access Memory Card	2,3,4,5,8
	4	—	Slot Available	
	5	—	Floppy Disk Drive Adapter	
PC01 - PC05			(standard)	
PC06	1	892874	(standard)	
		582h122	Letter Quality Nec 7710 Printer	
	2	66372	(standard)	
	3	671900	(standard)	
	4	822040	Asynchronous Communications Adapter Card for Hayes 1200 B Modem	
	5	803785	(standard)	

1. Insert switch numbers set to the "on" position only.

Table 2.11

SYSTEM BOARDS MAP

Date _____   Prepared By _____

ENCLOSURE		EXPANSION SLOT		
Device Name (1)	Slot # (2)	Serial # (3)	Status (4)	Board Switch Settings[1] (5)

1. Insert switch numbers set to the "on" position only.

3

Complete Your System Library: Beyond Hardware

UNIX. (Multi-user systems by nature tend to have more system files than networks do.)

System files are as unique as your data. It is unlikely your vendor has exact copies, so keep both original and backup copies for each configuration.

4. **Automatic processing files.** Your system allows you to set up your own files for automatic processing. You can write a series or batch of commands to perform repetitious tasks, which you then store in a file for later use. Each time you call upon the file, the computer follows your script, performing each command that you inserted in sequence. These batch (DOS) or script (UNIX) files are your own ''mini-programs'' which eliminate the need to enter command sequences again and again.

   You probably have a batch file that is executed automatically each time you start the computer. One of the simplest batch files for a PC sets the time and date. However lengthy or complex, batch or script files are as vulnerable as data files. And, like system files, they are unduplicated outside of your company. If you lose them, you have to recreate them from scratch. Keep original and backup copies of the important files to guard against the day your working copies are damaged.

5. **Data file originals**. Staff members might want to store data file originals on a diskette in the system library instead of on a hard disk or on diskettes at their workstations. Usually it is a matter of security when people prefer that you protect particularly sensitive information in the system library.

6. **Data file backup.** Your library should house current backup copies of all data files. These backups are the only insurance that your company has against disastrous loss of information.

   Keep two sets on site: (1) a ''full backup,'' a complete copy of everything residing on the hard disk on a given day; and (2) a ''partial backup,'' a set that contains current copies of files revised since the last complete backup. Store a second copy of your full backup at an off-site location. (Turn to Chapter Seven for a more detailed discussion about the backup procedure.)

7. **Data file archives.** Data file archives are historical files, copies of documents you should keep for a significant period of

time. An example is a successful grant proposal for a five-year project. You keep most archival copies for long, sometimes indefinite periods. For safety, keep both an original and a duplicate copy of each.

Table 3.1

CONTENTS OF DISKETTE AND TAPE PORTION OF THE SYSTEM LIBRARY

---

1. Software originals and backups
2. Installed versions of applications software: originals and backups
3. System files: originals and backups
4. Automatic processing files
5. Data file originals (in rare cases)
6. Data file backup
7. Data file archives

Keep Track: A Sample Method

In sheer volume and variety, library tapes and diskettes challenge every system manager. Rarely will you simply file them for posterity. When someone accidentally erases a file or when someone wants an archived spreadsheet to use as a template, you should be able to retrieve a copy from your library tapes or diskettes.

Organize yours now. This task is best done early in the life of a system, but it is never too late.

Several means are available to you. Partitioned storage works well, but only if you and others unfailingly return each item to its place. Both dots and color-coded labels are popular. Dots tend to adhere poorly until they find their way anywhere other than where you want them. One dot clinging to the innards of a floppy disk drive will make a label fan of you in short order.

Use your color-coded labels systematically. You could, for example, use one set of special colors to identify software and another for data files. Further code files to indicate varying levels of security, with bright red for high security documents and green for low security ones.

Be sure the scheme you select provides an easy way for you and others to retrieve and return home those multiplying numbers of tapes and diskettes.

Sample Method: Guidelines

Let's examine one way to organize the seven categories of information described in the previous section. The first step is to decide how to store the information on diskette or tape. Here are sample guidelines:

Guideline for diskettes. A single diskette should contain information from only one of the seven categories. This means system files will not reside on the same diskette as batch or script files, data files will not share a diskette with installed versions of applications programs, and so on.

Guideline for tapes. Tape is reserved strictly for full and partial backups of a hard disk.

Sample Method: The Detail

Next, enlist the help of labels, color codes, and printed directories:

1.   **Labels:** Use two categories of labels: one for software (Table 3.2) and one for data files (Table 3.3). Both can be duplicated on commercially available self-adhesive labels. (The typical label that comes with 5 1/4 inch diskettes is too small to hold the information you need.)

     Here's how to use each of the two sample labels.

     a.   *Software label.* The software label (Table 3.2) has six fields:

          1.   *Program.* Use this field to name the software program. Include qualifiers that apply, such as "XENIX System Files" or "Framework II Installed."

          2.   *Version.* Indicate the manufacturer's version of the software program, for instance 1.0 or 3.1. You need to know it because there can be significant differences among the various versions of a particular program.

3.   *Original.* Identify if the copy is an original or a backup. With an original, simply place an X in the space; with a backup copy, write *backup*.

4, 5.   *Capacity and Amount Used.* Indicate the capacity of the media and the amount used. This information will help you avoid overloading or seriously under using a diskette or a tape. With diskettes, you also will sidestep the deadly mixture of mistaking a 360K diskette for one that holds 1.2 megabytes.

6.   *Restrictions.* Note precautions in this field. For example, indicate an especially restrictive software license. Or, place a warning when a diskette contains a file that works nicely on one computer but would cause serious damage on another. For instance, you must alert yourself and others to a diskette that automatically erases files on drive C whenever you boot a computer with that diskette inserted in drive A. Otherwise, you risk losing everything stored on a hard disk.

Table 3.2
SOFTWARE LABEL

Program:		Version:
Original:	Capacity:	Amount Used:
Restrictions:		

Table 3.3
DATA LABEL

Date:	ID:		Custodian:
Original ____	Backup ____	Archive ____	Destroy:
Program:		Capacity:	Amount Used:
Restrictions:			

b. *Data label.* The data label (Table 3.3) has eleven fields.

1. *Date.* This field is handy for a couple of purposes that depend on the kind of information you store. Date backup copies according to the day you made them. To segregate archival data, use fiscal years.

2. *ID.* Assign a unique identifier. You could consecutively number library diskettes and tapes. Or you may prefer to use the identifier that you specify with the operating system, the volume label. The point is to have a quick and unquestionable means to distinguish each diskette and tape.

3. *Custodian.* This field is for cases when someone other than you is responsible for information in the library. (For example, you will want to identify individuals in charge of diskettes that contain data file originals.) Otherwise, you can ignore or eliminate this field.

4, 5, 6, 7. *Original, Backup, Archive, and Destroy.* Check the appropriate box to indicate if the data is an original, backup, or archival copy. For archival data, indicate the date beyond which you can destroy it.

8. *Program.* Identify the name and version of software programs used to create the data.

9, 10. *Capacity and Amount Used.* These fields serve the same purpose as on the software label. See the preceding explanation.

11. *Restrictions.* Insert details about the security requirements for the diskette or tape. For example, write "For Accounting Department Use Only" on the label for a tape that contains payroll information.

2. **Color codes:** The data label and software label are distinct enough to protect against confusion. That means you need only four colors to distinguish your seven categories of information.

Color code your labels with marking pens. Here is one scheme you might use:

Sample Color Codes

Color to Use: **To Indicate:**
  Blue   =   Backups of vendor-provided software
                 and data file originals
  Yellow =   Installed versions of software and
                 data file backup
  Orange =   System files and
                 data file archives
  Brown   =   Batch or script files

3. **Printed directories:** If you can, print directory listings. Labels rarely are large enough to hold a full description of what resides on a diskette or tape. To remove the mystery, keep a current paper copy of the directory for each diskette and tape. Store them in the diskette jacket or tape container. For this to work, you must always return system library diskettes and tapes to their original jackets or containers.

3.2 Take Control of Software

In the preceding section you saw one way to organize floppy diskette and tape portions of your library. This section helps you with your software.

You should know exactly what programs you have and how you set up each one to work with your system. The more applications you have, the easier it is to lose track. You will find the information you develop here invaluable when you are troubleshooting, reinstalling software, or making decisions about new programs to acquire.

Develop a Software Inventory

A software inventory is a bit like a system devices map. The inventory is a comprehensive list of your utilities, operating systems, applications software, and even programs staff members produce. But it is more than a simple inventory because it includes pertinent facts about each program, such as its license agreement and its RAM requirement.

You will find this information useful in a number of situations. For example, the fact that you have RAM requirements listed in one place will simplify the process of allocating RAM. (See Chapter Five for details.) The inventory can benefit others, too. Distribute it freely to let people know which time-saving packages are available to them. Also distribute it to inform people about software license agreements. Your company is less likely to suffer license violations if people understand the restrictions.

Steps to Complete a Software Inventory

To create your software inventory, use Table 3.4 and follow these step-by-step instructions:

Step One: Collect documents you need. Gather the documents you need to inventory each piece of software available on your system. Aside from the manuals your vendor provided, probably all you need is the collection of original software diskettes or the packing slip that accompanied the software when it arrived.

Step Two: Identify each package (Columns 1-3). Complete Columns 1 through 3 for all of the software available on your system. Include operating systems, utility programs, communications packages, applications software programs, and even programs you and other staff members have written.

Step Three: Insert the memory requirement (Column 4). When a software package is invoked, some or all of its program files are copied into RAM where they remain until you exit the program. (With some programs, a portion remains in RAM until you turn off the power or reboot your system.) Column 4 of the inventory is for you to record the amount of RAM each package on your system requires. (We'll see in Chapter Five how vital this information is to successful RAM management.)

Unfortunately, this is not a straightforward matter. Nevertheless, there is a simple way to calculate a ballpark figure for how much RAM a program needs. First, run a directory listing of a particular program's files. Then, add up the amount of space these files occupy and increase it by 15 percent. The result should be close to the amount of memory you need for the program.

Step Four: Add licensing information (Column 5). Software licensing is a sensitive matter, so you must be careful to abide by agreements your company has with the developers of your software packages. Because vendors offer such a variety of licensing

Table 3.4

SOFTWARE INVENTORY

Date _____   Prepared By _____

Program (1)	Version (2)	Serial Number (3)	RAM Requirement (4)	License (5)	Invoke With (6)	Comment (7)

terms for their products, use Column 5 to record licensing restrictions for each of your programs. Be explicit. For example, you might insert the maximum number of simultaneous users who legally can use a piece of software. Or you might indicate the device name(s) (see Section 2.2) of each workstation legally allowed to run the package.

Step Five: Identify how to invoke the program (Column 6). Use this column to specify the command which invokes the program. Information in the column is particularly useful when you keep more than one installed version of a program on the hard disk, each with different commands to load them. For example, you might have one name to invoke the version of a program that seasoned people use and another name for the version that novices use.

Step Six: Insert helpful comments (Column 7). This column is for comments. For example, if you have multiple installed versions of a particular program, use this column to describe each one, such as "for experienced users." Or if you use more than one operating system, use this column to name the operating system the program runs under.

Step Seven: Date and distribute. Date and distribute a copy of this inventory to every staff member. Keep a copy at your desk and a master copy in the system library.

How to Create Software Defaults Maps

Scan your software inventory and you will see packages listed that allow you to customize them to suit your needs. Usually the features you control have preset or default values which are called into play if you take no action. For example, the IBM PC Network permits more than one person to receive messages at the same workstation, allowing you to specify up to twelve additional names for each workstation. If you leave this feature alone, the network defaults to one additional name.

Chapter Two's sample local area network illustrates the point. Its system devices map (Table 2.1) shows that Suzanne's workstation, (PC05), is set up to receive messages for Suzanne and for two additional people, Theresa and Lydia. Michael's workstation receives them only for Michael.

Setting such features is one way to manage resources and to control how well the system performs. You probably can control selected features on every purchased program: your operating system, network program, utility programs, applications programs, and communications package.

Needless to say, the more control you take over the system in this way, the more essential it is to maintain clear records. Organize specialized information about how you have customized your software on a software defaults map (Table 3.5). Use the map to keep track of the range of allowed values, the original defaults, and the values you assign. Even if you retain original default settings, it is useful to have a defaults map when you are troubleshooting, developing procedures or making decisions about system resources.

Before you chart your software defaults maps, let's see how it is done. We will take a closer look at Suzanne's IBM PC (PC05) in the sample local area network (Figure 2.1). Her PC has its own custom default values for using the IBM PC Network program. Six of these defaults are documented on the sample software defaults map, Table 3.6.

At the top of the table, the IBM PC Network is identified as the program documented. Suzanne's computer is identified as the computer in question: an IBM PC with device name PC05.

The rest of the table lists each item (Column 1), its allowed and original default values (Columns 2 and 3, respectively), and its operative default (Column 4). The first item listed shows that the IBM PC Network would allow a range from one to thirty-two for the number of devices a workstation uses at a time. Suzanne's PC is set to use seven devices at one time, instead of the original default value of only five. The third item listed is the one described earlier: a PC in the network could receive messages for up to twelve additional people, but Suzanne's PC receives them for only two additional names, one more than the default value of one. Because more than one person receives messages on the PC, the system manager also set up the network to increase the temporary storage area, or buffer, for waiting messages (item two) from the original default of 1600 characters to 3200 characters.

Now, follow these steps to complete defaults maps for your software programs.

Steps to Complete the Software Defaults Maps

Step One: Collect the documents you need before you begin. You need a software defaults map (Table 3.5) for each package you have, whether or not you have changed its default values. You also need individual maps for personal computers that have unique default sets for particular programs. (For example, to produce reports with special formatting, an analyst using a stand-alone PC might need unique values on the word processor.)

With that in mind, the first step is to be sure you have everything you will want to consult while preparing your complete set of maps. You need the following:

1. Your software inventory (Table 3.4) to make sure you document defaults for all of your programs;
2. Your system devices map (Table 2.4 or 2.5) to identify PC's, if any;
3. Manuals for each of your software programs.

Step Two: Complete the subtitles. Identify the software and the computer (if applicable) in the spaces provided at the top of each map, Table 3.5. If your system has only one computer, or if all PC's use identical default values, ignore the spaces used to identify device type and device name and complete only one map per program for the system as a whole.

Step Three: Insert defaults and values (Columns 1, 2 & 3). List in Column 1 each item, or program feature, you can control. Next, for each of your programs, specify in Column 2 the range of values the program allows for each feature. Indicate in Column 3 the original default value for each feature.

You will find the information you need to complete these three columns in your manuals, either in a configuration section or in the installation guide.

Step Four: Insert the operative default value (Column 4). The operative default value is the one that the program is set up to use. If a particular item was never defined, the operative default should be identical to the original default. Otherwise, the operative default is the value specified when the program was installed.

You can determine the operative default values by running the program's installation procedure or by checking the appropriate system file, such as the CONFIG.SYS DOS file. (Before you do the former, please read about producing paper copies of the installation process on page 88.)

Step Five: Date and distribute. Keep a complete set of software default maps at your desk and in the system library. If you

---

Table 3.5

SOFTWARE DEFAULTS MAP
Date _____   Prepared By _____

[program name & version]

[computer type]   [device name]

Item (1)	Default Allowed (2)	Original Default (3)	Operative Default (4)

Table 3.6

SOFTWARE DEFAULTS MAP
Date _____   Prepared By _____

(sample)

IBM Network 1.00
[program name & version]

IBM PC   PC05
[computer type]   [device name]

Item (1)	Default Allowed (2)	Original Default (3)	Operative Default (4)
1. Number of devices station uses at a time	1-32	5	7
2. Size of buffer for waiting messages	256-60,000 characters	1600	3200
3. Number of additional names to receive messages for	0-12	1	2
4. Number of devices to share with others	1-150	10	4
5. Size of buffer for printing (for your shared printer)	512-16,384 bytes	512	512
6. Number of network computers to use your devices	1-25	10	10

have PC's, put copies of their maps near them. For example, the manager of the sample LAN would keep a copy of the sample default map (Table 3.6) nearby Suzanne's IBM PC.

Tip

Sometimes, vendors change the preset value before you take possession of the software. The reason is to tailor it for your system. In this case, you could use as "original defaults" the values your vendor set instead of those you find in your manual.

Three Invaluable Paper Copies

With your software inventory and defaults maps in hand, you have excellent records about your software programs. You know what software you have on hand and how you have customized it. This brings us to the final category of software documentation you need: paper copies (also called *hard copies*).

Yes, you need these too. Remember the seven categories of information described in Section 3.1? The diskette or tape copy of each category is your insurance against the day that the software or data is lost. But, you also need paper copies of these three categories: (1) application program installations, (2) system files, and (3) automatic processing files. (Turn to Section 3.1 to review these categories).

Your paper copies will be invaluable whenever you need to alter something or track down the source of a problem. Let's look at specific examples for each of the three categories:

1. **Application program installation.** The process of installing a program can be lengthy. In that case, you can be 99 percent sure that you need a hard copy of your responses to the sequence of questions you answered when you installed the program.

   Consider the following example. Suppose you decide to make one or two changes to how your word processing program is installed. Unfortunately, many programs do not allow you to make only one or two changes without also putting you through the tedium of scanning menu after menu that has no bearing on the changes you are about to make. Without a hard copy, you probably will find yourself considering each and every question, whether or not it pertains to your immediate task.

You would save time if you had a printed copy of the entire installation process, one that documents each question and highlights your responses. The time it takes to reinstall a program can be reduced by as much as 80 or 90 percent because you are able to focus on the changes and ignore areas you want to leave untouched. In fact, with this paper documentation, you can delegate the job of reinstalling or tailoring software to your backup person, with the confidence that all will proceed smoothly.

2. **System files.** Paper copies of system files can be a big help when the system is in trouble. For example, when you run into a problem with a terminal or a modem, you will have the paper copy of a system file to verify that the rate for data transmission (baud rate) is correctly set. (Like switch settings, baud rates frequently are changed "by accident.")

A paper copy also comes in handy whenever you make a change to one of these files. The reason is the same as the one mentioned for the installation programs mentioned above: You save time because you are free to focus on changes.

3. **Automatic processing files.** Keep paper copies of your batch or script files, particularly the long ones. Hard copies will be a welcome time-saver when you decide to change an existing file.

Paper copies of batch files bring an added benefit if you manage a system with personal computers. Use your judgment to funnel copies to people with PC's. This gives everyone the opportunity to share useful files, including those that people create themselves. Existing files can be patterns for new ones.

But, be very careful! Be sure people know what they are doing. The wrong batch file can destroy the information on a hard disk. If you are not sure staff members can handle batch files, send around a list that describes what your batch files can do, then install for people whichever files they select. It is a great way to increase productivity.

Producing Paper Copies

Now that you know the paper copies you need, let's see how and when it is most feasible to produce them.

1. Installation programs. The best way to produce a paper copy of your responses to questions in an installation program is to print the process while you run it. That way you will capture all of the program's prompts and each of your responses. Wait until the next time you run each program rather than do it for documentation purposes only. If you intend to adjust how one of your programs is installed, do it now and be sure to print the process. By all means, do not print the process for its own sake unless the process is short or you are about to go on vacation and you think your backup person will need a hard copy while you are away.

The typical response to a question in these programs is only one or two characters long. Searching for short responses in the midst of the program's verbiage can be tedious. So, it is a good idea to mark your responses with a highlighter pen as soon as you have a hard copy in hand. With your responses highlighted, the next time you run the program, your eye can jump rapidly from response to response.

2 & 3. System files and batch or script files. Print system files and batch or script files right away. You can accomplish this with ease and speed using the operating system print command followed by multiple file names to print a copy of each file you name. (With DOS, the command is PRINT; with UNIX, the command is **lp** or **lpr**.)

As soon as you print any of your paper copies, annotate them with identifying information. Date each one and make clear what it documents. Keep master copies in your system library.

3.3 Manage Your Library

The preceding sections show how to prepare most of the critical components of your system library. Earlier, in the introduction to Chapter Two, I stated that a system library takes time to build. By now, you probably agree. This section takes you nearly to the end of the final mile. When you complete it, you will have a library collection and a structure to manage it. That structure is neatly summed up in the system library motto:

"If it's worth keeping, keep track of it, keep it current, keep it available, and keep it safe."

Keep Track With a Library Inventory

Managing the system library implies that you know what it contains. You already know that system libraries collect a medley of information: manuals, custom documentation, various categories of diskettes and tapes, updates, and revisions. There is more: purchase, warranty, and insurance documents; books; magazines; catalogues; and internal procedures. Some of this material will appear as if by magic in your in-box. But because you must develop your own internal procedures, ensuing chapters will acquaint you with the indispensable ones.

Your library will contain a vast amount of information. At times, you might feel that the unending influx will be your undoing. Unless you can function with a jumble of material scattered across shelves, strewn on tables, piled on the floor or on filing cabinets, do yourself a favor: organize your system library *now*.

A system library inventory will help and it is easier to develop than the catalogues that your public library keeps. Your inventory is simply a comprehensive list of everything that you keep in your library.

There is no question that you need an inventory if you have a complicated system. Comfort yourself with the thought that to create the inventory is a smaller job than to develop the documents. If your system is simple, pulling together an inventory will be a snap, so easy, in fact, that you might be tempted to dispense with it entirely. Base your decision on the potential trouble for your company and for your successor if you depart without leaving behind a list of what should be found in the system library.

Tips To Create a System Library Inventory

Use Table 3.7 as a system library inventory form to list the contents of your library. The form provides space for four entries: (1) the title of the item, (2) a description that further identifies it, (3) a notation about access—the security requirement, and (4) additional comments.

Consider creating your library inventory with a database management program, using the four categories shown on Table 3.7.

Table 3.7

SYSTEM LIBRARY INVENTORY
Date _____   Prepared By _____

Title	Description	Access	Comment

That would allow you to print custom reports of library holdings that can be a real convenience for you and others using the system.

Tip #1: One reason to use a database program. People should know what tools and information are available to them, but that does not mean you have to advertise library materials that you cannot permit them to use or see. Few people want to know about something they cannot have. If you use a database management program, you can easily omit restricted documents from the published version of your inventory.

Tip #2: Specify access. If possible, be brief in noting the security requirement for each item. For example, a document that is freely available to all staff members could be identified as a "public" document. If an item has restricted availability, specify who has access to it. Mark items that cannot be taken from the library area with the words, "Library Use Only." We will discuss library access later in this section.

Tip #3: Distribute the inventory. Is distribution an issue? Yes. Publish the system library inventory so that people know what is available. Everyone assumes you have manuals in your library, but do they know you also have a small collection of readable books written about your system and your software? Someone having trouble with your database program who feels discouraged by the prospect of coping with a manual might feel comfortable prowling through a book written about the program.

Tip #4: Make copies. Treat the inventory as you would any other library document. Date it and keep a master copy in the library and one at your desk.

Keep Your Library Current

The size of your library inventory is testimony that computers create and attract a lot of material. All of the information you have will change or grow in volume and content as your system changes. As soon as a system is installed, it begs to develop. You'discover ways to fine tune it to get better performance from it. Maybe you add new equipment. Eventually, the operating system will be revised and at some point you might buy new software or updates of existing programs.

Those changes put demands on you. It means the library is in constant flux. You must add new material and update what you already have. On top of it all, you are on everyone's mailing list, so you are inundated with magazines and with unsolicited product and training program advertisements. Of these, you will toss out some, save others, and act on a few. Keeping your library up to date can be a formidable job. Follow these six rules to keep it current without spending all of your time doing it.

Rules to Keep the Library Current

Rule #1: When to be fanatical. Identify the items which *must* be kept current at all times. Typically, these critical documents show the current condition of your system. They include nearly all system files, hardware maps, and software documents. At the head of the list are your data file backups. Be a fanatic with these.

Rule #2: When to be reasonable. Assuming that you keep the critical documents current, you should be reasonable otherwise. Keep abreast of changes as best you can, but accept the fact that you may be unable to keep everything in the library current all of the time. Although three weeks might pass before you replace outdated pages of the operating system manual with the revisions, the system probably will not suffer.

Rule #3: Avoid creeping chaos. Do not permit the library to creep its way into chaos and deterioration. An outdated library promotes disaster in times of trouble and fritters away your time in calm moments. Keep your materials easy to locate and easy to update.

Rule #4: Keep the library in mind. Whenever a system-related "event" occurs, ask yourself if the goings-on bear on the contents of the library. See if you can add to the following list of events that require changes to a library document:

(1)   a service call
(2)   equipment replaced, moved, or sent out for repair
(3)   revisions to software packages
(4)   hardware or software additions
(5)   incoming or outgoing staff members

Rule #5: Keep valuable antiques. *Do not* discard documentation that you believe is obsolete after the system is upgraded. We saw earlier that you cannot predict when you must resort to an older version of software. In such an emergency, this documentation is priceless, so keep these and other valuable antiques.

Rule #6: Toss the trash. Keeping the library current means more than updating or adding material. It also sometimes means filling the waste basket. Because there is so much coming in, get rid of what you can. Destroy archival material after its destruction date. Discard whatever you do not need.

Keep Your Library Both Available and Safe

In this section we will look at the third and fourth pieces of the system library management puzzle. Aside from the usual measures to protect your library from environmental hazards (such as storing backups off-site in case of fire), safety and availability center mostly around access. This section describes how to strike the right balance between easy access and solid protection.

Encourage Library Use

When people know the type of information you keep in the library, when they know that they can count on its being current and well-protected, they want to use the library as borrowers and as depositors. People may stop by to check a minor point in documentation or to bring diskette copies of sensitive files that they want you to secure. Encourage people by making them feel welcome. Locate your library conveniently. Make it easy for people to use. If you can, have a desk available for them and provide access to the system.

Suggested Access Rights

Access to library material is more than a matter of physical arrangements. Access implies that you know who has the need and who has the right to see information. Keep a "public library" for unrestricted materials and a "private library" for the more sensitive things. Lock up whatever is confidential and control use of the rest.

Single copy materials, such as vendor-provided manuals, should stay in the library all of the time. That way people can count on finding information that is difficult to replace. Somebody trying to meet a deadline who runs into a snag with your spreadsheet program would be understandably angry to find the manual lost or otherwise unavailable. If people are going to check materials out of the library, keep duplicate copies, with one copy designated for library use only.

In the rest of this section, you will find ways to handle access to the various categories of information in your library.

1. **Vendor-provided documentaion for hardware and software.** In nearly every case, make vendor-provided documentation freely available to others, even if the material is for library use only. Exceptions might be documentation for system files, for software installation programs, and for debugging tools (software that allows you to poke around and alter program instruction code). All of these tempt people who want "to experiment" or who have malicious intentions. Otherwise, most vendor-provided documentation is important reference material for everyone who uses the system.

2. **Hardware and software maps.** Usually, problems do not arise from letting people see how you have configured hardware and software. In fact, remember that the final step to develop your hardware and software documents almost always advises you to distribute copies. But, you must be able to rely on one copy as accurate, so protect all master copies of hardware and software maps with full security.

   Prepare for the inevitability of someone losing a copy of this or that map. Make enough extra copies of each map for the library so that people can consult them and even take one back to their desks.

3. **Floppy diskette and streaming tape versions of valuable information.** Control these 100 percent. *All* system library diskettes and tapes are precious. Everyone will rest easy with the knowledge that you protect these primary copies.

   People can contact you when and if they need information stored on diskette or tape. When it happens, make a copy especially for them. You court trouble if you pass your originals around freely.

Assuming 100 percent control, the kind of access you allow still depends on the kind of information stored on the tape or diskette:

a. *Software originals and backups.* Under no circumstances should anyone have free access to original program diskettes. (The only time an original should be used is to make backup copies the day it arrives.) Otherwise, generally, there is no reason to restrict access to software (except for debugging tools that can be used to damage a program).

b. *Installed versions of applications software.* Treat master copies of your installed applications software the same as you do software originals and backups. Some system managers consider these more precious than the vendor's originals. Why? Because your installed versions represent the software as *your* system uses it, which in turn represents the time and thought that went into both deciding how the program best meets your system's needs and setting the program up to do just that.

c. *System files.* System files should be kept absolutely confidential whenever possible. You will avert no end of intentional or accidental trouble if you keep these files as far away as possible from prying eyes. So, unless someone justifies a need to see system files, there is no reason for anybody except you and your backup person to see these files.

d. *Batch or script files.* We looked at the pros and cons of distributing copies of batch or script files in the section about paper copies. For advice about access to these files, turn back to Section 3.2.

e. *Data file originals.* Chances are that you have no data file originals in the library. If you do, they are likely to be sensitive. People who ask you to store such files for them should specify who else is allowed to see the files. Or, you might prefer to allow access only to the person who brought the file to you.

f. *Data file backups and data file archives.* Access to these files depends on the sensitivity of the individual files. The issue of data file security is so complex that it is best to disallow access to data files through the library except in the case of lost files that must be restored from a backup. (Turn to Chapter Six for details about security.)

4. **System procedures, schedules, and logs.** Except for information someone could use to damage the system (intentionally or unintentionally), there is no reason to keep your procedures, schedules, and logs private. On the contrary, you want people to be intimate with system procedures, such as those that encourage them to change their passwords or to back up data files regularly. Also, it is good for people to understand the procedures you follow, particularly when the system is in trouble. The more that people know about your procedures, schedules, and logs, the more they will support, understand, and appreciate what you do.

5. **Publicly produced reference material.** This category includes books and articles written about your system as well as about related subjects. Make this type of information available to everyone and encourage people to browse through it. Somebody might see an article that describes a batch file others would find invaluable. Someone else might learn shortcuts for your database management program. The better educated people are, the more efficiently they can use the system.

3.4 Checklist of Recommended Library Materials

You have created many important documents for your system by following the instructions in this and the previous chapter. Hopefully, you will find the suggestions in the preceding section valuable as you manage your system library.

You already know that the documents you have collected thus far do not alone represent a complete collection, but be assured that yours is nearly that. In ensuing chapters, you will find just a few other documents to add.

To check your progress, compare your system library inventory with the items listed on the checklist of recommended library materials. You will recognize many of the items. Others are discussed in later chapters and some are not discussed in detail anywhere here. Those introduced in later chapters are identified with chapter references. Return to this list when you reach the last page of this book to double-check that you have everything you need.

Checklist of Recommended Library Materials

1. _____ Library inventory
2. _____ Documentation manuals for each piece of hardware
3. _____ Documentation manuals for each software program
4.   Hardware documents
   _____ System sketch
   _____ System devices map
   _____ Peripheral devices map
   _____ System boards map
   _____ Switch settings map
5.   Floppy diskette or tape library
   _____ Software originals and backups
   _____ Backup copies of installed versions of applications software
   _____ Backup copies of system files
   _____ Backup copies of batch or script files
   _____ Programs staff members write
   _____ Models or templates people develop to use with applications programs
   _____ Data file originals
   _____ Data file full backup
   _____ Data file partial backup
   _____ Data file archives
   _____ Data file storage policy and procedures
6.   Software documents
   _____ Software inventory
   _____ Software defaults map
   _____ Custom keyboard key assignments [Ch 5]
   _____ Paper copies of application program installations
   _____ Paper copies of system files
   _____ Paper copies of batch or script files
7.   Memory maps
   _____ Hard disk partitions map [Ch 4]
   _____ Reserved drive name scheme [Ch 4]
   _____ Random access memory calculations [Ch 5]

8.   System policies and procedures
- _____ Records management [Ch 4]
- _____ Disk housekeeping: data files [Ch 4]
- _____ Disk housekeeping: program files [Ch 4]
- _____ Data security [Ch 6]
- _____ Equipment security [Ch 6]
- _____ Software security [Ch 6]
- _____ File integrity check [Ch 7]
- _____ Equipment maintenance [Ch 7]
- _____ Equipment replacement [Ch 8]
- _____ Expendable supplies [Ch 7]
- _____ Emergency troubleshooting [Ch 8]
- _____ Reboot during a workperiod [Ch 8]
- _____ Full and partial backup [Ch 7]
- _____ Eliminate slow response time [Ch 4, 5, 8]
- _____ Handling problem devices [Ch 8]
- _____ Handling cryptic messages [Ch 8]
- _____ Move the system [Ch 8]
- _____ System development [Ch 7]
- _____ Staff training and development [Ch 7]
- _____ Vendor relations [Ch 8]

9.   Schedules and logs
- _____ Annual review [Ch 7]
- _____ Equipment maintenance schedule [Ch 7]
- _____ Expendable supply inventory [Ch 7]
- _____ Records retention and disposition schedule [Ch 4]
- _____ "To do list" of changes to make the next time the system is down or whenever you have time

10.   General reference material
- _____ Books
- _____ Magazines
- _____ Vendor catalogues

11.   Business operation documents
- _____ Purchase agreements and sales documents
- _____ Warranty agreements
- _____ Maintenance contracts
- _____ Insurance records
- _____ Software license agreements
- _____ Magazine subscription log

12. _____ Troubleshooter's survival kit [Ch 8]

Conclusion

With this chapter behind you, you have successfully built the foundation you need to manage your system. It will be a valuable reference for you to use as you proceed in developing the rest of your management program.

Building your library also has given you a comprehensive view of your system, so we can move on to the topic of how best to manage its resources.

Part II

Manage System Resources

4

Manage Disk Space
For Better System
Performance

Introduction

By now you know how much you depend upon thorough and up-to-date records. And you should have them if you completed each document described in Part I. Now you are ready to proceed with other areas of your responsibility.

This chapter introduces system resource management.

Chances are you will never encounter two systems with identical software and data files. But, to illustrate a point, let's suppose that you do and that the two systems function at remarkably different levels of performance. The difference would have little or nothing to do with who has the quickest finger action at the keyboard. Resource management would be the most likely reason.

Disk space is one system resource which, if managed properly, can transform your computer from a mediocre performer into one that is top flight. On the opposite side, if disk space is tight or if information is stored in a disorderly manner, your system's performance will suffer. In the following pages you will learn how to ensure that there is enough disk space for everyone and that data is stored on it in a way that supports optimal performance.

Disk space is an untidy and challenging resource to manage. That is partly because we cannot *see* it. But the main reason is the gap between your control and your responsibility. You have little or no control over the data files people create. Yet, when a disk is full, people probably turn to you for help. Techniques in this chapter will show you some of what you can do so that people have the space they need and your system performs at its best.

4.1 Control Data Files

This section will help you develop basic plans to avert disk-related problems and to encourage efficient use of disk space throughout your system. It is important to recognize that disk space is not an unlimited resource and that the potential trouble goes beyond how much disk space is actually free.

Hard disks may be larger and less expensive, but so are programs larger and data files proliferating. Data files are a primary source of trouble. They seem to multiply like rabbits, and as a result, they quickly become unmanageable. So, an important part of disk management is to control data files: what can be stored, where, and for how long?

Even simple file retrieval becomes difficult after a point. Assuming no employee turnover, a typical system will run for about nine months before it suffers from data file overflow and disorganization. During the first nine months, disk space probably is not yet scarce. People tend to recall file names without hesitation and will remember what is in their files when they scan a directory listing. No one realizes that behind the scenes, chaos is creeping into the system.

After about nine months, you confront the trouble. Disk space might be tight. People less readily recall file names and file contents. People confuse file names. They look in the archives for information that is still on the hard disk and visa versa. When one has worked with scads of files, file names, and directories, it is a rare person who can keep it all straight.

Review Your Records Management Plan

What can you do to avoid those problems? The first step in disk space management is to establish a policy and a set of procedures to control data files.

Did your company revise its records management plan when the system arrived? (You would be surprised at how often this process slips between the cracks.) If not, now is a good time to review your company's existing plan. Take a system manager's perspective and see that the plan defines how people should handle data from the moment it is created to the moment it can be destroyed.

Enlist Others to Help with the Review

Have others help you review your firm's records management plan. It is particularly important to involve other people if you find your firm's plan needs substantial revision. Ideally, include someone who can judge legal requirements and someone with records management expertise. If you are in a large organization, you might consult both department heads and people from various levels who directly process information (data entry clerks, etc.).

What To Consider During the Review

Throughout the review process, take the following into account:

1. **Procedures.** For every aspect of the system, you want procedures that promote rather than undermine desirable goals. With that in mind, assess existing records management procedures. Are there any you can streamline or eliminate? For instance, excessive reporting requirements can put such a burden on people that they are unable to keep their work current. I have seen many cases of data entry personnel so utterly bogged down with keeping track of how many x, y, and z's they complete every hour that they accomplish little actual work.

2. **Data file life cycle.** Data files are created, manipulated, and retired, like everything else. You put them through paces at every point. In addition to creating and retiring them, you store them, update them, protect them, produce hard copy from them, erase them, and purge them.

    If you keep track of what stage a data file is in, you will have an easier time managing it. You will know who is responsible for it and where it should reside at various points during its life cycle.

3. **A storage policy** Someone has to decide what can and what cannot be stored on the system. Files occupy little physical space, so you might be tempted to keep everything. One reason to resist the temptation is that cluttered disks are a cause of serious degradation in system performance. The alternative is to establish explicit file storage guidelines that you can distribute to everyone who uses the system.

    A critical question to ask is whether anyone uses the system for something that would be better done manually. (I once encountered a manager so carried away in his zeal for the computer that he used it for absolutely everything he did, including keeping his numerous "to-do lists" current. For that and similar projects, he persisted in tying up an inordinate amount of disk space until the day he ran headlong into a full disk crisis.)

    Decisions also must be made so people know how to handle their personal files. Can a scoutmaster use the hard disk to store the troup's mailing list? Will you keep games on the system for your son or daughter to use while you are working after hours?

4. **Ease of access.** Devise ways to make data file access easy. Consider possible filing procedures that would be helpful. You probably already use directory and subdirectory names to organize data for easy access. Two other methods you might use are file naming conventions and an index system.

First, establish file naming conventions that everyone will accept. For example, your system might provide for an eight-character file name followed by an optional three-character extension. Put both parts to work. You should find many ways to do it.

For instance, the last two slots in the first eight characters of a file name might identify the fiscal year the file pertains to. This sample would signify fiscal year 1987-88:

$$\_\,\_\,\_\,\_\,\_\,\_\,8\,8\quad.\quad\_\,\_\,\_$$

(8 character filename) . (3 character extension)

You might use the three-character file name extension to specify the file's format, such as ".ltr" for letter, or ".rpt" for report. Or you might prefer to use the three characters to specify the type of record: ".bud" for budget, ".per" for a personnel document, and so on.

Whatever scheme you choose, be sure it takes advantage of software programs that provide automatic extensions, such as Framework II's ".FW2" or SuperKey's ".MAC" for its keyboard redefinition files.

The second way to make data file access easier is to establish an indexing scheme. Even with a system like UNIX (its **grep** command enables you to find files by searching for specified words), it can be a time-consuming chore to locate which archival diskettes or tape you used to store a particular file. Software to help with indexing is available from vendors or from the public domain.

Establish a Records Retention and Disposition Schedule

Undoubtedly, you keep some records for years, while others are vital only for a few days. Fleeting files are fairly easy to keep track of if you follow good disk housekeeping procedures, (discussed later in this chapter). But, it is a different matter when it comes to critical and recurring documents that you must store for long periods (for example, tax returns and budget proposals) or historical documents that you might one day update (such as articles of incorporation). For these, you need a schedule.

A records retention and disposition schedule (Table 4.1) is the tool for the job. Use this schedule for important files so everyone understands how long a file should remain on-line, how long it resides in the archives (if at all), and when it can be destroyed (if ever). Use it to record who is responsible for each file. When you develop your schedule, consider each file on your system that is of more than fleeting interest.

Table 4.1 shows how one small corporation uses this schedule. It allows spaces for (1) a description of the item, (2) its retention period on-line, (3) its retention period off-line in the archives, (4) a date after which destruction is acceptable, and (5) the office or department official in charge of the file.

Table 4.1 is partially completed with only two entries: one for articles of incorporation and one for annual budget proposals. The firm, which operates on a July 1–June 30 Fiscal Year, keeps its articles indefinitely. Budget proposals are handled differently. The current proposal stays on the hard disk for one year to allow ready

Table 4.1

RECORDS RETENTION AND DISPOSITION SCHEDULE

Date _____   Prepared By _____

(sample)

Item (1)	Retention Period		Destruction Date (4)	Office of Record (5)
	On Line (2)	Archive (3)		
Articles of Incorporation	n/a	Indefinite	n/a	Administration
Budget Proposal	1 yr	5 yr	7/1	Administration

reference. After one year, the firm rarely refers to a proposal. As a result, each July 1 (the beginning of the firm's fiscal year), someone in administration—the office of record—shifts what has become the past year's budget proposal off the hard disk to an archival diskette or tape. The oldest proposal in the archives, now six-years-old, is deleted since it has aged beyond the required five-year period to retain it in the archives.

Use the blank schedule (Table 4.2) to record how your company handles its special files. See that people have copies and keep a master copy in the system library.

Tip #1: Archiving

Here is a tidy way to send files to the archives. Create a subdirectory (called "archive," for example) strictly for collecting files to archive. Instruct people to copy files to it periodically, say at the first of each month. (Once copied to this special subdirectory, files can be erased from their original disk or diskette.) Then, periodically move all of the subdirectory's files to archival diskettes or to an archival tape. With these files safely stored in the archives, erase them from your special subdirectory.

Tip #2: Destruction

Take every precaution to avoid the accidental and irreversible erasure of data files. Your records retention and disposition schedule will be a big help in avoiding this calamity, but be extra cautious. Devise procedures to handle cases of "ultimate destruction." For instance, specify one individual in the organization or in each office of record who is to be in charge of deleting files. Have this person develop consistent procedures for the process.

Table 4.2

RECORDS RETENTION AND DISPOSITION SCHEDULE

Date _____   Prepared By _____

Item (1)	Retention Period On Line (2)	Archive (3)	Destruction Date (4)	Office of Record (5)

4.2 Use Disk Housekeeping for Top System Performance

The preceding section will help you control data files. Now, let's look at what plagues hard disks and diskettes and what you can do to keep trouble at bay. We discussed earlier how important disk management is to promote top system performance and maintain free disk space. When disk space becomes tight, you are threatened with a full disk situation. In addition, a heavily populated disk puts a performance drag on any system.

In this section we will look at two disk space management strategies: to control the layout of individual files on *any* disk and to manage the amount of free space on hard disks. Both play a role in how well or how poorly your system performs. Of the two, data file disorganization on a disk is the more serious culprit, so we will look at it first.

Overcome Unavoidable Data File Disorganization

Each time someone updates a file on your system, it fluctuates in layout and in size on the disk. The result is unavoidable disorganization in the way the data file is stored. This has an adverse effect on your system's performance.

The problem creeps up on systems, so it typically goes undetected for a period of time. You cannot prevent data file disorganization, but you can counteract it. In order to do so, it helps to know how the computer stores information on a hard disk or floppy diskette and why data files become disorganized.

How Data Files Fragment

When you consider the amount of space on a disk (enough for about 80 million characters on a 80 megabyte hard disk), it is clear that managing it is a phenomenal task. Figure 4.1 shows a hard disk divided into what are called *tracks* and *sectors*. These enable the computer to keep track of disk space. Notice the disk drive head in the figure is positioned to read data stored in track 3, sector 4 on the disk.

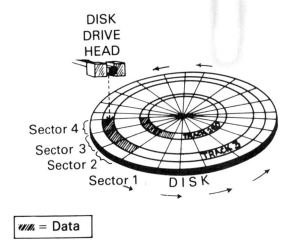

DISK
DRIVE
HEAD

Sector 4
Sector 3
Sector 2
Sector 1   DISK

///. = Data

Figure 4.1. How Disk Space is Organized in Tracks and Sectors. The disk drive head is positioned to read data stored in track 3, sector 4 on the disk.

Ideally, all parts of an individual file occupy adjacent space on disk for speediest system access. In reality, a file rarely is perfectly lined up sequentially on a disk because your computer stores a file wherever it finds free sectors. Such efficiency is possible because information is stored on disk in small segments, each one equal in size to one or more sectors, depending on the disk. That scheme allows the computer to allot space for your data files both as it is needed and as it is available, on a catch-as-catch-can basis.

Let's go back to Figure 4.1. Notice that data is stored in sectors 2 through 4 on track 3 and in sectors 1 through 4 on track 280. Conceivably, all highlighted data in the figure could be part of the same file. If *we* had to keep track of information in this manner, we soon would collapse under the strain, but the computer has no trouble finding every bit of your file for you when you need it.

Chances are that many of the data files on your hard disk are scattered across the disk like the data in the figure. Why? The first time you command the computer to save a new file, it might assign contiguous storage space to your file. (Figure 4.2 shows a file occupying four adjacent sectors on the disk.) But, you continually create and edit files all over the disk. The amount of space each one occupies expands and contracts. You also erase existing files.

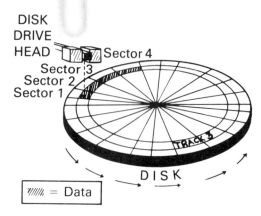

**Figure 4.2. Advantage of Data Stored on Adjacent Disk Sectors.
When the information is stored on adjacent disk space, the disk drive
head does not have to move again after it locates the first sector in
which the data file is located.**

All of this file activity disrupts the sequential allotment of disk
space for data files. So, when you add names to a mailing list, you
cannot be sure if the saved file will occupy adjacent disk space. Figure 4.3 shows four sections of a file, each stored on the same sector
but on different tracks. That is an unlikely storage pattern for one
file, but it illustrates why noncontiguous file storage puts a drag on
system performance.

Why Fragmented Files Slow Performance

A disk drive head moves above a rotating disk until it locates
the track it seeks in order to read or write information. The more
movement, the more time the search takes.

A fragmented file slows system performance because it demands that the disk head move wherever it must go to collect all of
the file's segments, no matter how far flung the tracks might be on
the disk.

Compare the head activity required for reading the files on
Figures 4.2 and 4.3. The file on Figure 4.2 occupies adjacent disk
space. As soon as the head locates the file's first sector, no further
movement is needed. The drive head sits motionless, reading data as
each sector spins into place.

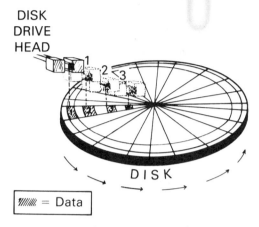

DISK
DRIVE
HEAD

DISK

////// = Data

Figure 4.3. Disadvantage of Data Scattered Across a Disk. The Figure shows four sequential sections, 1 through 4, of a file located on disk. Each section is on a different track. With the information scattered across the disk, the disk drive head must move three times to read all four sections after it locates the first.

The situation in Figure 4.3 is quite different. That one illustrates how an individual file scattered across tracks on the disk impedes system performance. The head has to move three times after it locates the first sector in which the file is located.

How Quickly Does the Problem Escalate?

Data file disorganization is a potential problem for files stored on floppy diskettes, on hard disks devoted to a stand–alone computer, and on shared hard disks. (In other words, expect it with all of your files, except the ones you keep on a streaming tape.)

In most cases, when the computer has to address a scattered file, system performance suffers. If your hard disk is shared, the problem might escalate rapidly. For an idea of how much this problem escalates daily, think about the number of files you personally create, edit, and save each day. Consider how many times you save each file while you are in the process of creating or editing it. Multiply this by the number of people who store files on the hard disk in question. This should give you an idea about the daily increase in potential file fragmentation.

How to Check the Extent of the Problem

You need not know how bad the problem is to solve it. But, if you want to, your operating system probably has a utility to check. DOS has the CHKDSK (checkdisk) program to tell you how bad file fragmentation is at a given moment.

Software developers offer utilities you can use to monitor the distribution of files on disk space. One such package is the well-known Norton Utilities, available for IBM PC's and compatibles, which allow you to map how disk space is used.

The Solution: Rearrange Data Files
In Contiguous Disk Space

If your system is sluggish and you suspect it is because files are fragmented, you can solve the problem easily. Generally, the solution is to remove files from the fragmented disk and copy them back to arrange them on contiguous space. (Check with your vendor about software that might assist you.)

It is possible to perform this procedure for selected files, but you are unlikely to gain very much. That is because unless you do it for every file on a disk, not all of the space freed will necessarily be contiguous. Removing and recopying selected files will alleviate the situation, but for the maximum benefit, this solution is an all or nothing proposition.

Warning

Before you implement this solution be absolutely sure that the disk you are about to reorganize does not contain a software program with a copy protection scheme that limits the number of times you can copy the program to a diskette or a hard disk. Check your vendor-provided manuals if you are unsure. For disks containing such programs, to avoid losing them, ignore alternative number one in step two below and follow alternative number two.

Step One. Copy files. Copy all files from the disk in question to floppy diskettes. (It is no good to copy them to a tape.) The exception, of course, is software with copy protection such as that described in the warning.

Your diskette copies are strictly for purposes of running this procedure. You will need them to replace the files you will delete in step two. *Do not* rely on the system's backup copies. If you did, it would mean you have some files in only one place. And that would mean you have no backup at all. Be very careful here. Before you go to step two, be absolutely sure the system backup copies are intact.

Step Two. Clean the disk. You have two options to clean files from your disk. The preferred method is to reformat the disk, alternative number one. *But,* if you have software on the disk with a nasty copy protection scheme like the one mentioned in the warning, follow alternative number two.

Alternative #1: Reformat the disk. Reformat the disk to obliterate everything on it. Take care. Some managers prefer to erase files (alternative number two), but reformatting the disk is better because it can bring an added benefit. If your disk has developed unusable areas, called *bad sectors*, reformatting will isolate them. With bad sectors unavailable, you are spared potential trouble later.

Alternative #2: Erase files. Use this alternative if you have software programs you cannot safely erase. Leave those programs intact, but erase all other files from your disk.

Step Three. Restore the files. The last step is to copy files from the floppy diskettes back to the original disk.

Perform the above process regularly to restore files to contiguous disk space. That will keep disk head movement at a minimum, reducing the time required to access information and improving overall system performance. By how much? System speed can be improved dramatically, up to 300 percent for some systems.

Contiguous data storage is desirable, but it takes you only so far in reaching your goal of optimal system performance. Now, let's look at another problem that plagues hard disks and how you can overcome it.

A Heavily Populated Disk Slows Performance

Hard disks and floppy diskettes need free space. An overpopulated disk undermines system performance, slowing down the system whenever the disk drive is needed for a read or write process.

Disk clutter is a particular problem on shared hard disks, but it also causes trouble on disks and diskettes that are not shared.

How much disk space is enough? It depends on your operating system. Follow the recommendation in your documentation. If you have a XENIX system, your documentation probably advises you to keep free at least 15 percent of total disk space. However, if the number of data files on your system fluctuates widely, you might increase that to 17 or 18 percent, maybe more.

Whatever percentage of disk space you decide to keep free, you will want to control it carefully to reduce the number of DISK FULL crises and to avoid most sudden system slowdowns. (Chapter 8 describes what to do if you encounter either problem.) How do you keep free space at the optimal level? There is more than one strategy to avoid overpopulation on disks. For starters, monitor the amount of free space frequently, as often as every day for hard disks if your system has high-volume file creation.

Tip #1

Too many directory entries put a drag on system performance. Your operating system manuals should advise you about the acceptable number of directory entries. For example, with XENIX, up to 286 directory entries is all right. Anything beyond that makes searches excessively time-consuming.

Tip #2

Lengthy directory paths, or subdirectories, have an adverse effect on system performance. Spot-check data file directories so that you can advise people if they are using unnecessarily lengthy directory paths. For most offices, two or three levels of subdirectories is optimal; five is too many.

The Solution: Getting It Down to Size

Your records management plan, which you were advised to review at the beginning of this chapter, specifies the kind of information people can keep on a disk. That plan helps you control disk space, but there are other steps you can take. For instance, some managers restrict the number of data files or the amount of disk space each person can use. Others treat disk space allocation more freely.

The most obvious way to increase free space on a disk is to depopulate it. Ask people to delete data files they no longer need. In particular, nudge people whose files occupy an inordinate amount of space. Identify and remove your own superfluous files.

The task of depopulating a hard disk can be tricky, so in the rest of this section, we will look at sample procedures to keep the numbers of both data and program files down to size.

Data files occupy the preponderance of disk space on most systems. You already know that data files multiply at alarming rates. So, make them your first candidates for removal when a disk is overpopulated. But, by all means, avoid ever taking the sole responsibility for deleting files that other people created.

You might find that people resist the idea of removing their own files, but most people will agree that data files in general should not proliferate to the extent that they clutter the hard disk and inhibit system performance. You will find it easier and safer to remove files if you establish a procedure to follow whenever disk space is in short supply. Use the following sample procedure to develop one for your system.

A Procedure to Delete Unneeded Data Files

Step One: Print directory listings. Print copies of directory listings to show every data file kept on your system.

Step Two: Identify each directory listing. Do you have more than one hard disk? Have you divided a hard disk into what are called *partitions*? (A disk will have partitions if you run it with more than one operating system or if you use partitions to segregate data files. Refer to Section 4.3 of this chapter for more information about partitions.)

Should the answer to either question be yes, be sure that you are able to match each directory with the proper location for its files. If the directory listings themselves do not make clear which hard disk or disk partition the files reside on, annotate this information on each printed directory.

Step Three: Prepare a note to staff members. Write a note that explains you are interested in speeding up the system for everyone. To accomplish this, people should identify files to archive on tape or floppy diskettes and remove from the hard disk. Specify a target, say a percentage of their files. Make it clear that these files will be intact in the archives in case they are needed again. If people understand that your goal is to make the system respond more efficiently for *them*, you should find them cooperative. Depending on the volume of files on the system, give people a reasonable amount of time to get back to you.

Step Four: Copy and distribute the listings. Distribute a copy of the directory listings along with your note to each person who uses the system.

Step Five: Archive and delete. When the deadwood is identified, archive it and remove it from the hard disk. You might prefer to have people archive and delete their own files. Whoever does the job, be absolutely sure that a file is not removed until first copied to a diskette or a tape for the archives. This precaution protects everyone from hasty decisions and inadvertent erasures.

Step Six: Rearrange files to contiguous disk space. If you have removed a lot of files, the disk probably has many non-contiguous unused sectors. So, now is an ideal time to perform the three-step process to overcome data file disorganization described earlier in this chapter. But it is not required. And, in fact, skip it for the moment if you are about to delete program files from the hard disk because the three-step process is also part of the program file deletion procedure we will look at next. There is no need to perform the process twice.

Step Seven: Document what you have done. Date and store the annotated directory listings in the system library. They will be your record of files people marked for removal.

Surprisingly, people sometimes forget their decisions when it comes to deleting data files. You will avoid headaches all around if you give people copies of the directory listings they used to mark their files. This step is particularly important if the people do not remove their files themselves.

Print new directory listings of your archival diskettes or tapes to store in each medium's container.

Data is not the only needless clutter on a disk. Program files can be just as guilty. The idea of removing a program from a hard disk,

Tip

A common problem when staff members depart is that they disappear without letting you know what they left behind on the system. Screening these files later can be an overwhelming task. It happened to me only once. I thought I might go blind scanning the directory listing of mysterious files left behind.

Establish a practice for departing people to do some disk cleaning and to give you an annotated directory of their files that remain.

particularly a shared hard disk, is disconcerting initially. But nearly every system manager discovers a few programs that are idle much or most of the time. Such programs may not warrant space on a hard disk. You might decide to delete unused or rarely used programs.

As with data files, deleting unnecessary programs from a hard disk has its hazards. For example, you must know the names of each file your word processing program needs to function. Otherwise, you run the risk of accidentally erasing an essential file. Invariably, the loss becomes evident when someone reaches a critical point in an editing session. This means lost work for them and time wasted for you in restoring the file.

Program file deletion is one job you should do yourself. To avoid pitfalls and to accomplish the task with relative ease, use the following procedure. It assumes that the disk in question is shared. You should find it easy to adapt the procedure for your stand-alone computers, if you have them.

A Procedure to Delete Unneeded Program Files

Step One: Establish guidelines. The first step is to set guidelines. Involve other people. That way you will avoid the mistake of deleting a program somebody needs or the game your boss uses after hours. If you have an in-house users' group, raise the issue of guidelines with them. Otherwise, consult with others on an *ad hoc* basis. Talk with key people, including departmental managers, secretaries, analysts, and clerks.

Whatever guidelines you use, be very clear about them and write them down. The sample procedure follows these two guidelines:

Guideline #1: Delete all unnecessary program files, that is, those characterized by the following:

* rarely or never used
* redundant
* not essential to a needed program
* not business-related

Guideline #2: Consider all programs for possible deletion. No program is automatically inviolate.

Step Two: Print associated directories. Print directory listings to give yourself a road map of the disk. If you keep programs in subdirectories, print them also. The more complicated your disk storage scheme is, the more vulnerable you are to a mixup.

Printed directories simplify the selection and deletion process because they are a picture of how programs are arrayed on the disk, showing you which files reside together. That information will be helpful if you happen to delete a program inadvertently. You will know exactly where to restore it.

Step Three: Identify possible candidates. Use the printed directories to identify files you might erase. Scan the listings and mark program files you will consider deleting. Remember, at this point you are only proposing to yourself that you might delete a particular program. You will make final decisions later.

Think about each type of program separately. For instance, look at all application program files before you look at your utility programs. The prime candidates for deletion listed on Table 4.3 should help you to do that.

Step Four: Establish if each program is a viable candidate. Convince yourself on a case-by-case basis that the programs you selected in step three are viable candidates. If you are unfamiliar with a program, check its documentation to find out what purpose the program serves. You might discover a program you or someone else would have been using all along had you known you had it.

Be sure that the file is not part of a program you want available. Watch out for auxiliary files that your program files need in the course of operation. Such files include help files that you will want to retain on the hard disk.

Step Five: Take care with multiple copies of program files. You might discover multiple copies of a program. Before you assume you have run into duplication, find out if the copies are simply different installed versions of a program or if they are identical but necessary to keep on the disk in duplicate.

Help files are a common case in point if you use tree-structured directories. Some programs require that their help files be duplicated in various subdirectories. If you delete the help files, they will be inaccessible to people working outside of the main or root directory.

Step Six: Select preliminary candidates. Now compare your tentative list of program files to delete with the guidelines you developed in step one. Re-examine your guidelines if you have to. Programs that fall within the guidelines will stay on the list. Eliminate the others from your list or revise the guidelines.

Step Seven: Involve others in the final selection process. Every rule has its exceptions. No matter how many people contributed to your guidelines, no matter how carefully people thought about them, there is a chance that somebody agreed to them without understanding that it meant the loss of a favorite program from on-line access.

Each person who uses the hard disk in question should participate in the final selection process. Stress that a deleted program will not disappear, but will be safely stored on a floppy diskette should anyone wish to use it again. If you ensure that the entire group participates at this stage, you will avoid disrupting critical work. You might find someone happens to be making heavy use of a program that usually is idle. If so, ask the person to estimate how long the program should stay on the hard disk. Mark that program for possible deletion later.

Step Eight: Identify programs for deletion. Run through your list a final time. Look at the programs you intend to delete. You might have second thoughts about a program or two yourself.

At this point, you may be asking yourself whether the net gain in system performance justifies the time you will spend deleting files and restoring programs used only occasionally.

Table 4.3

PRIME CANDIDATES FOR DELETION

Do not waste valuable disk space. Here are four types of program files to consider erasing from a hard disk.

1. **Rarely used operating systems.** If your system has more than one operating system and one of them is used rarely, consider removing it from the hard disk. Whenever you need a rarely used operating system, you can boot it from a floppy diskette.

   Be aware that deleting an operating system has implications beyond simply erasing its program files. First, earlier we mentioned that a disk with two operating systems will be divided into partitions. If you decide to eliminate the operating system, you also will have to adjust your disk partitions (see Section 4.3.)

   Second, if the operating system in question has been used at all, chances are that you have applications programs and data files in the operating system's partition. These, too, must be saved and removed if you delete their operating system from the disk.

2. **Utility programs.** Utility programs you might delete include infrequently used diagnostics or utilities that you consider dangerous to leave on the disk. An example of the latter is one mentioned earlier, debugging tools, programs that permit people to inspect or alter program code itself. In the hands of the wrong person, such a program can be used to destroy or plant an insidious bug in one of your application programs. Store these programs on floppy diskettes until you need them.

Table 4.3

PRIME CANDIDATES FOR DELETION

(continued)

3. **Outdated script or batch files.** People sometimes update script or batch files without removing previous versions. As a result, these files occupy disk space long after they are current and useful.

 Most obvious are batch or script files based on an outdated system configuration. For instance, do you have a discarded batch file that you previously used to streamline your task of backing up data files before you added a second hard disk?

 Delete batch files only after you copy them to a diskette. In Chapter Three, I cautioned you that one day you might want or need to use such files. There may come a time when you have to resort to an old configuration for one reason or another. As an example, suppose you send out one of your hard disks for repair. While the disk is gone, it certainly can help to have available the batch or script file that you used to backup data when your system had only one hard disk. Or someday you may want to resurrect an old batch file. Even if you revise the file, your task is easier than it would be were you to recreate the file from scratch.

4. **Applications programs.** It is common to find at least one unused program on a hard disk. Maybe no one uses your system's calendar program. If that is the case, why allow it to clutter disk space?

Before you decide to eliminate files from the list, ask yourself how severe your free space problem is. Weigh its severity against the fact that deleting and restoring files involves simple commands that you can execute quickly.

Step Nine: Preparing for deletion. *Before* you delete a program, be sure that you have both its original floppy diskette and backup copies. That way, if ever you want to use one of the deleted programs, you can use the backup copy without jeopardizing the original.

Most important, be sure none of the programs you are thinking of deleting have one of the copy protection schemes discussed earlier which limit the number of copies you can make. Some schemes allow you to copy the program to a hard disk only once. After that, should you try to recopy the program, you will be unable to. Obviously, leave such programs intact on the hard disk.

Step Ten: Delete each program selected. Erase each program only after you are entirely sure that everyone is better off with it removed from the hard disk.

Step Eleven: Rearrange files to contiguous disk space. This step is optional. If you have deleted very many files, the disk probably has a multiplicity of the non-contiguous unused sectors mentioned earlier. That is especially true if you have just done a housekeeping job on data files. Follow the three step process to rearrange files to contiguous disk space described earlier in this chapter.

Step Twelve: Document the process. To record what you have done, date and store each of the following items for the system library:

1. The file scheme on the hard disk prior to starting this process. This scheme is best represented by the directories you printed in step two. If you deleted a program by mistake, its directory will show exactly where to return the file.
2. The list of files deleted. Annotate your directories from step two to show which programs you deleted.
3. The file population scheme on the hard disk after completing this process. Obtain this by printing a fresh copy of each directory.

For most systems, putting a lid on program files is a one-time procedure. Once you have removed the unnecessary ones, plan to make only annual spot checks. (Someone might be prone to copying a game or two to the disk.)

Tip #1

Periodically check the amount of free space on the system. (Managers of UNIX systems will use **fsck***; managers of DOS systems will use CHKDSK.) Take action before it gets tight. A frontline tactic for UNIX systems is to remove temporary files and clear the contents of system log files.*

Tip #2

If you backup files to diskettes, an uncluttered disk saves you time during that process because you do not have to wait while the deadwood is being backed up.

4.3 Eliminate Confusion with Specialty Disk Storage Maps

Thus far in this chapter we have looked at key techniques to manage disk space: what gets stored on it, how long files should stay there, and how best to remove files when their time has come. In this section, we will look at two documents that can help you with disk management, depending on the type of system you manage and how you have it set up.

If you manage a system with more than one operating system that you run from one disk, you need the first document, a hard disk partitions map. If you manage a system with PC's hooked up to another computer or to a local area network, you need the second document, a reserved drive names scheme. If you manage *only* stand-alone PC's, you need neither and can skip ahead to Chapter Five.

Develop a Hard Disk Map

Earlier, in the procedures to remove data and program files from disks, we briefly mentioned disk partitions. Remember that hard disk space is divided into tracks and sectors, shown in Figure 4.1.

Another way (not mutually exclusive) to divide a disk is to partition it. Partitions isolate parts of a disk and there are two reasons you might use them. You already know that you have to partition your disk if you run more than one operating system from it. You also might partition a disk to assign more than one partition for selected data files.

Because you can control—within limits—the size of a partition, you will want to keep track of how you have assigned space to each partition on a disk.

Cylinders and Partitions

Partitions are not always immediately clear, so let's take a closer look. Figure 4.4 shows a hard disk with two platters. Each platter has two surfaces, one on top and another on the bottom, for a total of four surfaces where information can be stored on the disk.

A single track on each of the four surfaces, when taken together, make up one cylinder. Cylinders are identified by number,

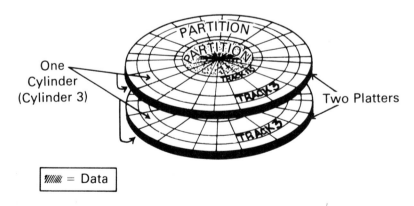

Figure 4.4. Cylinders and Partitions on a Hard Disk. Data is stored on both sides of each platter. Track 3 on all four surfaces makes up one cylinder. Cylinders 0 through 115 make up one partition.

just as tracks are. The figure highlights Cylinder 3, which is made up of Track 3 on all four surfaces.

You can isolate a series of cylinders into partitions. The disk in the figure has two. The first partition begins at the outer portion of the disk and isolates cylinders 0 through 115; the rest of the disk is devoted to the second partition.

Hard Disk Partitions Map

You can document where your disk partitions begin and end with a hard disk partitions map (Table 4.4). Most likely, you will use this map rarely—probably only to view or to change how you divide disk space between operating systems that you are running.

For example, earlier we saw that you would have to rework your partitions if you delete one of your operating systems and its partition from a disk. A partitions map also is helpful when you want to alter the amount of disk space (the number of cylinders) assigned to each partition. Some operating systems have minimum amounts of space you must assign to their partitions, so you have less than total control over the size of partitions. (XENIX is a case in point.) Your hard disk partitions map will make it immediately clear if excess space is available in any of the existing partitions.

But, even if you never change disk partitions, you should have a hard disk partitions map in your system library because it describes a basic part of your system's configuration.

What the Map Tells You

A hard disk partitions map provides useful information about your disk and its organization. Refer to the sample map, Table 4.4. Let's see what it tells us.

The device name identifies the disk in question as PCAT01. Using the codes from Chapter Two, this means that the hard disk is located inside of the first PC-AT on the system.

The disk has three partitions, one for the DOS operating system and the two required for the XENIX operating system. The DOS partition is the "active partition," that is, the one that controls the computer when it is turned on or reset. XENIX is nonactive. The sample map shows where each partition begins and ends, its size in cylinders, and the number of bytes it occupies.

Table 4.4

HARD DISK PARTITIONS MAP
Date _____   Prepared By _____

(Sample)

Device Name: PCAT01

PARTITION NUMBER (1)	STATUS (2)	OPERATING SYSTEM (3)	CYLINDER			NO. BYTES (7)	COMMENTS (8)
			START (4)	END (5)	SIZE (6)		
1	Active	DOS	000	151	152	5 Megabytes	
2	Nonactive	XENIX Root	152	428	277	9 Megabytes	Minimum
3	Nonactive	XENIX User	429	613	185	6 Megabytes	Minimum
TOTAL DISK SPACE			000	613	614	20 Megabytes	
TOTAL SPACE USED			000	613	614	20 Megabytes	
Unused Disk Space			–	–	0	0	

Table 4.5

HARD DISK PARTITIONS MAP
Date _____   Prepared By _____

Device Name:

PARTITION NUMBER (1)	STATUS (2)	OPERATING SYSTEM (3)	CYLINDER START (4)	END (5)	SIZE (6)	NO. BYTES (7)	COMMENTS (8)
TOTAL DISK SPACE TOTAL SPACE USED Unused Disk Space							

The DOS partition starts at cylinder 000 and ends at cylinder 151, for a total of 152 cylinders in the partition. That partition has five megabytes of space. (In a moment, we will see how to calculate the number of megabytes that your partitions contain.)

The XENIX operating system has its two required partitions:

1. The root partition, which contains the XENIX programs you use to manage the system and user directories, occupies nine megabytes.
2. The user partition, which contains user files and application programs, occupies six megabytes.

The amount of space allocated to both of the XENIX partitions is the minimum allowed. Not one cylinder can be deleted from either XENIX partition.

Finally, the sample map accounts for all of the space on the disk, showing that the disk has a total of 614 cylinders and 20 megabytes of space, all of which is used.

Tips To Create a Hard Disk Partitions Map

Tip #1. Use Table 4.5 to create a partitions map for each hard disk on your system, even for those with only one partition. That way, you will have comprehensive information about all of the disks on your system when it comes to planning changes.

Tip #2. Identify the hard disk in question. Extract the device name from your system devices map. If you have no devices map, turn to Chapter Two for instructions.

Tip #3. You might recognize the sample hard disk partitions map (Table 4.4) for an IBM PC-AT running both DOS and XENIX. The map is similar to a screen you might see when you use the DOS FDISK program. That screen (Table 4.6) is not identical to the map (Table 4.4). Compare the two and you will see that the hard disk partitions map contains needed additions.

However, for each partition you can draw information for Columns 1 through 6 on the partitions map from this particular FDISK screen.

Next, add comments as needed. Then, complete the rest of the map by performing arithmetic (see Tip #4).

Table 4.6

DOS SCREEN TO COMPARE WITH HARD DISK PARTITIONS MAP

Display Partition Information

Current Fixed Disk Drive: 1

Partition	Status	Type	Start	End	Size
1	A	DOS	000	151	152
2	N	nonDOS	152	613	462

Total fixed disk space is 614 cylinders

Tip #4. Calculating the number of bytes in a partition can tease the brain. If you wished to, you could become hopelessly bogged down with minutiae. I suggest that you use round figures.

The hard disk on Table 4.4 has 20 megabytes of space. I have never seen a hard disk with exactly 20 megabytes (or 10, or 80). You probably have not either. Usually, they have a bit more than advertised, say 21.4 megabytes on what is advertised as a 20 megabyte disk. But, for our purposes, I made the disk an even 20.

The hard disk on the table has 614 cylinders available for partitions. On a 20 megabyte disk, this means 30.7 cylinders per megabyte (614 / 20 = 30.7). If you divide the size of the DOS partition (Column 6) by 30.7, you find that you have a 5 megabyte partition: (152 / 30.7 = 5). Once you have the number of bytes for each partition (Column 7), completing the rest of the map is a matter of addition.

Tip #5. For the comments section, check your documentation to see if your operating system has special requirements. We have already seen that XENIX requires a partition at least 9 megabytes of space for the root directory, for instance. You should easily locate that kind of information because disk partitions should be listed in your manual's index. If they are not listed, check the manual's installation section.

Develop a Reserved Drive
Names Scheme

This section presents the second disk document, the reserved drive names scheme. If your system has PC's connected in a local area network or PC's that use another computer's disk drives, this document will save you headaches.

When you use a lone PC, you rarely if ever mix up disk drive names because you are working with only three or four drives. But, as soon as you hook the PC up to a larger system, there is the potential for conflict and confusion.

For example, if you manage a network similar to IBM's PC Network, you already know that file servers share disk drives and even directories with other workstations. And you can assign a drive name specifier (A, B, C, etc.) to each shared disk drive and directory. For instance, you might assign the drive name E to a directory that contains boiler plate correspondence that the server shares with others.

So far, so good. But what happens if one of the PC's in the network already has its own E drive? In that case, the local drive E will be out of reach whenever the person uses the network's E drive. That can pose quite an inconvenience.

Conflict of that type is easy to avoid if you carefully assign and then keep track of how each workstation names the disk drives it has access to. Simply reserve a block of drive names for local devices and separate blocks for each server on your network. Table 4.7 shows a sample reserved drive name scheme for the sample local area network from Chapter Two. As you recall, the sample LAN has two file servers (Figure 2.1), so in addition to the block for PC's to use locally, the table shows a block of names reserved for each of the two servers.

Drives A through F are reserved for PC's to use locally, allowing a total of six possible drive names for local hard disks, floppy disk drives, and RAM disks (see Section 5.2). Every PC on the system will use these names, including the server PC's. This means that when people use your servers as workstations, under this scheme they, too, would use A through F to name local drives.

Table 4.7

RESERVED DRIVE NAMES SCHEME

For Sample Local Area Network: Figure 2.1

Date _____   Prepared By _____

Drive Names	Reserved For
A - F	Each PC's Local Drives
G - J	PCAT01: Server #1
K - N	PCXT01: Server #2

Four drive names, G through J and K through N respectively, are reserved for each file server to name the drives and directories it shares. That means that for instance, that the PC-AT (Server #1) can share drives or directories as G through J with other PC's on the network. The PC-XT (Server #2) would use K through N. (Notice that each server is identified here by its device name assigned on the system devices map in Chapter Two.)

Develop a reserved drive name scheme for your system. You can add the information to the system library database you developed in Chapter Two or use Table 4.8. In either case, distribute the map to others using the system and keep a master copy in the system library.

Tip

With DOS, you can assign any letter of the alphabet, A through Z, as a drive name. Table 4.7 for the sample local area network uses the IBM PC Network default, A through N. You can change the default by using the network's LASTDRIVE command. Check your documentation for instructions.

Table 4.8

RESERVED DRIVE NAMES SCHEME
Date _____   Prepared By _____

Drive Names	Reserved For

Conclusion

The information in this chapter can help you to bring system disks under control. You have seen how clutter and file fragmentation on a disk impede system response. And you have collected techniques to counteract these problems so that your system will maintain its high level of performance. If your system has disk partitions or networked PC's, you will find the specialty disk documents you created to be useful additions to your system library.

The next chapter covers strategies to manage yet another important system resource, random access memory.

5

Capitalize On Random
Access Memory

Introduction

As discussed in the previous chapter, good disk management practices will improve system performance. However, as fast as computers are, they have bottlenecks that even a well-managed disk cannot overcome. Disk drives and printers are the most notorious bottlenecks, but there are others. This chapter will show you how clever use of RAM can help you overcome typical impediments to achieve significant increases in productivity.

RAM has always been a challenge to manage. It is one system resource that seems perpetually in demand. First, it was so costly that people were hesitant to load their systems with the maximum amount allowed (at the time, 640K on a PC, for example). Then the price dropped. Vendors developed ways to put RAM to work, many requiring notable chunks of RAM for optimal performance. As a result, the maximum amount of RAM allowed, previously considered far more than anyone would possibly need, became a frustrating limitation.

That, too, changed. Today, new software and hardware stretch the amount of RAM allowed and push its utility beyond the old limits. An important hardware advance that allows PC's to break the previous 640K limitation is expanded memory, such as that provided on Intel's Above Board. With four fully populated Above Boards, a personal computer has the equivalent of over 8 megabytes of RAM, a staggering figure compared to the 64K available to early mainframe computers.

The extra space allows us to build larger files than ever before, to take greater advantage of specialty programs that increase our productivity, to work with even greater efficiency than we previously could, and to run concurrent operations.

Those advances complicate RAM management. This chapter will show you how to use RAM wisely, for no matter how much you have, it remains a limited resource. We will review specific ways that you can put RAM to work for optimal system performance and high people productivity. In addition, we will look at common pitfalls to avoid, and finally, we will see how one calculation can help you exploit RAM to its limit.

5.1 What Competes for This Valuable Resource?

You probably have heard people refer to RAM as the computer's desktop, the place where things happen. Virtually everything that you do with your computer flows through RAM at some point because the computer cannot "speak" directly with hard disks or with diskettes. Your computer first must copy programs and data files into RAM before you can use them. Then, when you are ready to save your work, you copy it from RAM to a hard disk or diskette.

In this section we will look at the major contenders for RAM. Four basic needs must be met. After that, you have a range of options to select from which can transform your system into a much more powerful tool than it otherwise would be.

Meet Basic Needs

Whenever you use a computer, its RAM is called into service for a few basic tasks. Let's look at an example. Suppose you arrive at work to edit a one page letter drafted yesterday just before you shut down the system. Figure 5.1 shows the four categories of information that require space in RAM while you complete your editing task.

First, when you power up the system, a portion of the operating system is copied from a disk (or loaded) into RAM, where it remains until you power down or reboot the system. That portion of the operating system is called its *resident portion* because it resides in RAM until the system's power is cut. The resident portion performs basic functions, knows where to locate other operating system modules and programs when you need them, and knows how to retrieve required data. Next, when you invoke your word processing program, it, too, is loaded into RAM. Finally, when you call up the draft of the letter begun yesterday, its contents are copied into RAM.

With these three elements present in RAM—the resident portion of the operating system, the word processing program, and your draft text file—you are ready to go to work rewriting, deleting, and editing portions of the letter. That leaves only one more basic contender: you need space to work on your letter.

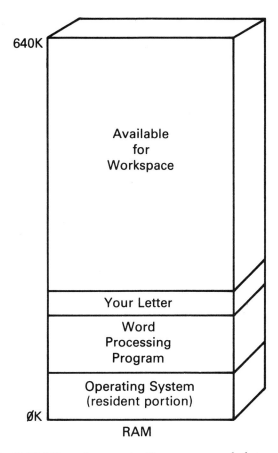

Figure 5.1. Basic RAM Requirements. Programs and data must be copied into RAM in order for you to use them. The figure shows the basic RAM requirements when you start the system and edit a letter created previously.

Figure 5.1 shows one example of how RAM is needed for basic requirements:

1. the resident portion of the operating system,
2. the applications you run (a word processing program in the figure),
3. the portion of your data files you work on (a letter in the figure), and
4. additional work space.

Tip

There might be times when you simultaneously run more than one application. So, for example, were the computer in the figure connected to a network, you would need space in RAM for the network software, thereby increasing the system's basic RAM requirement.

Exploit the Power of Available RAM

Your system probably has RAM in excess of what is required to fill basic needs. If so, you owe it to yourself and everyone using your system to implement ways to exploit idle RAM.

A broad range of optional software products are designed to make your work easier. Some add features to operating systems or standard programs to improve their performance or ease of use. Others work alone to overcome typical bottlenecks mentioned earlier.

We will use the terms *specialty* or *productivity program* to identify software that allows you to get more mileage out of your system or your application programs. Rather than describe all of the useful productivity programs on the market, we will look at three popular applications in the next section.

First, let's address three characteristics that productivity programs generally share.

Learn Three Characteristics of Specialty Programs

To begin, productivity programs may appear optional before you use them, but once you have experience with the best of them, you soon will consider them essential.

Second, after you have loaded one of these programs, it typically is ready for you to use at a moment's notice. Like the resident portion of an operating system, many specialty programs stay entirely resident in RAM. As a result, you can use other programs while the specialty program waits in the background for your call.

Third, unfortunately, productivity programs are not always coordinated to work with one another. This incompatibility is no surprise, considering that these programs are developed by different companies. But, vendors are making a concerted effort to see that their software does not conflict with major products on the market.

You should have little or no trouble with the way your productivity programs relate to one another if they are developed by the same vendor and if you follow the instructions in the documentation. Three cases in point are SuperKey, Lightning, and Sidekick from Borland International, which co-exist beautifully if you follow Borland's instructions to load first SuperKey, then Lightning, and finally Sidekick.

Problems can begin when you mix products from different vendors. Section 5.3 of this chapter describes what you can do to maintain some measure of polite behavior among your software programs.

5.2 Take Advantage of Specialty Programs

Several popular productivity applications have been developed to eliminate three of the most insistent, nagging, and frustrating delays we encounter with microcomputers. You probably should avail yourself and your office of every one of the special applications discussed here. Each one can be used on personal computers and on many multi-user systems, but if you are unsure about whether your system can take advantage of them, contact your vendor.

Use a Supercharged Disk Drive

If I had to choose just one program to enhance productivity, it would be one that creates a supercharged disk drive: RAM disk software. We will discuss this application in detail. Personal preference aside, the discussion will establish concepts and principles that apply to subsequent sections in this book. And, just as important, many people who use RAM disk software misunderstand it. As a result, they use their systems inefficiently and sometimes lose files without knowing why. The information here will help to avoid those problems.

In Chapter Four we saw how neglected hard disks and diskettes impede system performance. For instance, a text file stored on non-contiguous disk space can take longer for a disk drive to read than if the same file were located on contiguous blocks of space. The delay occurs because the drive head must travel to the tracks on the disk where the file's fragments are located. If you follow the disk management techniques presented in Chapter Four, your disk drives will perform at their best.

But, no matter how fast you enable your disk drives to be, their efficiency is inherently limited because they operate mechanically. Whenever your computer needs information from a hard disk or a floppy diskette, the disk drive head mechanically must locate the required data and copy it into RAM. Although associated waiting might seem insignificant, with most systems the aggregate is unacceptable, particularly if you are running programs that repeatedly pursue information on a disk.

While you cannot always avoid the need to access information on a disk, you can eliminate having to wait while the information is fetched. RAM disk software is *the* solution, particularly when the alternative is a diskette drive. But, even hard disk speed can be

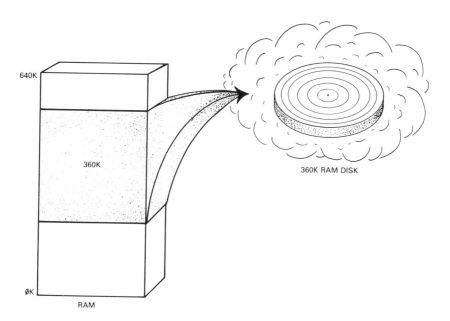

Figure 5.2. Your Disk Drive in the Sky. RAM disk software dedicates a portion of random access memory to function like a disk drive.

meaningfully outstripped by the speed achieved with this software.

Figure 5.2 illustrates that a RAM disk mimics a physical disk drive. (IBM calls this solution *virtual disk*, but we will use *RAM disk* because that term describes exactly what the software accomplishes.)

RAM disk software isolates a specific portion of random access memory to behave like a disk drive, joining the electronic speed of RAM with the function of a disk drive. Consider the RAM disk your "disk drive in the sky" which allows you to copy both data and programs to it.

Figure 5.3 demonstrates the speed advantage that a RAM disk's electronic transfers have over the mechanical process that your physical disk drives use. The figure also illustrates that a RAM disk does not eliminate disk access: it simply replaces the mechanical pro-

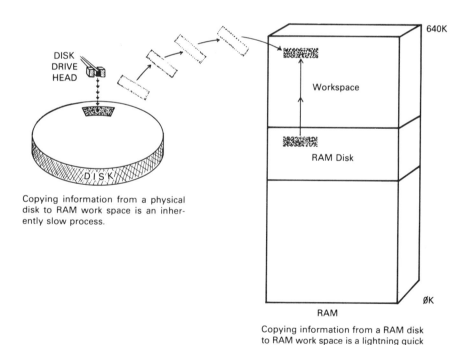

DISK
DRIVE
HEAD

DISK

Copying information from a physical
disk to RAM work space is an inherently slow process.

640K

Workspace

RAM Disk

ØK

RAM

Copying information from a RAM disk
to RAM work space is a lightning quick
electronic process.

Figure 5.3. The Advantage of a RAM Disk. The figure illustrates the advantage of a RAM disk, comparing electronic and mechanical processes of copying information into the computer's workspace.

cess with an electronic one. For some systems running certain processes, a RAM disk can boost system speed by a staggering 20:1.

How to Judge What to Use It For

A RAM disk improves the speed of many programs and processes that people run, but not all. People with huge amounts of RAM are tempted to use a RAM disk for all of their programs and data files, but this is a poor use of resources because nothing is gained from running certain types of files and programs from a RAM disk. Also, no matter how much RAM exists, it remains a precious and limited commodity.

Consequently, you must bring judgment to the question of which programs and files you should run from a RAM disk. How, then, do you decide? The determining factor is whether it will save time. The goal is to reduce or eliminate disk accesses because they impede system speed.

If a process requires repeated disk access, it will save time if the disk accessed is a RAM disk instead of a physical disk. Such processes are referred to as *disk intensive*. A disk intensive process is easy to identify because each time a disk is being read or written to, its indicator light flashes. Both floppy and hard disk drives have indicator lights, usually located on the front of the drive itself. Hard disks located on expansion boards typically have an indicator on the display screen that appears whenever the drive is used. If your hard disk is housed completely out of sight, you can easily verify whether or not a process is disk intensive by running it from a floppy disk drive.

Considering this information, let's see when you and those using your system will benefit by running data and programs from a RAM disk.

Generally, you will save time if you run data files from a RAM disk. See that your data files are accessed from a RAM disk whenever you sort a database, run a spelling checker, or merge information from two data files. Processes like those typically require the disk drive head to hop all over a disk for information.

In a few cases, you also will save time by running program files from a RAM disk. First, let's see when you gain nothing. As you know, your operating system has a resident portion. Most specialty programs (including RAM disk software) and many other application programs are entirely memory resident. Obviously, it would do no good to run these programs from a RAM disk because they already are 100 percent in RAM as soon as you invoke them. No further disk access is required.

So when do you run a program from a RAM disk? Consider doing so with programs that are not entirely RAM resident. When you invoke such a program, the main program file is copied to RAM. But certain modules of the program are omitted. As a result, the program has to fetch its modules whenever they are required. If you use a RAM disk to run a program that repeatedly accesses a disk for its modules, you eliminate the need and extra time required for a disk drive head to seek the modules on a physical disk.

If you are unsure whether a data file or a program would be most efficiently used from a RAM disk, try it both ways and see if you notice an improvement with the RAM disk.

Three Points For a Trouble-Free RAM Disk

Point #1: RAM disk is not RAM. Think of a RAM disk as just another hard or floppy disk. Figure 5.2 illustrates that a RAM disk is storage space, not work space. Files stored on a RAM disk are as idle as they are on a hard disk. They must be copied to random access memory workspace before they can be used.

Point #2: RAM disk is not a disk. The preceding point advises you to think of RAM as a physical disk drive. Do *not* do so from the standpoint of storing data permanently. Otherwise, it would be as if your janitor throws out all papers you leave on your desk each evening. Anything you want to keep must be filed. Likewise, anything stored on a RAM disk vanishes as soon as the system is turned off or otherwise loses power. To save information permanently, you must copy it to a physical disk drive. (That is not always the case. Check with your vendor for information about products that enable you to retain information in RAM even after the computer's power is cut.)

Point #3: RAM disk itself is temporary. A RAM disk itself is temporary, disappearing along with everything else in random access memory whenever the system is rebooted. If you turn off the system, you have to re-establish the RAM disk. Likewise, if you want to change its size or eliminate it entirely, you have to reboot the system to extract it from RAM.

A Warning About Copy Protection

In Chapter Four we mentioned that some software developers add copy protection schemes which limit the number of times a program can be copied. For obvious reasons, do not copy such programs to a RAM disk until you verify that you will not put your investment in jeopardy.

Print with Dispatch

RAM disk software is among the most useful specialty applications available, but there are others to consider. Printing from a personal computer and from some multi-user computers is inherently slow, whether your printer produces 20 or 400 characters per second. The reason lies in how the computer handles the fact that the printer is unable to print data as quickly as the computer can process it.

Whenever you send a file to be printed, it goes into the printer's own temporary internal storage area, called its *buffer*, on the way to be printed. Printer buffers typically are too small to store most documents in their entirety, much less a series of documents. Your printer's buffer might store a total of only 2000 characters, the equivalent of about one page of text. If your file is larger than the printer's buffer can hold, the computer compensates by transferring only so much information and then watching for when the buffer is empty before sending another batch. Whenever you print a document, you have to wait while the computer performs its traffic control role with the printer.

It is easy to find out if you are being detained. Evidence of the problem during a printing process includes (1) a slowdown in system performance and (2) a flashing disk drive indicator light which notifies you that the system is fetching data for the printer from the disk at intervals during the printing process. (The latter assumes the file is being printed from a hard disk or floppy disk drive rather than from a RAM disk.)

One way to overcome being dragged down by slow printing processes is to use a print spool program. Print spool software sets aside a portion of RAM to function as an extension of the printer's own buffer. As far as the computer is concerned, the data to be printed is safely and entirely dispatched to the printer much earlier than it would be were you without the extra storage space that the print spool provides, freeing the computer's attention for other processes.

Before you buy print spool software, see if you already own it. Some systems come with print spooling capability. Memory expansion cards for personal computers often include spooling software. Some word processing programs include a print spool option. Further, some systems, such as an IBM PC-AT running XENIX or the IBM PC Network, automatically spool print jobs.

If you have to buy a print spool software package, first check whether it will allow your files to be printed exactly as they would be printed without the software. For example, if you use the bold-face option when creating a document with your word processor, you want to be sure you are able to print in boldface through the spooler. With some programs, that might be impossible.

Whether or not you have to buy a separate software package, check your documentation to learn the control you are allowed over the spool. For example, IBM's PC Network has a print buffer, 512 bytes in size, on the network's server. You can increase the size of this buffer if you need a larger one.

| Tip |

The print spool is temporary storage, just like other RAM. For this reason, you must be careful to keep the computer on until all printing is completed. Otherwise, you might derail a job before it is fully printed.

| Another Solution |

Another way to print with dispatch is to install an external printer buffer. These units are devoted entirely to adding temporary storage and are readily available for just about all systems.

Create Custom Keyboards

However fast disk access or print processes are, our potential productivity can be reduced by the amount of time it takes us to tell the computer what we want it to do. It is not that human beings are slow. The issue is that the communication lines between you and the computer are needlessly slow, unless you take action to change the speed.

You can reduce frequently used commands to a single keystroke with the help of a keyboard redefinition program. Programs such as Borland International's SuperKey let you specify the meaning of single keys or key combinations. With those programs, you can get the computer to "memorize" anything from one character to a series of commands that will be executed when you hit the defined key(s).

You can redefine nearly all of the keys on your keyboard. Most key redefinition programs permit you to control the meaning of keys whether you are striking them from within the operating system or from within an application program. You even should be able to store in one keystroke a lengthy task that you perform frequently and that makes use of several programs.

The potential time saved by using powerful productivity boosters like SuperKey is staggering. In addition to improved efficiency, these programs can be used as a training tool and to help temporary employees get to work in minutes, regardless of whether they know how to use a particular program.

However, things can become complicated when you are confronted with competing key assignments. Suppose you use both your spreadsheet program and your word processor during a work session. Further suppose that your spreadsheet program itself allows you to define the meanings of keys, but when you use the word processor, you must use a program like SuperKey to define them. In that situation, while working on the spreadsheet, you easily might run into trouble if key definitions you previously established with SuperKey remain operative.

The problem can be solved with SuperKey and other programs which permit you to save key definition sets in individual files. That means you can create one keyboard to use with your word processor, another to run with your database program, and so on. Simply invoke the special key files to activate the keyboards of your choice. The solution to conflicts is to clear the active key assignments when you are finished using the first program and to activate a new set of key assignments to use with the second program.

Another way to avoid conflicts is to develop standard keyboard sets for office or company-wide use. Table 5.1 shows how the ten function keys on a PC might be assigned for everyone to use with WordStar. The key assignments are stored in a file named WS.KEY, which can be called up whenever a person uses the WordStar program.

Rules for Creating Standard Keyboard Sets

Follow these rules to create top notch keyboards for you and other staff members.

Rule #1: Do not do it alone. Gather a small group of imaginative employees to develop a standard keyboard for each program. (In my experience, large groups tend to spend excessive time in discussion.)

Rule #2: Keep key assignments you should retain. If your applications come with ready-made key assignments, leave them intact *unless* you specifically decide to override them. Likewise, avoid assigning common typewriter key combinations like Shift-A. If you assign this combination or others like it, the first time you try to produce a capital letter, you will be surprised with the results.

Rule #3: Make your keyboards similar. Keep keyboards relatively similar so people are not stymied when they have to use another person's workstation. Take as an example the ten function keys on a personal computer (Figure 5.4). You can set aside the first seven or eight function keys on a personal computer for commands that vary according to the particular application being run. You might take consistency one step further and assign to the F2 key, for instance, the necessary command to save a file to disk. Under this system, striking the F2 key on each of your custom keyboards would save the file in progress, regardless of the program being used.

Rule #4: Leave room for personal preference. Leave available specific keys or key combinations so that people can assign them to meet special needs or personal preference.

Rule #5: Test before releasing. After you have agreed on common keyboards for your programs, establish the keyboards and then test them. *Do not* test them with original work. This precaution will protect your data should you inadvertently have omitted a

Table 5.1

KEY ASSIGNMENTS

Date _____   Prepared By _____

Sample Key Assignments for the Ten Function Keys on a PC For Use with WordStar

Program <u>WordStar</u>
Key Filename <u>WS.KEY</u>

KEY	KEY STROKES STORED	COMMAND
F1	ˆU	*Stop a process/Cancel a command
F2	ˆKSˆQP	*Save and continue working Return to previous position
F3	ˆQC	*Move to bottom of file
F4	ˆQR	*Move to top of file
F5	ˆQF.<CR><CR>[1]	Move to end of sentence
F6	ˆQF.<space><space><space><CR><CR>[2]	Move to end of paragraph
F7	ˆPBˆQDˆPBˆOC	Boldface and center a line
F8	[unassigned][3]	
F9	[unassigned]	
F10	[unassigned]	
[etc.]		

* = signifies a COMMAND that appears on *all* keyboards, even though the actual keystrokes stored will vary.

NOTES:

1. <CR> signifies a carriage return
2. <space> signifies striking the space bar once. The sample command for the F6 key works only if you insert three blank spaces at the end of each paragraph in your WordStar text file.
3. Staff members are free to use the unassigned keys as they wish.

Table 5.2

KEY ASSIGNMENTS
Date _____   Prepared By _____

Program _____
Key Filename _____

KEY	KEY STROKES STORED	COMMAND

Ten
Function
Keys

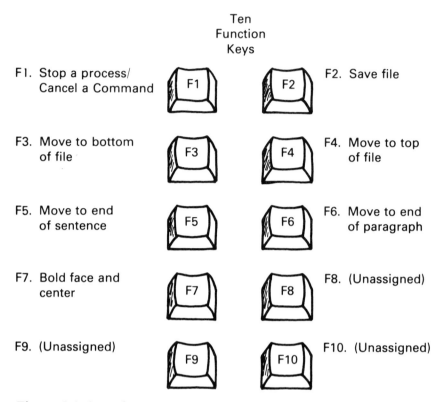

F1. Stop a process/
     Cancel a Command

F2. Save file

F3. Move to bottom
     of file

F4. Move to top
     of file

F5. Move to end
     of sentence

F6. Move to end
     of paragraph

F7. Bold face and
     center

F8. (Unassigned)

F9. (Unassigned)

F10. (Unassigned)

Figure 5.4. Sample Key Assignments. Function keys 1 through 7 on the sample IBM PC have standard meanings, regardless of the program being used. Keys 8 through 10 are available for people to assign as they wish.

needed character or otherwise mis-typed a command. A simple example illustrates the point. Suppose you want to store in one key the commands both to save your WordStar text file and to return your cursor to where you left off in the file. The series of commands you should be storing would be ^KS (to save) and ^QP (to return to your previous position in the text). If you run the test using original work and you had the misfortune accidentally to store ^KQ^SP, you would lose changes made to the file since the last time you saved your work because the ^KQ command abandons the file and bumps you into WordStar's opening menu. Protect yourself and your data: save your worksheet, text file, or database before you test or experiment with new key assignments.

Rule #6: Document your keyboards. Document the standard key assignments for each program on a form similar to Table 5.2. Use the sample on Table 5.1 as a guide. Pass copies of your completed charts to others for general use and personal adaptation. Be sure to keep a copy of each chart in the system library.

Tip

When you store a lengthy process in one key or key combination, such as a process that makes use of several application programs, print the series of commands to document the key assignment.

5.3 How to Cope with Misbehaving Specialty Programs

A single productivity program rarely causes problems when it is the only program you are using during a work session, but some of these programs will run amok in the company of an application, such as when you have trouble running your word processing program with a productivity program. Be on special alert when you use more than one utility simultaneously (i.e. when you have at least two concurrently loaded in RAM). Utility programs often collide or otherwise misbehave in one another's company. The resulting clash—whether between two utility programs or between one such program and an application—can be as harmless as a chirping computer or as serious as a deadlocked system.

Software developers are fairly successful keeping their own programs out of one another's way, less so with programs that other companies develop. Unfortunately, the various specialty applications you want to use probably are unavailable from a single company. If that is the case, you will have to mix programs from different companies and anticipate a few fights among them.

Prevent Collisions

You are not helpless in the face of such problems. Developers frequently know what hitches you can expect when using their products in conjunction with those of another company.

The best way to avoid collisions is to read and follow the instructions in your documentation. Most firms are conscientious about advising you. For example, Borland International describes the oddities of using Sidekick with some of the better-known programs, such as Framework. Borland also advises (1) that you load its programs last and (2) that Sidekick be the very last program loaded. We will see why later in this section.

Advice in software company documentation can be very useful, but it is not enough. First, for obvious reasons, few will make a point to publicize that their programs clash with a famed product, although they will tell you if you ask. Hence, you have to ask and also read product reviews to find out where deadly incompatibilities exist. (If you are interested in a product that fails to run peacefully with one of your existing software programs, the incompatibility might be eliminated in a subsequent version, so check with your vendor.)

Also, no software company can anticipate all the combinations of programs you might run. Contact the company's technical support division for their advice. If they are unable to help you, conduct your own tests before releasing specialty programs for office or company-wide use. (See Section 7.4 for suggested tests.)

The Importance of Loading Sequence

As things are today, the sequence in which programs are loaded into RAM is extremely important for avoiding trouble. That is because of the way some operating systems (such as DOS version 3.1 and earlier) allocate RAM. It is different from the way we have seen that files are copied to disk space on a hard or floppy disk. Recall from Chapter Four that DOS, for example, stores data on a hard or floppy disk wherever space is available. If need be, a single file can occupy space "miles apart" on the disk.

The case is different with information copied into RAM. DOS, for example, needs contiguous RAM for loading programs and data. If no contiguous block large enough for a program is available, the system refuses to load the program. Moreover, just one blank space in the middle of RAM confuses DOS. (Note that multi-user systems do not have this problem because their operating systems typically are designed to store information in non-contiguous RAM as a matter of course.)

Suppose that when you were editing the letter we discussed earlier in this chapter, you first loaded two specialty programs, both SuperKey and Sidekick, to use during the work session. Figure 5.5 shows how RAM would have been allocated had you loaded everything in the proper sequence.

Let's take the letter example one step further. You have finished editing your text file. Now you want to make space in RAM to edit a large spreadsheet that you previously created. Both Sidekick and SuperKey will allow you to delete them from RAM without flipping off your computer. If you delete only SuperKey, you will leave

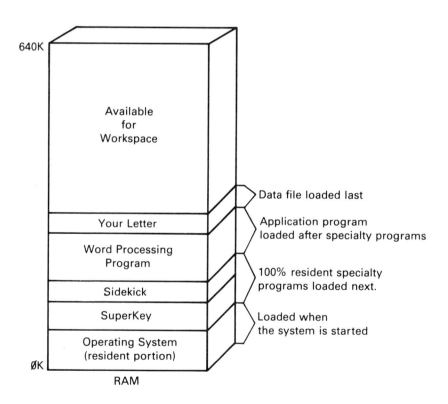

Figure 5.5. Proper Software Program Loading Sequence.

a blank spot between Sidekick and the resident portion of the operating system. (Refer to Figure 5.5.) The blank space is a time bomb that may be your undoing, one that might not explode immediately. In fact, you might load your spreadsheet program and your worksheet without mishap and spend fifteen minutes editing with no sign of trouble until you try to save your file. One poor soul had this experience and lost the better part of an important data file stored on his hard disk because DOS went crazy over that blank space.

To avoid collisions, pass on these rules of thumb to the others using the system:

1. After you boot your system (in order to load the resident portion of your operating system into RAM), load all other resident programs (RAM disk, print spooler, keyboard redefinition program, etc.). Be careful to load once and only once any utility program that stays resident in RAM. A well-written program such as SuperKey will not duplicate itself, but you cannot be certain that every utility program you use will behave as well. Next, load your application programs as you need them.
2. Always follow software manufacturers' instructions for loading their programs.
3. Leave no gaping holes. If you want to delete programs from RAM, *always* delete them in last-in-first-out order.
4. Once you have determined the proper loading sequence, write it into a batch file to prevent future mistakes.

Some Conflict is Inevitable

You can be familiar with your documentation and dutifully follow its advice and yet still encounter roadblocks when you mix specialty programs.

One reason is that sometimes programs handle basic communications inside of the computer differently. Software developers are not trying to cause anyone grief. The incompatibility usually is an unavoidable by-product either of improving processing speed or of bypassing the shortcomings of an operating system designed to orchestrate only one task at a time.

One example of that type of incompatibility is in how programs handle putting information on the video display screen. To illustrate the point, we will look at an example of a specialty program run with an application program. Your system can misbehave when you run Framework and Sidekick (version 1.56A). Suppose while viewing a graph with Framework, you decide to use Sidekick's notepad. As soon as you activate Sidekick and as long as you keep it activated, your graph will be replaced by a pattern of meaningless characters or will disappear entirely. When Sidekick is returned to the background, your graph reappears because Framework has recaptured control of how things are displayed on the screen.

While that is no serious problem (unless you need to see the graph to write your note), it illustrates what can happen when you combine programs that handle the system differently. In this case, when you display the graph with Framework, the monitor is in graphics mode and when you bring up Sidekick, the monitor is switched to text mode. The result turns the graph into gibberish or blanks it out entirely. (This result is not peculiar to Framework and Sidekick. You will have a similar problem whenever you simultaneously use a program that displays information in text mode with one that displays it in graphics mode.)

Another problem you might encounter—one that is much more serious—occurs when a program takes control of the system and refuses to let go of it. Not every program is well-mannered enough to release control.

Find the Offender
When Programs Collide

When you have inexplicable problems running an application program along with specialty programs, it could be that there has been a collision of the sort described above. It should be easy to identify the offending program. Run through the following steps.

Step One. Reboot and run the application program by itself, without loading the specialty program. See whether the application runs problem free. Trouble at this juncture indicates trouble with the application, so contact your vendor. Otherwise, continue to step two.

Step Two. Conduct this eight-part test.

1. Boot to load the operating system.
2. Load into RAM your favorite or most essential specialty program.

3. Invoke the specialty program and see if it works. Do something simple with it. For example, with a program like Sidekick, write a one-line note or add two figures with the calculator. With a RAM disk program, log on to the RAM disk and run a directory of its contents.

4. Exit the specialty program, (i.e. put Sidekick away, log off of the RAM disk, and so on).

5. Load the application program, and see if it functions.

6. Run the application along with the specialty program and see if they work together. For instance, with a program like Sidekick, enter the application program before you invoke the notepad. With RAM disk software, run the application from the RAM disk.

7. Create a short test file using your application. Save the file. Then, reopen the file and see if it is intact. Keep in mind that you are out of the woods only after you successfully save a file to a disk.

8. Continue to step three if you have as yet run into no trouble.

Step Three. Reboot and repeat parts 2 through 7 under step two, adding utility programs, one by one, on top of the first. Reboot each time you finish part 7 and need to add a new program to the test. Keep adding specialty programs until you encounter trouble.

As soon as you run into a problem, it is likely to be associated with the last specialty program you added. Try loading your specialty programs in a different sequence; double-check your documentation.

Unfortunately, you might learn that you have a combination of programs that are unavoidably incompatible. If the source of the problem remains a mystery, call your vendor as a last resort.

5.4 Keep Track of How You Use RAM

By now you should have a good grasp of important ways to squeeze top performance from your computer with programs that enable you to use RAM for all it is worth. How well you do so depends partly on your knowledge of how your system uses RAM, regardless of how much or how little you have.

There was a time when 64K of RAM was comfortable for a mainframe computer. Today, some consider ten times that to be paltry for a personal computer. Even some who use PC's loaded with 8 megabytes feel themselves held back.

But, the amount is less important than the need to manage it sensibly. For example, the 640K system in Figure 5.1 has a significant percentage of idle RAM when the PC is used for editing letters. The system's manager could use some of the available RAM to improve productivity by adding a print spool. Likewise, imagine a PC with a full 8 megabytes of expanded memory. Suppose that the personnel manager uses this PC to maintain a 7.5 megabyte database file of employee information. Further suppose that he creates a RAM disk of equal size for work sessions that involve extensive updates to the database. This leaves but a small—and possibly insufficient—percentage of RAM for other simultaneous needs, such as those mentioned earlier in this chapter. RAM management techniques should be applied to both of these systems.

No matter how much you have and despite industry advances, RAM remains a limited resource. This means you have to figure out how best to allocate it, how best to fit your most needed and functional programs while leaving room for data files, and how best to take advantage of specialty programs designed to increase productivity and those designed to make your work and that of other staff members easier.

The first step in practical RAM management is to understand how the system's existing RAM is used. With all of the possible contenders for RAM, you want to establish how much you require for basic needs, how much for the specialty programs you find valuable, and how much for data files.

Managing RAM is an Art

The worksheets in this section are not meant to imply that managing RAM is a science. No ironclad rules exist because too many elements are involved and too many are far too difficult to pin down. Several components cloud the issue.

Generally, whenever you ask the computer to do something, the task may require RAM for program code and for task execution. Information is constantly shuffled in and out of RAM, and it is impossible to pinpoint how much RAM is needed at a particular moment. For example, your operating system might create temporary files as it conducts its work, and you cannot calculate exactly how much RAM these files occupy at any point during the day. Certain productivity and application programs automatically bring an overhead RAM requirement that is quite difficult to calculate. Furthermore, the amount of RAM needed can fluctuate from version to version of the same program!

In addition, your software might have modules that it loads from time to time during a work session. With insufficient RAM, a program can halt the system, or "crash." Also, integrated programs, such as Framework, can bring a special RAM overhead on top of what you might expect them to need for data. These programs might need more space for a five-page text file than your word processor would.

Finally, the entire issue is complicated when you add concurrent processing, which we will look at separately at the end of this section.

In most cases, then, you have no way of knowing how much RAM each program needs at a given moment, unless you contact the programmer(s) who wrote it. However, you need not go that far, and you need not despair. Estimates will carry you through.

Instead of an exact science, managing RAM is something between a guessing game and an art. Although it is doubtful that you will establish precise figures, you need a sense of how well the resource is being used. What can you expect to learn? Maybe you will find that productivity could be increased dramatically if you add additional RAM to accommodate a particular specialty program. Maybe you will discover that you are using RAM just short of the limit and therefore are perilously close to system crashes. Or maybe you will learn that a substantial portion sits idle much of the day, waiting for you to engage it productively.

Understand the Minimum RAM Requirement

You probably are familiar with the minimum RAM requirement software developers state in documentation. The first step in evaluating how a system uses RAM is to understand that you cannot learn the total space needed simply by adding up the minimum

RAM requirement for each and every program you want to run during a work session.

For example, suppose you run both Sidekick and SuperKey. Borland International recommends a minimum of 128K of RAM for each program. Does that mean you need twice the amount in order to run both programs successfully during the same work session? No, because the 128K includes some duplication. Then what does the company's recommendation tell you? First, each product will run on a system that has a minimum of 128K; try either one on a system with less, and you probably will be out of luck. Second, the 128K minimum assumes that the program is being run with DOS only; add another program, and the system will require more RAM. These facts tell us that minimum requirement figures generally account for four categories of information:

1. **The resident portion of your operating system.** We discussed the meaning of residency in Section 5.1 of this chapter.
2. **The resident portion of the program itself.** As explained earlier, while many of your application programs may be entirely resident, some programs have only certain portions that remain resident while you use them. In such a case, other program modules are fetched as needed.
3. **Program overhead (if needed).** Most programs need extra space for their own processes. The amount of overhead varies, depending on the program and how it functions, but the amount is generally modest and in fact can be quite negligible. However, program overhead can be as large as 10 or 15 percent of the RAM needed to accommodate the program's resident portion.
4. **Space for data.** You also need space to accommodate the whole point of using computers: data files. The amount of space needed for data files obviously varies a lot.

Calculate Reasonable Estimates

While we cannot break down minimum requirement figures to specifically account for the four elements that need RAM, we can use the categories themselves to calculate reasonable estimates.

Considering that all you can do is to establish estimates, some of them very rough, let's look at how you use RAM. In this section, complete a RAM worksheet for each computer on your system to compare the amount of memory it has with the amount needed to run your programs during a single work session. The process will enable you to judge approximately how effectively RAM is used on each computer.

Use a spreadsheet or database management program to complete your worksheets if you can. That way, your figures will be calculated automatically. In addition, should you find that you could improve the way RAM is used, the computer will perform calculations for you as you experiment with various allocation schemes.

Two worksheets are provided. Use RAM Worksheet #1, Table 5.3, for computers without expanded memory. As you work through your calculation, refer to Table 5.4, a sample Worksheet #1 completed for a PC with 640K of *conventional memory*, conventional memory being RAM that the operating system can access directly. Use RAM Worksheet #2, Table 5.5, for computers that contain expanded memory. (Before completing Worksheet #2, read the section "If Your System Has Expanded Memory.")

Each worksheet has four parts. The first identifies the total amount of RAM the system has. The second identifies the amount of RAM the computer will use for resident programs. The third identifies the amount of RAM your applications need when you run them. The fourth is for you to keep a running balance of available RAM on the far right-hand side of each worksheet.

A Sample Calculation: Conventional Memory Only

Follow the steps below to complete Worksheet #1 for your personal computers that have conventional memory only. If all of your PC's have the same amount of RAM and if they always run identical programs, prepare this worksheet only once for your standard configuration. At the other extreme, if you have PC's that run different combinations of specialty and application programs during various work sessions, prepare several worksheets for each PC. You will want to do that if a computer sometimes is used exclusively for word processing with a print spool and other times strictly for spreadsheet analysis and word processing.

Refer to the sample Worksheet #1, Table 5.4, which is completed for a PC loaded with 640K RAM and running these programs:

1. The DOS 3.1 operating system;
2. Three specialty programs: a RAM disk, SuperKey, and Side-kick; and
3. WordStar

Step One. Computer ID. First, identify the computer in question with the device name you assigned it in Chapter Two when you completed your system devices map. The computer Table 5.4 describes is PC01, Michael's PC in the sample LAN from Figure 2.1.

Step Two. How much RAM does the system have? Insert the computer's total amount of RAM in the blank. The sample PC has 640K.

Step Three. How much RAM is used for resident programs? Here you are concerned with the amount of RAM needed for programs that stay resident until you reboot the system or power down. Begin with your operating system.

a. Operating system. Insert your operating system's name and version in the space provided. Next, insert the amount of RAM your operating system's resident portion occupies.

There are two ways to find out approximately how much space the resident system needs. First, calculate it by increasing the size of the program by about 15 percent. With DOS, you also might boot your system to load *only* the operating system. Then, issue the CHKDSK command. The screen will tell you both the total amount of RAM on the system and how much of it remains. The difference between these figures is the space the resident portion of the operating system needs. DOS 3.1 on the sample system occupies about 37K.

Let's continue with the worksheet. Now, subtract the resident portion from the total amount of RAM to derive the running balance figure under item 4 on the worksheet. (If you ran CHKDSK, the running balance at this point should be the same as the available balance shown on the screen.) On the sample system, 603K is available after the operating system is loaded.

b. Resident specialty programs. The worksheet provides room for four specialty programs that you might run simultaneously. Add spaces if you need them. For each program that remains resident in RAM until you reboot, first insert the program's name and version. Then, insert the space the program needs. Remember that some specialty programs will require space for more than program code alone. For example, RAM disk software will need (1) space for the program and (2) space for the RAM disk itself, (4K and 256K, respectively, for the system documented in the sample worksheet).

The simplest way to figure out the total amount of space each specialty program needs is to perform the following process. For DOS systems, load each program, one at a time. Issue CHKDSK after you load each one to see how much additional space has been used.

Otherwise, first figure out the space needed for the program itself by adding 15 percent to the size of the program (as described earlier in this step). To the resulting figure add the additional space needed. This depends upon the program, such as the size of a RAM disk, a print spool, a notepad, and so on.

Notice the three programs and their required space listed on the sample worksheet.

> | *Tip* |
>
> *Some specialty programs, including a few RAM disk and print spool programs, do not use system RAM. They come with an expansion board that sets aside RAM specifically and exclusively for the program. Others use hard disk space instead of random access memory. If you have programs that bring a dowry like this, ignore them on your RAM worksheets.*

Step Four. Running balance. Insert the new running balance of available RAM after you account for the space each program needs. Notice that about 215K is available after the sample system accommodates all of its specialty programs.

Step Five. How much RAM is needed for applications? With this step, your calculations move squarely into the area of artistry or guesswork, whichever term you prefer. It is likely that a given PC on your system is used for several applications. To complete this section, select the program that requires the most RAM. Let's see why.

Unless you are running concurrent applications, usually, only one application program uses RAM at a single time: as soon as you exit a program, it frees the space it occupied in RAM. But while the program is in use, it demands its share. If the RAM it needs is unavailable, the shortage can be fatal: the system might crash inelegantly and lost files can result. Thus, it makes sense to know the maximum RAM the computer must provide to a program. Your best bet is to use your hungriest application program for this part of your calculation, but before you proceed, take note of the tip.

Tip

You could tailor how you use RAM depending on the program or constellation of programs being run. That can be a bad practice whenever it changes the way people use the system. For example, it might confuse people if you establish a RAM disk for times when Program A is run and eliminate it when Program B is run. If you constantly change the way the system is set up, people will be after your head, and understandably so. The only exception is when people both prefer and fully understand the implications of the various configurations and know how to use them without mishap.

With a program selected, note that this part of the worksheet provides space for RAM required for the program itself and for RAM required for the data you will manipulate while using the program.

Derive the approximate amount of RAM the program itself needs by using the following process. Look at a directory listing of the program's files to find out the size of the main program and increase it by 15 percent. (With DOS systems, these files typically have the extension .COM or .EXE.) On the sample worksheet, WordStar occupies about 22K on disk, which inflates to about 25K when increased by 15 percent.

Table 5.3

RAM WORKSHEET #1

Date _____   Prepared By _____

For computers with conventional memory only

_____
Computer ID

1. How much RAM does the system have?

_____K
Conventional Memory

2. How much RAM is used for resident programs?

Program Name & Version	RAM Needed
a. _____ Operating System	_____K Resident Amount
b. _____ Resident Specialty	_____K
_____ Resident Specialty	_____K
_____ Resident Specialty	_____K
_____ Resident Specialty	_____K

4. Running balance

_____K
Balance

_____K
Balance

_____K
Balance

_____K
Balance

_____K
Balance

3. How much RAM is needed for applications?

	Prog Size	Data Space Needed
_____ Program Name & Version	_____K	_____K

_____K
Balance

Table 5.4

RAM WORKSHEET #1

Date _____   Prepared By _____

For computers with conventional memory only
(Sample)

_____PC01_____
Computer ID

1. How much RAM does the system have?   _____640_____ K
_____Conventional Memory

2. How much RAM is used for resident programs?		**4. Running balance**
Program Name & Version	**RAM Needed**	
a. PC-DOS 3.1 / Operating System	37 K / Resident Amount	603 K / Balance
b. RAM Disk / Resident Specialty	260 K	343 K / Balance
Superkey 1.11A / Resident Specialty	64 K	279 K / Balance
SideKick 1.56A / Resident Specialty	64 K	215 K / Balance
_____ / Resident Specialty	K	K / Balance

3. How much RAM is needed for applications?

	Prog Size	Data Space Needed	
WordStar 3.31 / Program Name & Version	25 K	168 K	22 K / Balance

To figure out how much space the system needs for data, run a directory of data files created with the program. Insert the figure of the largest file in the space "Data Space Needed." That figure for the sample system is 168K.

Be sure to insert the running balance after you account for the RAM needed for both the application and data. Notice the sample system has a final running balance of 22K.

What to Do with Your Calculation

Although your calculations are estimates, each worksheet offers valuable information. It provides a good map of how RAM is used on a particular computer, based on the programs it has to run during the neediest work session. A worksheet also shows the approximate bottom line balance of available RAM. With that information, you can better decide if you should make adjustments to how you have set up the computer. And, if change is needed, the worksheet should help you decide where it can and should be made.

For example, if I managed the PC whose RAM distribution is displayed in the sample worksheet, I would feel uneasy. The 22K bottom line is less than 4 percent of the total RAM on the system. That amount is too tight for my comfort. I would adjust the allocation immediately to avoid the risk of a system freeze and lost work.

Turn to your own completed worksheet. No matter what the bottom line, you will want to analyze the figures.

If you are comfortable with the bottom line. Satisfaction with the bottom line does not necessarily translate into a system that uses RAM most effectively. Take a closer look at each category of use. Do the allocations make sense? Or would you be better off to increase the size of your RAM disk and decrease the print spool? Should you eliminate a specialty program entirely? Would the system be more efficient if you were to add a new specialty program?

If there is plenty of room. If you find a huge amount of RAM unused on the system, find a way to use it to increase productivity or improve system efficiency. Consider adding a useful specialty program or increasing the amount assigned to your existing specialty programs.

If space is tight. Your system should have more breathing space than the one in the sample. When little RAM is available, you have two alternatives. You can add RAM to the system or you can adjust the existing allocation. In addition to the questions raised above, ask yourself if there are any unneeded programs occupying valuable RAM. Maybe you need to arrange programs to work in groups, depending on the particular applications you run (but *only* if people are willing to use various configurations). For instance, you could pull out the print spool for times the database management program is in use.

In making these decisions, work jointly with the people using the system. Your RAM worksheets will assist you with the process. Store them in the system library. Whenever you add RAM or software to your system, update your worksheets to evaluate whether further change makes sense.

If Your System Has Expanded Memory

When you add expanded memory to a system, RAM management has even more ifs, ands, and buts than systems with only conventional memory because a program can handle expanded memory in several ways. To begin, not every program is able to use expanded memory. (You can be sure programmers are scurrying around to modify code in existing programs so that they will not be left behind.) Another variation is that some programs can use expanded memory before conventional memory is exhausted, while other programs will use expanded memory only after the first 640K is unavailable.

Regardless of how a program *handles* memory, expanded memory is used for the same purposes as conventional memory. One is direct use for data, as a program would use any RAM. Another is to use it with utility programs, such as a print spool or a RAM disk. Print spools and RAM disks in expanded memory function as do their counterparts occupying conventional memory. Third, the programs themselves can reside in expanded memory. (At the time of this writing, the last way is possible only as long as a small portion of the program is in conventional memory, the only place that the operating system can find it. For example, a popular outlining program requires 130K of space, but it is constructed so that it needs only 3K of conventional RAM; the rest can reside in expanded memory. The average program does not yet allow that.)

Your programs may use expanded memory in one or more of the above ways, although all undoubtedly can access a RAM disk located there. The way your programs use expanded memory has an impact on how you will complete your RAM worksheet. For each program that uses expanded memory, you have to ask for what purposes it does so.

That means you need a worksheet different from the one we already have examined. First, you want to keep two running balances: one for conventional memory and another for expanded memory. Second, you have to account for programs that use expanded memory only for data. For instance, the Above Board's RAM disk software resides in conventional memory, while the RAM disk itself can reside in expanded memory. You want to be able to break out the amount of space specialty programs need for program code itself from the amount their data occupies. ("Data" for specialty programs refers to a number of possibilities: with a RAM disk or print spool it would be the actual size you specify for the RAM disk or print spool. With a keyboard redefinition program, it would be the space set aside to store key definitions.)

Refer for a moment to Worksheet #2, Table 5.5. Notice the addition of a column for both expanded memory and its running balance at the right side of the worksheet. Also notice that item 2 enables you to distinguish between the space specialty programs use for themselves and the space needed for data.

To complete the worksheet, follow the same steps described for Worksheet #1 above, with only two changes. First, estimate the size of the resident specialty software program by increasing the size of the program itself by another 15 percent, as you do with application programs when following the instructions for Worksheet #1. The only other difference comes with your running balances. For each demand on RAM, ask yourself which type of memory is needed: conventional memory or expanded memory. Subtract the amount of needed RAM from the available balance in the appropriate column. For example, if you use a 4K program in conventional memory to establish a 2 megabyte RAM disk in expanded memory, reduce the amount of available conventional memory by 4K and the amount of available expanded memory by the 2 megabytes of space set aside for the RAM disk.

Review the results of your calculation using the same process described above for systems with only conventional memory. (Refer to the information in the section immediately preceding, "What to do with Your Calculation.")

There is one additional bit of advice to follow for systems with expanded memory. Some software developers graciously include

Table 5.5

RAM WORKSHEET #2

Date _____   Prepared By _____

For computers with expanded memory

_____
Computer ID

1. How much RAM does the system have?

_____K _____K
Conventional Expanded
Memory   Memory

2. How much RAM is used for resident programs?

4. Running balance

Program Name	RAM Needed		
a. _____	_____K	_____K	_____K
Operating System	Resident Amount	Balance	Balance

	Prog Size	Data Space Needed		
b. _____	_____K	_____K	_____K	_____K
Resident Specialty			Balance	Balance
_____	_____K	_____K	_____K	_____K
Resident Specialty			Balance	Balance
_____	_____K	_____K	_____K	_____K
Resident Specialty			Balance	Balance
_____	_____K	_____K	_____K	_____K
Resident Specialty			Balance	Balance

3. How much RAM is needed for applications?

	Prog Size	Data Space Needed		
b. _____	_____K	_____K	_____K	_____K
Program Name & Version			Balance	Balance

recommendations for the amount of space you should set aside for their programs. For example, when you install Intel's Above Board Print Spooler and RAM disk, the installation software checks the amount of memory your system has and calculates the probable "best size" for your print spool and your RAM disk. As useful as such suggestions are, you might want to change the recommended value. Elaborate calculations are not required. Just take some time to consider whether the recommended size makes sense for your system. For example, suppose an accountant, who uses an IBM PC with 640K of conventional memory and 2048K of expanded memory, manipulates database files in the neighborhood of 1.5 megabytes. A 192K or 256K RAM disk, about the recommended size, would be feebly small in that case.

RAM and Concurrent Processing

We have to digress briefly to understand what concurrent processing is and what it has to offer before we can see how it affects your system's use of RAM.

When you add a software program to your PC's that establishes what is called a concurrent processing environment, the program takes control of how system resources (CPU time and RAM) are used. You can load multiple applications which you can use and switch among as you wish, without exiting any of them. The environment divides CPU time among the programs you have loaded, so you often can have a task take place with one program while you work with another. For example, you can have your mailing list sorted while you write a letter. When you resume work with a previously loaded program, you can return to the precise point where you left off.

Concurrent processing software does even more. Typically, you can move information stored with one program to a file created with another program. For example, you can join a graph created with your spreadsheet program with text created with your word processor. Further, some programs stretch your RAM because they allow you to run more applications than otherwise would fit into RAM. How? By sharing what the computer has among all of the programs. As memory is needed, the software in charge of the environment temporarily removes from RAM (or "swaps out" of RAM) what need not be there at that particular moment.

As wonderful as this capability is, these programs have their drawbacks. The first and most obvious is that they require a huge amount of RAM to run, in the neighborhood of 120K to 200K. Another problem you might find when you run programs under one of these environments is a degradation in system performance. The degradation can be negligible, depending upon the application you are running. You also might encounter compatibility problems. Programs you have today may work or may bomb when operating under these environments. Collisions similar to those mentioned earlier in the chapter may very well rear their heads when you try to run your programs under a concurrent processing program.

Check with your vendor before you buy. Investigate the product thoroughly. (See Section 7.4 for advice about developing your system.) Control the fervor you might feel about new possibilities. It may be that you and your colleagues are better off switching between programs manually. The decision depends on your office environment, the programs you run, and people's preferred style of working. There are people who operate well in frenetic worlds, people whose productivity or peace of mind would be increased were they to have concurrent processing capability, and people who lust after the ability to use more than one program at a time. A concurrent processing environment might be the right one for any of them. But, there are people who have no need or desire for such an environment. Remember that concurrent processing might not be the answer for everyone just yet.

Concurrent Processing and Your RAM Worksheets

The calculations in the foregoing pages purposely exclude the issue of concurrent processing because, as we've just seen, concurrent processing usually turns RAM allocation on its head, treating memory in sophisticated ways that differ from program to program. Concurrent processing environments provide their own memory managers that can defy the artistry you are attempting with your RAM worksheets.

The exception is when you are using a program that uses RAM in much the same manner as the application and specialty programs discussed earlier. In that case, to use the RAM worksheets, consider the concurrent processing program as you would any other resident program, and be sure to account for application programs that will occupy RAM simultaneously under the concurrent processing environment.

Conclusion

In this chapter you learned principles to manage random access memory and discovered its role in influencing system performance. You now have tools to evaluate how efficiently your system makes use of this important resource.

Memory is one of the foremost areas in which technological advances are being made. Watch the developments carefully. As you discover hardware and software products that use memory to increase system power, come back to this chapter so that you can integrate where you plan to take your system with where it already is.

Part III

Prevent Crises
and Solve Problems

6

Secure Your System

Introduction

In this chapter we will switch gears from resource management to resource protection. Whatever business or industry you are in, somebody considers your equipment, your computer time, your software, or your data a desirable target for trespassing, theft, or vandalism.

Companies have always taken security measures, no matter how minimal, such as locking office doors and following generally accepted accounting practices. Some companies have security programs that include elaborate procedures and electronic screening devices to monitor visitors and even employees.

Whatever level of security your company historically has needed, most likely security became more difficult when you installed its computer system. Did your company revamp its security program at that time? Would a person intent on stealing a sensitive report find it easier to copy the report from a hard disk to a floppy diskette than to get his or her hands on a paper copy? It is only a matter of time before someone attempts that or some other security violation.

Your responsibilities include protecting the value of the system and its data. Take action now, rather than wait for something to happen. Use this chapter to identify threats to your system, to evaluate your options, and to implement the ones you select. If your firm needs top security, supplement this chapter with one or more book-length pieces on computer security. Possibly, you need a professional risk manager.

It takes time to develop or fine-tune a security program. Furthermore, security measures can be expensive. Thus, whatever level of security your system requires, you need management support to have the resources and cooperation to implement it. If you see that management must be convinced how important your program is, demonstrate how easy it is to violate the system's security. One system manager convinced the company owner only after presenting a purloined list of employees and their confidential salaries. If you cannot make your point short of committing a crime, simply acquaint people with the threats described in Section 6.1.

6.1 Appraise the Situation

To design a security program, you need to know what you are up against. What do you have to lose? Who are possible culprits? What are they after? How might they get to it?

You have much to lose through someone's machinations. Usually, the motive is financial gain; sometimes it is malice. The right data can command a hefty sum and it is said that revenge is sweet. Anything on your system is a potential target. Aside from the equipment itself, typical targets are your company's bank account, receivables, payables, client lists, client data, and employee files.

The Range of Threat to Your System

The range of violation is as broad as the range of perpetrators, from petty infractions committed by otherwise honest individuals to major criminal acts. Here are five actual cases:

1. An employee snoops in unguarded personnel records to learn someone's marital status.
2. A salesperson transferring to another firm leaves with an unauthorized copy of the company's entire client list.
3. A employee marks as paid a relative's outstanding debt to the firm.
4. A legal assistant to a defense attorney alerts the prosecuting attorney's assistant when to tap into the communications line for critical documents that will be transmitted to the courthouse.
5. A secretary sells information describing well-guarded company financial trouble to an unscrupulous stockbroker.

People always have had access to company information and have committed such acts long before computers arrived. But, computers—particularly unguarded systems—not only make these violations easier to commit than before, but also they make it less likely for the perpetrators to be caught. Compare how times have changed, using the first four of the five situations mentioned above as examples:

1. Unprotected personnel records are available to anyone who has access to a terminal on the system. Before the computer

was installed, these records were less accessible because they were housed in the personnel manager's office.

2. A salesperson can copy the company's client list to a diskette and walk out with it hidden in a briefcase. In pre-computer days, each salesperson had private lists or the complete list was quite secure in the sales manager's office.
3. Unlike before, clever and determined employees can adjust receivables without leaving their desks, possibly even without leaving an audit trail.
4. Finally, before the days of transferring data over telephone lines, sensitive legal documents would have been taken across town under the protection of a special messenger.

What You Protect

Despite the range of security violations, most companies are vulnerable and need protection in these six areas:

1. **Investment in the system.** Your firm probably has a substantial financial investment in its system. For starters, there is the expense of the system itself: the equipment, the software, and the installation. Remember also the cost of staff training and time spent to configure the system and develop data.

    Microcomputers might be less expensive than they were five years ago, but they still are not cheap. And, the cost of staff time is ever on the rise. With an unprotected system, a night's work by thieves or vandals puts your firm's entire investment in jeopardy.
2. **Money on hand today.** Embezzlement of funds is a crime made ever so much easier with the advent of computers. Without detection, a shrewd person might be able to provoke your system to initiate a false overtime payment or to process a bogus insurance claim.
3. **Future income and productivity.** Your firm's future income and productivity depend on your security program. When software or data files are compromised, the price can be lost productivity and lost income. The employee in the example who made a false adjustment to the accounts receivable file might as well have put a hand in the firm's cash register.

4. **Trade secrets.** Is your data valuable to others? Competitors might pay a substantial sum for files that describe a new product design or the findings of a sensitive research project. The secretary in the example who leaked confidential company information to the stockbroker had much to gain by participating in the high stakes crime of insider stock market trading.

5. **Lawsuit.** Every system contains information that can be used improperly, even to the extent of provoking a lawsuit. At the very least, your firm is vulnerable in the area of software theft (no small concern). Your firm probably is liable to maintain the confidentiality of information kept on individuals or other companies.

    The legal assistant who provided the prosecuting attorney's office with secret documents bearing on a case set up both lawyers for what could be an endless lawsuit, not to mention the obstruction of our legal processes.

6. **Reputation.** Computer-related crime will do more than embarrass you. It well may damage your and your company's good reputation. The more serious the violation, the greater the damage. Even the case of an employee spying into personnel files to learn someone's marital status hurts the firm because it undermines employee trust.

Common Culprits and Contact Points

Obviously, you have much to protect. Now, let's briefly consider how your equipment, your software, and your data are vulnerable from the standpoint of who might violate them and at what contact points.

With computer-related crime, there is no single category of common culprit. Anyone and everyone is capable of it. The examples mentioned thus far in this chapter indicate that you should consider the possibility that even an insider might violate security. In fact, according to some studies, over 70 percent of computer-related crimes are committed by insiders: accountants, clerks, managers, janitors, and owners. But, anybody is a potential security violator, from a company vice-president to a stranger three states away who taps into the system through a modem.

Contact points are not as various as the people who take advantage of them. Every system is exposed through its keyboards. Consider the manager who forgets to log off before going to a meeting. The manager's level of system access is available to anyone who passes by.

Access to your system has a lot to do with the type of system you manage. Table 6.1 shows the relative difficulty in securing different types of systems. Generally, stand-alone PC's are the easiest to secure; systems allowing access through modems are the most difficult.

Table 6.1

SYSTEMS AND THEIR RELATIVE DIFFICULTY OF SECURING

RELATIVE DIFFICULTY OF SECURING	SYSTEM
LOW	
	Stand-alone PC's
	Multi-user or LAN
	Multi-user or LAN with modem access
HIGH	

Your stand-alone PC's probably are least difficult to secure because they are self-contained and have a relatively small radius of vulnerability. To violate security, a person would have to come to the PC itself. Securing your multi-user system or local area network is a greater challenge because both have points of access at every terminal or workstation.

Local area networks are vulnerable when information is passed between workstations. Unprotected data travelling along network cables is easy game for an unauthorized person, even someone otherwise authorized to log on to the network.

Vulnerability increases further when you put a modem on your system. A modem is every system's Achilles' heel, bringing the added concern that anyone with a computer, a modem, and the willingness to play password guessing games can break security from literally anywhere on the globe. Imagine how quickly and secretly your most precious file might be copied to a disk on a remote computer.

Identify What Your Firm Has at Stake

Let's take an odyssey through the land of system security so that you can identify more specifically what your firm has at stake. A sound security program begins with knowing what you are up against; so indulge your imagination as you consider each of the questions below. Explore your greatest fears about possible violations to your system's security. Put yourself in a criminal's shoes. Acknowledge every threat.

Equipment Theft

1. How easy would it be for someone to walk out of the office with a terminal or a modem?
2. How long would it be before you found out a memory board was missing from a personal computer?
3. Are you sure that every piece of equipment is where the system devices map says it should be?
4. What equipment might you personally steal without being detected?

Unauthorized Access to Data

1. Who might covet your data or wish to destroy it?
2. What system data can be stolen easily?
3. What if someone wanted to sell sensitive data to a competitor?
4. How easily might someone sabotage your system or erase critical files?
5. Can your firm's accountant keep two sets of books without detection?
6. What if a staff member wanted to write an unauthorized overtime check?
7. What transactions could you hide if need be?

8. How easily might the firm's most valuable records be compromised?
9. Do staff members have access to information that they do not need to do their jobs but that they might be able to turn to their personal advantage?

Unauthorized Access to Software

1. How easy would it be for a staff member to alter the data transmission speed for a remote terminal?
2. What if someone decided to make a copy of the company's spreadsheet program for personal use at home?
3. What changes can you and others make to system files?

General

1. What motives might insiders have to violate security?
2. How difficult would it be for someone to make the system manager look bad?
3. What if an angry former employee decided to sabotage the system?
4. Are you comfortable with the current level of security?

| Tip |

Systems have their particular areas that require special security measures, so ask your vendor to identify your system's special vulnerabilities.

6.2 Understand Your Security Options

Does the exercise in the previous section have you feeling uneasy? Relax. There is much you can do to protect your system.

Each security violation has two ingredients: motive and opportunity. You have little control over people's intentions; so your best defense against security violations is to keep a potential culprit entirely away from the target, or at least to make access very difficult. This section describes various ways to do that. In Section 6.3, we will look at tips and strategies for using the various security measures described in this section.

Equipment theft is touched upon only briefly because your firm should have a well-established and effective plan to protect all of its equipment against theft, from its forklifts to its floppy disk drives. The focus here is on means to prevent unauthorized access to data and software, with the exception of software theft, the subject of Section 6.4.

Prevent Equipment Theft

There are several ways to prevent people from stealing your equipment. Consult the police and your insurance company about security systems that they recommend. Otherwise, secure the work place after hours with locked doors and an alarm system. Locked doors pose no barrier to former employees who still have office keys, so see that an office key assignment program is in force to control who has access to the premises without sounding off alarms. Keep your system devices map (see Section 2.2) current and use it to conduct an annual equipment inventory. If you allow employees to use company equipment in their homes, keep an accurate record of who has borrowed it. Be watchful of suspicious behavior of visitors or employees during office hours.

Further protect equipment by bolting it down. Install locks on the equipment itself, particularly enclosures that house expensive removable components. Store equipment in cabinets that lock. Mark equipment as your company's property so that it can be identified easily in case of burglary. You will find many security products offered in computer supply catalogs. Browse through them for ideas.

Finally, impress upon people the importance of reporting all thefts so that you can investigate each loss.

Prevent Unauthorized Access to Data
and Software

In this section we will look at four techniques you should consider to protect information and software on your system. Although each one offers good protection, no single technique is sufficient alone, and, as we will see, each has its drawbacks.

Use Access Permissions

Your system probably has built-in protection features that allow you to control what people can do to files after they have accessed them and maybe even whether people can access files at all. These features might not stop a technically educated and determined culprit, but they work wonders for controlling what most employees can do with the system. With 70 percent of violations perpetrated by insiders, you might short-circuit many problems when you put access permissions to work for you.

What kind of control you have depends on your operating system and what version you use because file access comes in many forms, and the complexity of access permissions is correlated to the complexity of the system. Let's look at examples from DOS, the IBM PC Network, and XENIX.

DOS 3.1 and Stand-alone PC's. Stand-alone PC's have bottom line access permissions. One allows a person to both read and modify the contents of a file, (read/write access). Another allows a person to read a file, but not to change its contents, (read-only access). DOS 3.1 allows you to protect files with the ATTRIB command when you turn on the read-only attribute for files you select. If you open a file with its read-only attribute on, you only can view its contents because the system prevents you from modifying them. To change the file, you must turn off the read-only attribute. The ATTRIB command does not distinguish among the people accessing files: everyone allowed to open a file has identical access to it. Read-only permission is one way to protect files, such as application program files, from being overwritten or damaged.

IBM Network. When you set up files and directories to share with others on the IBM Network, you have control over read and write access plus control over whether a person can create or delete files. In addition, you can share the same file with different access permissions, depending upon the person who asks to share them. For example, you could allow a department manager to see but not modify the time/leave records of the department's employees. You might give the company payroll clerk permission to read and add to every departments' time/leave records, but not to delete a file or create new ones.

Xenix and Multi-User Systems. Multi-user systems typically allow the greatest control over access permissions. With XENIX, you can specify these:

1. Read permission, which allows a person to read the contents of a file or the names of files in a directory;
2. Write permission, which allows a person to modify a file or a directory; and
3. Execute permission, which allows a person to execute a program file or search a directory for specified files.

(Some UNIX systems also allow the system manager to make a file accessible only through a command or a program. Check your **chmod** command for details.)

Moreover, XENIX offers a scheme of file ownership and groups that allow greater access control because you can specify different permissions for each of these categories of people: the file owner (the person who created the file); the owner's group (the file owner's user group); and other users (anyone else logged on the system).

Assessment. Access permissions are a primary security option that every system manager should implement. Even with stand-alone PC's you would find the DOS read-only option useful, if only to protect someone from mistakenly erasing or overwriting a file, such as COMMAND.COM. Implementing that security measure on stand-alone PC's is virtually trouble-free. But when you control access permissions on a local area network or multi-user system, you might run into a few procedural difficulties while you figure out who should have the various types of access to the information stored on your system. On those systems, once you establish permissions, you probably will not run into further trouble.

Control Access with Passwords

Passwords are a traditional way to control what people can do. By restricting who is allowed to log on, computer systems use passwords to ensure that only those with the right one are allowed access to the system and its files. Some systems, such as IBM's PC Network, allow you to put passwords on disks, directories, and even printers. Some systems allow password protection on individual records in a file.

Assessment. Passwords have their drawbacks. Unfortunately, an unauthorized person in the possession of a valid password can do whatever the password allows. Conversely, passwords can backfire. If employees forget their passwords, no amount of cajoling or logical argument will convince the computer to permit them to log on. One frustrated system manager put a password on the system files a few days before going on vacation. When she returned and needed to adjust a system file, the password escaped her. Because she did not have a backup of the current system configuration, she had no choice but to proceed with a tedious installation task.

But the most serious drawback of passwords is that they cannot effectively thwart someone intent on mischief. To circumvent password protection, sometimes all one must do is take advantage of another person's carelessness. People frequently are far more casual with passwords than they are with the keys to the office. Employees sometimes find it expedient to share a password with colleagues. Or, to guard against forgetting a password, they jot it down where others can find it. Sometimes they key in their passwords just as someone with unethical intentions is passing by.

When people protect their passwords, a determined person still can successfully break into a system. Guessing passwords frequently works. Furthermore, passwords even can be bypassed entirely by someone who has the technical ability to get at disks directly instead of going through the directory and file system.

Despite the drawbacks, passwords provide good protection; but alone they are insufficient. Other security means are available that you can and should add as you see appropriate.

Mask Data with Encryption

We have seen that access permissions and passwords will not stop all people intent on breaking into your system. However, you can foil those who get in by making the data unintelligible once they have it. The way to establish this security is to scramble, or encrypt, the data so that what once was readable information becomes a string of gibberish. The only way to return an encrypted file to its original state is to use the right keyword or phrase, similar to a password.

Encryption is accomplished either with a software program alone (Borland International's SuperKey offers two separate encryption schemes), or with the assistance of a device, some of which automatically encrypt every data file on a disk or every file sent over a network.

Some programs overwrite the original readable file with the encrypted version; others write the encrypted version to a new file, leaving the original file intact. The latter is useful when you need to transmit a file over a communication line because you have both a readable file on disk that you can use and the encrypted version that you can transmit with relative safety.

Assessment. File encryption is a good way to protect sensitive information, but like passwords, the method has shortcomings. First, keywords are as vulnerable as passwords. You can get around that particular drawback to some extent if you use a combination software/hardware encryption system. With one such scheme, each person has a small device which provides a fresh keyword for each encryption transaction. The person in possession of the device does not know what the next keyword will be, but for each person's logon identification, the computer is programmed to anticipate what the correct new word should be. This scheme provides double protection because the individual's password alone is not enough, nor is possession of his or her device. A successful intruder would have to have both.

Encryption has two other serious drawbacks which you should consider before you use it on any particular file. First, it typically takes a lot of time and computer attention to encrypt or decrypt a file. Second, encrypted files need as much as three times the disk space required by their unencrypted versions. If disk space is a problem, be judicious when you select files to encrypt.

Consider Two Hardware Alternatives

Two hardware security devices worth mentioning are the dial-back modem and a special device designed to protect information stored on hard disks.

A hardware alternative for systems with communications lines is a dial-back modem which identifies authorized callers, breaks the connection, and dials back the caller at a predetermined telephone number. Such devices provide a double layer of protection by requiring verification of both the caller's identity (via the person's logon password) and the number where the caller should be dialing in from. Some modems disconnect callers who try a specified number of passwords, discouraging people trying to access your system by guessing passwords.

The second hardware product works with hard disk systems. Each evening the device first copies the contents of the disk to a tape which can be locked in a safe and then formats the disk to eradicate its contents. The next morning, everything on tape can be restored to the disk. Certain copy protection schemes on your software might render this choice unwise for you. Check with your vendor.

Also check with your vendor to learn about other security measures to consider. Before you decide the combination of security measures you want to implement, it helps first to review the following:

1. Acknowledge the drawbacks inherent in each solution. (This section introduced you to a few options and their drawbacks.)
2. Weigh the financial costs to implement a solution. They range from zero (for solutions you already own, such as the access permission scheme that your system includes) to costly solutions (for new purchases, such as locked cabinets for every one of your PC's).
3. Consider the inconvenience each solution might pose to personnel. A solution is only as effective as the procedures designed to implement it, and procedures are effective only to the extent to which people follow through. There is a correlation between follow-through and convenience. And, the convenience factor varies from work place to work place as a result of company personality. For example, I have seen programmers in one company never use the locks on their equipment, even when they depart for the day; and I have seen others religiously lock their equipment whenever they expect to be away from their desks for more than fifteen minutes.
4. Eliminate impractical solutions. Certain solutions might be clearly impractical for you and your firm. For example, consider how ineffective it would be for travelling sales personnel to use call-back modems that dial specified telephone numbers, unless they would also carry special devices to circumvent the obvious problem.

6.3 Implement Your Security Plan

By now, you understand the security risks your system is up against and what measures you might implement to reduce them. Now is the time to develop a security plan that makes as much trouble as possible for would-be violators.

In Chapter Four you enlisted the help of others with your records management plan. Implementing a security plan that is unique to your system is another task that requires the efforts of a small group. A critical element of every successful security program is company-wide support, based on an attitude of seriousness toward the security program. Because people have a tendency to be casual about security, you have to take extra measures to see that everyone understands its importance.

An essential component of a security program is the security officer, regardless of your firm's size. One individual—preferably not yourself—should be appointed to supervise security and to see that procedures are followed. It is better to have someone other than the system manager to ensure a division of responsibility. Since you already have substantial control over the system, having another individual in charge of security protects you by providing the firm with checks and balances. You need an individual with as much integrity as you have, someone who sets high standards by example, someone able to conduct investigations with both grace and firmness.

Five Rules of Security

The following five rules of security will help you to meet these two goals: first, to foster a climate where security is taken seriously, and second, to reduce the number of attempted violations.

Rule #1. Publish the security policies and the procedures you expect people to follow.

Rule #2. Enforce security measures to reduce the number of attempts.

Rule #3. Urge people to promptly report *all* violations and *all* losses.

Rule #4. Investigate each violation or loss, no matter how small.

Rule #5. Periodically audit the security system and test security equipment.

Those rules should form the foundation of your security plan. To assist you in planning a security program, check with your professional counterparts to see how your business or industry typically handles computer security. The following information will make it easier for you to implement the specific strategies described in the Section 6.2.

Design a Scheme for Access Permissions

The steps in this section will help you establish proper access permissions for data and software stored on your system. The more complicated your system, the more important it is to take advantage of the control your system allows by establishing access permissions as a bottom-line security measure.

Rule of Thumb

A rule of thumb with access permissions is to give people the access they need in order to do their jobs, no more.

Managers of Stand-alone PC's. If you manage stand-alone PC's, you should work with the people who use them to identify files that no one should modify, such as system files and others you will establish as read-only files.

Managers of Local Area Networks or Multi-User Systems. Recruit others to help you to assign permissions. Enlist a small number of people who are knowledgeable about your firm's operations. If possible, include people from various departments and various levels in the organization. Be sure that everyone, yourself included, understands the types of access permissions available. If necessary, prepare an explanatory chart.

Step One: Collect directory listings. You need a list of files on the system. Your printed directory listings most likely can include existing access permissions. For example, with DOS 3.1 systems, use the ATTRIB command to display them. With UNIX, use the **ls -al** command.

Step Two: Establish permissions for software. Determine the proper access permissions for system files and software program files. There are three levels of access to a system file or software program:

1. You can install or configure it (create access)
2. You can alter the program code (write access)
3. You can simply view it (read-only access)

Following the rule of thumb that people should have access to tools and information they need in order to do their work and no more, in most organizations, only the system manager and the manager's backup should be able to install, configure, or alter system files and software program files.

That means you are the only two people who should have access to installation programs or programs that allow you to modify, or "patch," program code. Delete installation and debugging programs from the system's hard disks. Store them on floppy diskettes in the library until you need them.

To protect system files, take write permission off of all system files for safety. The only time you should change it is when you personally need to modify the file. When you are finished, put the restriction back on.

Set software application programs to read-only or execute, so that people can use them but are unable to modify them.

You want to avoid the grief one system manager had when an employee decided to follow instructions in a magazine and blundered badly in an attempt to patch the system's word processing program.

Step Three: Mark files with potential security risk. Identify all of the files on each directory listing that might pose a potential security hazard, including those you believe are well-protected.

Step Four: Determine who needs data file access. For the data files you marked in step three, use one of the following two methods to determine who should have the various access permissions your system allows.

Method #1: Track the path of each file through your organization from its creation to its destruction. Whether or not you use a flow chart, the following questions will help you determine who needs access to each file:

What prompts the need for the file?
Who creates the file?
What information do they use to create the file?
What happens to the file next?
Is the file updated?
If so, what prompts the update and who enters it?
What reports or decisions are made based on information in the file?
Who deletes the file?
What prompts the deletion?

Method #2: Take a mission or task-oriented approach. Survey people in the organization for the data that they need to do their jobs. Remember to include the firm's decision-makers because they too need access to information stored on the system. Ask staff members about their functions, about the data they need, and about what they do with it. A marketing vice president may need access to the spreadsheet program to read the most current sales figures. A clerk may need only write permission in order to update personnel records. Do not overlook anyone.

One or both of these methods should allow you to determine the best scheme of access permissions for files. For instance, the person who posts incoming checks will have only write access to the accounts receivable file. The person responsible for reconciling the general ledger will have read-only access to it. Decision-makers may have only read access to files that bear on their responsibilities.

Step Five: Double-check. With tentative access permissions in hand, double-check them to ensure that you do not deny valid access or allow inappropriate access.

Step Six: Implement and document your new access permissions. Follow the instructions in your manuals to set the access permissions as determined in step five. When these access permissions are set, reprint the directory listings to document the access permissions allowed. Store this set of directory listings in the system library.

Protect Passwords

Your access permissions are in place. If you elect to use passwords as an additional level of protection, follow the suggestions in this section. You increase the effectiveness of passwords if you exercise care.

Password Selection

A circumvented or forgotten password is at best a big inconvenience, at worst a disaster. Advise people to select passwords carefully. Unfortunately, the tendency is to pick an obvious word for a password because it is remembered easily, such as the name of a pet. The advantage is that the person is not tempted to write down that kind of password. But, another person could soon stumble upon such an obvious password. People should be advised to pick something that they can remember easily but that is not readily guessed.

You too should be careful when you select passwords, particularly those you use to protect the system. Managers of UNIX systems must be extremely careful with the password to the super-user account, which allows free reign over the entire system. The system manager of a national company picked the name of the company's chief competitor to use as a password to protect access to the directory where system files were kept. The password was easily and accidentally guessed by a company employee. Luckily, in this case, the employee was "exploring" with no malicious intentions and was quite shaken to find himself in unknown and obviously forbidden territory. He logged off as quickly and unobtrusively as he could, without causing trouble.

Changing Passwords

The longer a password remains in effect, the more likely it is to be compromised. Establish a procedure for people to change their passwords on a regular basis. However, passwords should not be changed too often because people will write them down in order not to forget them. For most people, a monthly change of password is best.

Help from the System

Your system probably offers at least one way to assist with password management. If your system offers electronic mail, use it to remind everyone when it is time to change passwords. Some systems offer even more help by allowing you to force password changes (**pwadmin** for XENIX systems) or otherwise expire passwords unchanged for a specified period. With some systems, a person whose password has expired may still log on, but cannot access the system until after putting a new password into effect.

Some systems allow you to lock workstations automatically whenever no keyboard activity has occurred within a specified period of time. With this feature, the only way to unlock a workstation is to enter the password that was keyed upon logon. If you use this tactic, implement it with care. Your firm might have employees who would find it tedious and annoying to have to key in their passwords whenever they leave their workstations idle for, say, five minutes.

The audit features on some systems allow you to track the number of password attempts made by particular persons or from particular workstations. That feature can be a fairly good deterrent to insiders who otherwise might be tempted to try guessing passwords as a means to gain access to forbidden regions.

Direct Action You Can Take To Protect Passwords

There are two other procedures that you can implement to protect your system's passwords.

First, you would not allow a staff member to depart with keys to the office or, worse, with several signed checks. Be sure that former employees do not walk away with "keys" to the system. Delete their passwords and change any they knew. When an employee transfers to another position in the company, review that person's logon access permission and see that it is consistent with his or her new responsibilities.

Second, if you are a new system manager, change *all* passwords in effect when your predecessor left.

Tip

As with files, so with passwords. Do not put a password in an unprotected place. Many a password has been discovered innocently stored in a batch file, game for any eyes to see.

Take Precautions with Encryption

Given the trade offs mentioned in Section 6.2, file encryption is a security method you will choose only after careful thought. Encryption is a must whenever the threat to security is substantial and you are transmitting sensitive files over a telephone line or over communication cables in a local area network.

Should you add encryption to your security plan, the precautions listed here will help you to avoid some of the problems associated with implementation.

If your encryption scheme uses keywords, quickly review the immediately preceding paragraphs about passwords; most everything said about protecting passwords applies to encryption keywords.

As with any software, there are problems you will encounter with file encryption if you are not cautious. First, be thoroughly familiar with the encryption documentation. Next, establish careful encryption procedures. Sloppy procedures might result in obliterated data. No one, not even your vendor, can recapture data lost through careless encryption. Then, identify files to encrypt. In addition to sensitive information that will travel over communication lines, you should consider encrypting high security documents that reside on a hard disk, shared disks in particular. Review the directory listings you marked in the section on access permissions to see if there are any files that you want to secure further with encryption.

Think about encryption in tandem with various access permissions. Encryption can be a roadblock if you want to give people different types of access to the same file—unless you have an encrypted version for each level of access. That process often is not worth the trouble, the time, or the disk space, but you and your security team must be the judges. Because encryption is so demanding of system resources, carefully consider whether or not to use it, especially when it comes to files that are frequently read. The idea of having to decrypt and encrypt a file on a regular basis would give most people a migraine.

Warnings

Minimize the possibility of destroying data inadvertently by adhering to the following rules, unless your documentation tells you otherwise:

1. Do not encrypt an encrypted file. You gain nothing by encrypting a file twice. (If a file is inadvertently encrypted twice, you might be able to restore it by reversing exactly the steps you followed.)

2. Never decrypt a file that is not encrypted: you run the risk of losing it.

3. Do not change the name of an encrypted file or you may never be able to restore it to its original state.

4. Discourage using wildcards to identify files you wish to encrypt or decrypt. Imagine opening a file one day to find it was accidentally encrypted weeks earlier when someone used a wildcard specification to encrypt a group of files! If you must use wildcards, use them with great care.

6.4 Prevent Software Theft

Software theft, the unauthorized copying of programs for either company or personal use, is the last topic in this chapter about security. Some people estimate that as many as eight illegal copies exist in the corporate world for every legal one. You will find many estimates, few of them verifiable. But most people agree that software theft is a crime that is both serious and alarmingly prevalent.

Several factors contribute. First, the crime generally is called "software piracy," an unfortunate term. The word *piracy* connotes the romance of masterful deeds on the high seas. Terminology is largely responsible for the attitude that the crime is no crime at all, or if it is, then it is not one to take very seriously.

Second, stealing software does not seem like real stealing because the licensed owner is not being deprived of property. A thief can walk off with a copy of your word processing program, leaving your company's legal copy behind.

Third, the crime is simple to commit and difficult to detect. Technically, your system probably does not prevent you or anyone else from making illegal copies of software. Usually, you can make as many copies as you like. As far as I know, every copy protection scheme devised to date has been broken.

Despite the ease with which programs can be copied illegally, software theft *is* serious because people—namely, software developers—*are* being deprived of funds rightfully theirs, and your company can be liable for instances of theft on its premises.

It is your duty to try to prevent this predictable crime. Firms with local area networks are particularly vulnerable on this issue. Many networks, including IBM's, allow shared use of software programs that legally should not be shared. Copyright laws for these programs are enforced with the honor system. Although bottom-line prevention remains with the honor system, there is much you can do.

Five Steps to Protect Your Firm

Step One: Know your license agreements. Know well the terms of license agreements your company has for each of the software programs it owns. There is no standard license agreement. Here is a sampling:

a. Most strict are those manufacturers who require that full price be paid for each computer or CPU that uses the program. So, if you have five PC's in a network, you need five copies of a software package sold under this license agreement, even if you are running the program from a shared network hard disk.

b. Other firms provide a discount, sometimes offering what is called a *site license*, which allows companies to use the package at a specified site for a specified sum. Site licenses sometimes cover the entire company, sometimes just departments within a company.

c. Other agreements specify the number of people licensed to run the program at any one time. If such a license states that five people are authorized to use the program and you have ten people on staff, it would be legal for half of the people to use the program in the morning hours and the other half in the afternoon.

d. Borland International has an unusual and provocative twist on licensing agreements. Its agreement states that buyers should treat its products "just like a book," not tied to any one person or any one computer, to be shared as desired so long as the product is not used simultaneously from two workstations. Backup copies are allowed.

e. Most lenient are developers of software placed in the public domain. These developers sometimes actively encourage you to copy and disseminate their products. In return, they request a modest sum in the event that people who use a program find it useful.

If you are unsure about the terms for any of your company's programs, check with your vendor. With such a range of licensing agreements, it is a challenge to juggle your company's rights: to pay fairly for software, but not to pay for more than it legally should; to prevent theft and avoid liability while using its programs within the law.

Step Two: Establish a policy. Write a policy that states your company's position against software theft. Specify what constitutes a legal backup copy for your programs and denounce their unlawful copying. Include action the company will take against persons found to have violated copyright laws.

Step Three: Inform people. Publish both your company's policy and its various licensing agreements. You want to educate employees about the problem and discourage them from adding to it.

Step Four: Do not tempt anyone. Be sure that your firm has the number of legal copies it needs of each program on the system. If twenty copies of your spreadsheet program are required, see to it that you have them. Too few resources is an incentive to theft. You might find people passing around unlawful copies of programs if you do not provide them with the tools they need to do their jobs.

Step Five: If it happens, take action. In the event a software license violation occurs, you must take action. Treat the situation as stated in your written policy about software theft.

Ultimately, all you can do is take reasonable precautions. Would your boss or a judge expect more?

Conclusion

A realistic attitude is a prime component of a successful security plan. You must accept the fact that it is impossible to secure your system 100 percent. The key is to be sure that the risks you take are calculated. Remember, the more trouble you can give to would-be thieves or vandals, the more protection your system has. But the advantage has to be balanced against the trouble also given authorized users who have no intention of sabotaging the system.

7

Avoid Trouble
with Your System

Introduction

Introduction

Computers are prone to any number of evils that you can keep to a minimum. In the previous chapter we looked at ways to protect your system from human beings intent upon doing it harm. In this chapter we will move on to how you might counterbalance threats or troubles that can arise from other quarters. Those range from power line trouble to happenings that take place inside of the system itself. We will look at tips about basic equipment protection and maintenance, how you can protect data, and how you should handle system development. The key is in taking preventive measures. The recommendations in this chapter will help you minimize system downtime, avert avoidable system-related problems, and spot brewing trouble before it becomes a calamity.

7.1 Keep the System Running

A computer needs a good environment. It needs enough, but not too much power. It even needs clean air and regular care. In this section we will look at ways to ensure that your system continues to function. You will learn to protect it from damage that environmental hazards might cause. Equipment care is one of your most effective strategies to avoid trouble with the system, and it begins the moment the system arrives, when you return warranty cards and you see that the system is insured. Your dedication to equipment care should extend much further. Static electricity might erase precious information, air pollution from cigarette smoke eventually will muck up disk drives, and dust on a diskette can obliterate data. In addition, because even the best cared for system comes to a halt when its supplies run out, we will look at how you can simplify the ordering process.

Protect Against Three Power Demons

Power line trouble poses major problems for computer systems, such as the potential to blow out a hard disk. Electrical power surges can do serious damage to circuitry. Unexpected power failure can mean the demise of information not yet saved on a hard disk or floppy diskette. Electrical noise can garble data, sometimes as effectively as deliberate file encryption. Guarding against these power demons is a matter of installing one or more devices that provide the following:

1. **Surge protection.** You need surge protection to impede overvoltages from reaching your system. All you need is one encounter with a serious power surge to be struck by the critical difference this protection makes. The most extreme situation that I have seen was a mighty power surge during a mild electrical storm. The surge was followed instantly by a total power failure. People in the firm reported seeing miniature nuclear explosions on their display screens. Until power was restored—some thirty minutes later—the company had no idea whether or not it had lost any of its system's electronic parts or data. The system's manager installed surge protection that same afternoon.

   Before you install it, you should know that surge protection is not only for computer systems that might be used during fierce electrical storms and it is not only for systems located in geographical areas noted for unstable electrical power. Power surges of a magnitude to damage a computer can occur in a residential area in San Francisco on a mild spring afternoon.

   You also should know that surge protection is available in varying degrees. Plug-in adapters with surge protection typically shunt off voltage that is more than 400 volts and less than 500 volts. That might be too little protection for your system. Certainly, if your company is located in or near a heavy industrial or commercial area where power requirements range far beyond 110 volts, you need better quality surge protection, maybe one that prohibits anything over 150 volts from reaching your system.

2. **Power line filtering.** AC lines have a tendency to pick up electrical noise from other devices, such as a copy machine. That noise can interfere with your system. All but the low end surge protectors provide power line filtering.

3. **Uninterruptible power supply.** We discussed in Chapter Five that RAM is cleared of its contents when the system loses power. Any work done after the last time work was saved must be reconstructed. That may or may not pose a serious threat to your company. If it does *or* if your firm is

located in an area with frequent power failures, consider adding an uninterruptible power supply. These devices are battery backed to keep your system running up to thirty minutes if you lose commercial power, enough time to save work in progress and power down the system in an orderly manner. Such devices run from a few hundred dollars to $1,000 and on up; so for some firms buying them can require a fair amount of justification.

To handle any of the potential power line problems, check with an experienced electrician before you determine the level of protection you want and need for your system.

Design an Equipment Maintenance Schedule

Once your system equipment is properly installed and your AC power line conditioners are in place, it is time to plan your equipment maintenance program. Probably, you will want to follow regularly the manufacturer's recommendations for each component on your system. Somewhere in your documentation—however massive it is—you should find preventive maintenance information for your equipment. The manuals probably recommend that you provide proper cooling, keep equipment clean inside and out, regularly examine cables, and so on. Some of this advice might appear unnecessary. Take it seriously. There was a time when I considered interior dust balls relatively harmless, until I encountered a system suffocating from a two-year accumulation.

Your system will thrive with routine testing and preventive maintenance. An equipment maintenance schedule will help you to follow through on your good intentions. The best schedule is one designed to help you both plan and track maintenance activities.

There are any number of ways to design an equipment maintenance schedule. Whether you manage a multi-user system or a local area network, Table 7.1 offers the flexibility you need: it allows you to organize your schedule by piece of equipment, by computer, and even according to the frequency of activities (one schedule for tasks to perform annually, another for monthly ones, etc.).

Table 7.2 shows how the form might be used for a personal computer. But, no matter how you organize your schedule, at all times you will know at a glance what is already done and what

Table 7.1

EQUIPMENT MAINTENANCE SCHEDULE
Date _____   Prepared By _____

Equipment (1)	Task (2)	Special Precautions (3)	Recommended Frequency (4)	Completed Date By (5)	Comment (6)

Table 7.2

EQUIPMENT MAINTENANCE SCHEDULE
Date _____ Prepared By _____

(Sample)

Completed for a personal computer

_____PC01_____
(device name)

Equipment (1)	Task (2)	Special Precautions (3)	Recommended Frequency (4)	Completed Date By (5)	Comment (6)
System Unit	Fan inspection		Annual		
	Eliminate dust	POWER OFF	Annual		
	Circuit boards seated	POWER OFF	Annual		
	Examine Cables		Annual		
	Interior		Annual		
	Exterior		Annual		
Disk Drives	Check alignment		Biennial		
	Test drive speed		Biennial		
	Clean floppy disk drive heads		When sign of trouble		
	Eliminate dust	POWER OFF	Annual		
	Examine Cables		Annual		
Monitor	Examine Cables		Annual		
Keyboard	Eliminate dust		Annual		

needs to be. The point is to establish a comprehensive equipment care program that makes the job painless for you and others.

Steps to Create an Equipment Maintenance Schedule

Develop your schedule using Table 7.1. You will want to verify that your schedule accounts for all of your equipment, so have your system devices map (see Section 2.2) on hand.

Step One: Plan the format. Select an organizing principle, (i.e. by device or frequency of activity). Your firm's physical layout and the assignment of maintenance responsibility probably bear on how you might best organize your schedule. How far flung is your equipment? Is one person responsible to maintain it or do people take care of equipment they personally use? Should you have multiple schedules?

Step Two: Complete Columns 1-4. Use the first two columns to identify equipment and to specify tasks required to maintain it. Column 3 is for special precautions to protect people and equipment. In Column 4, indicate how often each task should be performed.

Refer to your vendor provided documentation for the information you need to complete these four columns. In some cases, it might be inappropriate for you to follow the manufacturer's recommended frequency for a given task. For example, if your work place is especially prone to dust and airborne debris, schedule to eliminate dust more often than your manuals suggest.

Step Three: Make master copies and working copies. Be sure to have two copies of each schedule you develop: (1) a working copy for you to track both when and by whom each activity is performed, and (2) a master copy which you keep in the system library so that you have a complete set on hand for reference and for making working copies.

Tip

Store working copies with the equipment itself so that they are readily available to you and service personnel.

Step Four: Use the schedule. See that maintenance is performed according to your plan. The final two columns on the schedule should be filled in as tasks are completed. Column 5 is for the date and the initials of the person performing the task. Column 6 is for pertinent comments you want to include.

Three Tips for Successful Maintenance

Equipment maintenance is one task that is easy to let slide. Set aside a special day and time for maintenance, for example, 4 p.m. on Fridays. Use this time to perform regularly scheduled tasks, whether they are weekly, monthly, or quarterly.

If maintenance activities make the system unavailable, let people know ahead of time that the system will be down and for how long. This forewarning allows them to adjust their schedules and avoids resentment and lost work.

Keep historic copies of each completed schedule either in the system library or in binders located near the equipment. These records will help you and anyone else with an interest in the equipment when trouble occurs.

Tips for Equipment Care

The following tips describe simple steps you and other staff members can take to avoid some common mistakes and to protect your firm's expensive investment.

Tip #1: Equipment arrangements. Observe how your equipment is set up. You do not want to copy showroom displays and promotional literature that unwittingly mislead you into damaging your system. For example, you probably have seen a dot-matrix or daisy wheel printer sitting on the same surface as disk drives. (I have seen it in computer furniture showrooms, in industry magazines and, unfortunately, in many offices.) Printer vibrations will knock a drive out of alignment in short order. Another common sight is a paper tray blocking air vents on top of a monitor. Without freely flowing air, monitors can overheat and melt down. Beware of following either of these two examples.

Tip #2: Cables. Cable trouble means system trouble, so when you inspect cabling, always replace cables that have even the most minute tear. One rip in the wrong place can take the entire system down (and hours to discover).

Tip #3: Circuit boards. Whenever you check to see that a removable circuit board is seated properly, inspect the contact points. A cotton swab and alcohol will clean corrosion without damaging the circuit board. (CAUTION: as stated earlier, to protect yourself and the system, *never* touch a circuit board unless the power is *off*.)

Tip #4: Monitors. Whenever you (or others) step away from a workstation, turn down the intensity of the monitor to avoid burning an image on the screen. Some systems have software that automatically dims a monitor's intensity if a certain amount of time passes with no keyboard action. Borland International's SuperKey has that option. Software for this purpose also comes with the series of monitor cards produced by Hercules Computer Technology. If your system lacks that option, protect your monitors by manually reducing their intensity when they are idle.

Tips for Disk Drives

Chapter Four describes the delicate and precise job that disk drives perform. Being extremely vulnerable, drives warrant extra care and attention. These four tips will help:

Tip #5. In Chapters Four and Five, we looked at ways to boost system performance. Two of them have the added benefit of saving wear and tear on disk drives. First, if you see that files are stored on contiguous disk space (see Section 4.2), you will spare your drives the work of travelling all over a disk to find information. Second, whenever you use a RAM disk (see Section 5.2), you give your disk drives a vacation by reducing disk access. Both strategies prolong the useful life of your drives.

Tip #6. The adage "If it works, don't fix it" spells potential trouble when it comes to disk drives. Drives drift out of alignment imperceptibly. They appear to work as long as they regularly read information from the same disks or diskettes. With a floppy disk drive, you might discover the problem only after you try to use a diskette formatted on another disk drive or read information you stored on a diskette six months earlier, before the drive went out of alignment. So, for drives, change the adage to "If it works, it *may* need fixing." Check drive alignment as regularly as the manufacturer advises, even when there is no discernible sign of trouble.

Tip #7. System documentation probably advises that you clean the heads on each floppy disk drive regularly. Do not overdo it.

Disk drive head cleaning kits that use an abrasive can wear down the drive head, so use them sparingly. Some system managers clean drive heads once a year. Others do it *only* when the drives are not working properly. The first sign of a dirty head is a read or write error. If the problem is with only one diskette, then the trouble probably is the diskette itself; but when it is with multiple diskettes, the problem is likely to be with the drive.

Tip #8. Be gentle with the plastic doors on the floppy disk drives. Rough handling can result in a broken latch and a broken latch means that you cannot use the drive. I have seen this happen only twice, but when a little care avoids a problem it makes sense to use it.

Keep Your Supply Room Well-Stocked

Every system manager wants to avoid the embarrassment of a deadline missed for lack of paper or a printer ribbon. It can happen to you unless you keep a well-stocked computer supply room (or cabinet, whatever it takes).

However large or small your firm, presumably it has procedures to procure, inventory, and dispense the supplies people need to operate their equipment. Those procedures depend on your company's size and organization, but most likely they are out of your immediate control.

Whatever the case, integrate the system's supply requirements with the firm's existing scheme if you can. I have seen a few cases where purchasing personnel fail to assume the responsibility of ordering supplies for a new system because they were uninformed from the outset. A year later you can ask them about computer supplies and they almost invariably say "I know nothing about those things." This response is understandable when you browse through a computer supply catalog. The volume of cryptic descriptions for diskettes and ribbons alone is confusing until you know how to decipher them.

The person in charge of purchasing and inventory at your firm might welcome your assistance in ordering and storing computer supplies. That assistance comes in the form of information. You can be of immense help if you delineate exactly what your firm needs. In addition to providing the person with correct descriptions and stock numbers, recommend a vendor for each item. Set minimum and maximum quantities that must be kept on hand.

Table 7.3

COMPUTER SUPPLIES SUMMARY
Date _____   Prepared By _____

Quantity Max. Min. (1) (2)	Item (3)	Specifications (4)	Vendor (5)	Stock # (6)	Comments

Table 7.4

COMPUTER SUPPLIES SUMMARY
Date _____   Prepared By _____

(Sample)

Quantity Max. Min. (1) (2)	Item (3)	Specifications (4)	Vendor (5)	Stock # (6)	Comments
8 bx 3 bx	Diskettes (PC-AT)	1.2 Megs DS-HD 5¼"	IBM	#6109660	
20 bx 6 bx	Diskettes (PC, PC-XT)	360K DS-DD 5¼"	IBM	#6023450	
5 bx 1 bx	Diskettes (Displaywriter)	985K DS-DD 8"	IBM	#4498959	
5 ea 2 ea	Printer Ribbons (FX-80)	nylon	IBM	#7034623	Buy in quantity *only* if sealed in airtight packages

A smart purchasing manager takes advantage of volume discounts, so warn him or her about items with short shelf lives. A six month's supply of nylon printer ribbons might be a wise purchase *only* if each ribbon is sealed in an air-tight container. Otherwise, you will be far from opening the last box when you encounter the first dried out ribbon.

A smart purchasing manager also takes advantage of lower cost whenever possible. Lower cost sometimes involves buying a brand other than your usual, and this sometimes means unacceptably inferior products. Before the situation poses itself, identify acceptable brands to head off misunderstanding and poor purchases.

Summarize your needs in one place, such as the computer supplies summary in Table 7.3. With a completed table in hand, anyone can safely order needed items in your absence. If, by chance, you are the person who orders supplies for the system, the table will help you too to keep things manageable.

The sample computer supplies summary in Table 7.4 describes ribbons for Epson FX-80 printers and diskettes for these IBM Computers: PC-AT's, PC's, PC-XT's, and Displaywriters. For each item, Columns 1 and 2 show the maximum and minimum quantities to keep on hand in the supply area. Each item is identified in Column 3, with specifications listed in Column 4, such as the 5¼" double-sided, high-density (DS-HD), 1.2 Megabyte diskettes for the PC-AT's. Vendor name goes in Column 5 and the stock number in Column 6. Column 7 is for comments, such as the warning to buy only sealed nylon ribbons when purchasing large quantities.

Complete your supply summary using Table 7.3. Include both expendable and non-expendable supplies. Here is a list to get you started:

1. Expendable supplies: anti-static spray, diskettes, labels, paper (i.e. forms, letterhead envelopes and paper, non-letterhead envelopes and paper), printer ribbons, print wheels and print thimbles, tape.
2. Non-Expendable supplies: binders for printouts, copy holders (non-magnetic!), diskette cases and cabinets, printout trays.

Give both your backup person and the purchasing department a copy of your completed computer supply summary. Use it to conduct a regularly scheduled inventory of supplies. As with other documents, store a copy in your system library and update it whenever you add equipment to the system.

7.2 Avoid Trouble with Your Information

Now, let us turn to data protection. Electronically stored data is vulnerable. For example, if the system fails during operation or is improperly shut down, you cannot trust the integrity of your files. Under either of these two situations, your data could be beyond repair, but more commonly the system will have developed errors in keeping track of your files. It is rare that an entire disk will be damaged (though it happens). In this section, we will look at two ways to minimize or altogether avoid trouble with information on the system.

Check and Restore File Integrity

All is not lost if something happens to damage your files or to disrupt the way a disk keeps tabs on the whereabouts of files. Your operating system should provide a means to repair both damaged files and disk directories. But, the first step is to determine if there is a problem. If there is, it will only grow worse, so the earlier you detect and resolve it, the better.

When to Check

Checking file integrity is an ongoing responsibility. We will see how to do it in a moment. But, first, how often should you check? Do not wait for power failure or improper shutdown. If your system is UNIX-based, check daily, particularly if you shut down the system each day. IBM's PC manuals recommend "occasional checks" for its systems, but it is good practice to check these and other DOS systems at least weekly. A researcher neglected to check the integrity of his data for a month, although he religiously made his daily backup copies. When he finally discovered some of his files were damaged, he had lost 15 percent of his current project. Worse, he had backed up the damaged files on top of his good files, so even his backup copies were useless. Do check files on your hard disks every week.

Advise people periodically to check the condition of information stored on their floppy diskettes every six months. Check the integrity of information in the system library twice a year.

In addition to routine checking, verify the integrity of data whenever *any* of the following occurs:

1. You power up the system (UNIX).
2. The system behaves mysteriously.
3. You suspect someone tampered with the system.
4. Power surges or other power line troubles occur.
5. Hardware fails.
6. The system sends you a hardware error message, such as this one: "PARITY ERROR."
7. Available disk space is significantly below what you expect from reading the directory listings. Garbage files are not always named on a directory listing. For example, when there is insufficient disk space, your operating system might save part of the file on disk space without completing the process and assigning a filename.

Tip

See that your backup knows how to check and repair files for times you are unavailable.

Precautions For Running a Check and Repair

Procedures to check and repair trouble with files or file systems range from the simple to the maddeningly complex, from the relatively harmless to the downright dangerous.

The simplest and most harmless method is the automatic checking some operating systems perform each time the system is started or powered down. An example is XENIX for the IBM PC-AT, which checks if the file system is clean each time the system is started. Likewise, whenever the system is powered down with the **shutdown** command, XENIX automatically invokes a command (**synch**) to ensure file integrity.

But you need to run checks at will, which most operating systems do allow. Unless you know what you are doing, you can do more damage than good when you take control. Running check and repair processes is an art, so take these precautions to protect your files:

1. If possible, prior to encountering actual trouble, become familiar with how your system handles file inspection and repair. Check your documentation thoroughly before you have to cope with file integrity questions.

    Each system offers its own options for checking and restoring file integrity. For example, DOS has these commands that relate to check and repair operations: CHKDSK (Checkdisk), RECOVER, and VERIFY. If you manage a network similar to IBM's PC Network, you must stop sharing what you want to check before you can use the DOS commands to check and repair, (see NET SHARE). With XENIX for the IBM PC-AT, the key command is **fsck**. If your UNIX system does not have **fsck**, it probably uses **icheck**, **dcheck**, and **ncheck**. Typically, the program you run to check integrity also makes repairs, such as with both CHKDSK or **fsck**.

2. Be prepared to accept the possibility that your corrective action might result in lost data. If possible, back up data to a tape or on diskettes before you repair anything when there is a chance the check and repair procedure might muck up data or if you feel uneasy about performing the procedure. This backup should be in addition to your regular system backup. (You do not want to replace perfectly good files on a backup with damaged files.)

3. If possible, do not inspect or restore file integrity while others are using the system. Before you begin, bring up your multi-user system in single user mode; stop sharing disks or directories on your local area network.

4. Fix trouble as soon as you find it. Minimize file creation or updates made subsequent to discovering damage. Otherwise, the problem might pollute what are believed to be perfectly good updates made to affected disks or directories. Whenever data integrity is compromised, halt all new work until the problem is corrected, if you can.

5. Whenever you repair damaged files or file systems, consider the job done only after you have run a final check that indicates no further problem exists.

Tip for managers of UNIX systems. With XENIX and other UNIX systems, it is critical that you dismount file systems before you check and repair them. When the file system being checked is the root file system, usually there are complications, stemming from the fact that the root file system cannot be dismounted. Carefully read your documentation to be sure that you fully understand how to check and repair the root file system. In fact, when you need to repair the root file system, consider bringing up a backup system either (a) to allow you to repair the damaged root file system dismounted or (b) if the two systems are identical, to replace the damaged system with its problem-free backup.

Tip for LAN managers. If you have a network, such as IBM's PC Network, there is an additional step to check the file integrity on disks shared with the network. If the disk is on a network server, you must PAUSE the server before you can successfully run CHKDSK on it. If the disk is simply shared, you must stop sharing the disk to run CHKDSK.

A Practical Backup Procedure

Suppose you are unable to repair a damaged file or file system. Or suppose someone accidentally erases an entire directory or an entire disk. What if your hard disk becomes completely unusable? If your system is not backed up, these dangers can be fatal. A California department store experienced this ultimate system tragedy: it lost its hard disk and no one had copied any of its files to tape or diskettes. Without a backup, they lost everything: data files (including accounts receivable!), system configuration, and a few employees. Recreating data files can take weeks, even months or more.

You cannot afford to be lax or careless about making backups. Inevitably, some day you will lose data from hardware or software failure, from serious human error, or maybe even from sabotage. The whole point of backing up information is to minimize the losses you will incur when that day arrives. Backup is the most cost-effective insurance any system can have.

Backup Procedures

Because having a current backup is so critical, make the process as easy and as painless as possible to perform. Start with a policy that states your commitment to backup and that specifies responsibility, timing, and how the backup should be stored.

These details will depend on the kind of system you have. For instance, the manager of a multi-user system might be responsible for backing up the central hard disk. With a LAN, people using personal computers might be responsible for backing up information on their hard disks, even if these disks are shared. Another variation is to have the system manager's backup person perform the job for the entire system. Whatever scheme you choose, consider the security issues involved.

As far as timing goes, your motto should be "no day ends with unique files on the system." At the end of each day, back up the day's work. Your operating system should be able to identify files modified since the last backup, making this kind of backup, called a "partial backup," relatively easy. You should back up everything ("full backup") once a week. With this plan, you will always have current copies of everything stored on the system. The most ever at risk is one day's work.

For trouble-free backup, incorporate these seven recommendations into your procedure:

1. **Plan your time.** Set aside enough time to perform the entire backup at one sitting, particularly when you are making a full backup. A major factor in determining how much time a full backup will take is the media you use for storing backed-up data. Backing up to tape is much quicker than to floppy diskettes. You also will avoid having to feed diskettes into the machine as it needs them. You can fully back up a 20 megabyte hard disk to tape in under 10 minutes. Unless you have a software specialty program to speed up the process with diskettes, it will take more time (about 50 minutes) and more of your attention to back up the same hard disk to 1.2 megabyte floppy diskettes.

2. **Schedule the process.** Perform the back up when no one else is using the system. First, backing up files requires substantial computer attention so, if the disk is shared, the process probably will put a drag on system performance. More important, you want to avoid the data integrity threat posed by backing up files people might be in the process of updating. You can schedule the backup outside of normal work periods. Or you can have everyone off of the system 50 minutes before the end of each day so that

you can safely perform backup and other system maintenance procedures.

3. **Gather materials.** If you back up to floppy diskettes, be sure
you have the number of diskettes you need before you begin,
to avoid being caught without enough when you are in the
middle of the process. You can easily calculate the required
number. For example, if you are doing a complete backup,
find out the total amount of space occupied on the disk and
divide that amount by the capacity of your diskettes. If you
are using 360K diskettes, you will need about 60 formatted
diskettes to back up 20 megabytes of information.

4. **Prepare diskettes and tapes.** Keep six sets of tapes or floppy
diskettes, one set for each day's partial backup (Monday
through Friday) and a sixth for your full backup.

Clearly identify each diskette or tape. Chapter Three introduced a means to keep track of them, using color codes
and labels (see Section 3.1). Table 7.5 is a sample label completed for a partial backup to diskette for an IBM PC-XT.
The label tells us that it is Monday's #1 partial backup diskette for PCXT01 (the device name for the PC-XT), that the
system manager is responsible for performing the backup,
and that the diskette has a capacity of 360K bytes, with 250K
occupied with backup files.

Table 7.5
SAMPLE LABEL FOR PARTIAL BACKUP

DATE: <u>Monday</u>   ID: <u>#1: Partial for PCXT01</u>   Custodian: <u>Sys Mgr</u>
Original ___   Backup <u>X</u> Archive ___   Destroy:
Program: Capacity: <u>360K</u>   Amount Used: <u>250K</u>
Restrictions: *USE FOR BACKUP AND RESTORE ONLY*

5. **Clean the disk.** When you are about to do a full backup,
remember that there is no point backing up files that should
be removed from the disk, whether the files should be
archived or just erased. Before you start a full backup, clean
your directories and ask others to do the same (see Section
4.2). Clean directories minimize the time required for
backup, especially if you are copying files to floppy diskettes.

Littered directories are not such a problem with partial backups because you are backing up only recently modified files and by definition these are not deadweight.

6. **Print a record.** The contents of your backup diskettes and tapes change with each backup. For this reason, it is especially important to store paper copies of their directories with them. Check your documentation to find out the most efficient way to print a record of the backup. With DOS, the BACKUP command displays the name of each file being backed up and you can print a list using redirection of output to the printer. With XENIX, use the **sysadmin** program to get a printout.

7. **Verify integrity of backups.** Verify that the backup was successful, especially when you do a full backup. Indeed, some operating systems offer you the option to check integrity as part of the backup process. (See Section 7.2 on checking data integrity.)

8. **Store backups in a safe place.** The system library is the logical place to store backups safely. Keep a second full backup away from the premises as extra insurance against fire or other catastrophes. Rotate this copy with the one kept in the system library. Depending on the volume of system activity, you also might rotate on-site daily backups with a copy kept elsewhere.

Take proper security measures with backup copies. A top security document demands top security, whether it is on a hard disk or floppy diskette.

Tip for A Special Backup

There is always a chance the system will be entirely out of service as a result of breakdown. This possibility causes some system managers to keep a very special backup, a hard copy of data that absolutely must be available at all times. This course of action is wise for firms which must resort to hand processing rather than halt work in the event of a system failure. If your firm has activities that are as urgent, identify and make paper copies of the needed data. Store one set off site as an extra precaution.

7.3 Supervise Processes

Certain processes require extreme care, either for purposes of system safety or optimal system performance. In the previous section, we mentioned that the backup procedure puts such a demand on system resources that you should schedule it for times when people are not using the system. We also have touched on the various causes of a system freeze, resulting in lost work and hot tempers. In this section, we will identify operations to avoid and processes to schedule carefully. Follow the recommendations below to put your system ever-closer to a trouble-free state.

Be Cautious with Hazardous Processes

Exercise caution and warn others about these situations:

1. Some day you or someone else might find yourself in one of those no-win situations in which the system asks you to hit any key to activate a process that you must not allow, such as when you inadvertently ask the operating system to format your hard disk. In a situation like that, *do not* hit Ctrl-Alt-Del or whatever keys you depress to reset or reboot your system. If you strike these keys, you might precipitate damage.

   The best response is to flip off the system's power. Go right ahead if the problem is on a stand-alone PC. Take extra care if the problem happens on a multi-user system or a network server. You will be very unpopular if you shut off the network server when people are working on files that they expected to save on the server's shared disk. So, warn the others using the system before you cut the power. They will be able to save their files without mishap because keystrokes on their keyboards will not bear at all on what is happening on yours.

2. Caution others about the perils of using random diskettes to boot the system. Although this was mentioned earlier, it bears repeating. Frequently, bootable diskettes contain a batch or script file that automatically executes whenever the system is booted with the diskette. Depending on the commands in such a file, booting with the diskette can be perfectly harmless and even desirable on one personal computer while it can be disastrous on another, erasing its hard disk.

Remember the precautions recommended while you were building your system library: carefully mark such diskettes and encourage others to use them cautiously.

3. People sometimes want to remove a diskette from a floppy disk drive while in the middle of using an application or a productivity program and sometimes even while the disk drive is whirling and its indicator light is on. Removal in either case threatens files stored on the diskette. Never interrupt a disk drive by removing the diskette it is accessing. Even with the drive light off, when you remove a diskette while using a program, your operating system can become confused about what should be on the diskette and where it should be. Change diskettes only from the operating system unless a program instructs you to do otherwise.

Carefully Schedule Touchy Processes

You already know that some processes you must run are touchy and that others put a drain on the system. This section describes the major ones to schedule for a time when they will have the least impact on the system and the people using it. If you manage only stand-alone computers, read number 3 about unattended printing and then continue to Section 7.4 of this chapter.

1. **Processes known to crash the system.** Programmers probably understand more than anyone else how it can be possible that you have to run a process despite the fact that it is known to bring down the system. But, it is not exclusively a programmer's problem. My earliest experience with it was with a multi-user system that completely froze each time an employee opened a particular spreadsheet file. Solving the problem meant risking further system freezes. The problem had to be tracked down, but not at the possible expense of other people losing their work or being denied system access. If you can, see that troubleshooting and other processes known to crash the system are run outside of working hours or at a scheduled time when others will not be inconvenienced.

2. **Processes that drain the system.** Certain processes slow down the system. The backup process is a case in point. Other such processes are operating system features that ask the system to look around and make notations or frequent

checks. For example, your system may offer an audit function that puts a heavy, on-going demand on system resources. It takes a lot of system attention to continually note who is using the system, for how long, and for what purposes. Other processes that typically drain a system are restoring the system or its data files, encrypting and decrypting files, searching and sorting a data base, running a lengthy spelling check, and performing extensive calculations. In fact, run too many such processes simultaneously and the system will not simply slow down, it may well stop running altogether.

Determine which processes slow down *your* system's performance. Once you have identified them, distribute them throughout the day or to times of minimal system use, if practicable. Careful scheduling of such processes will promote top performance for everyone.

3. **Unattended printing.** Perhaps you find it expedient to print files overnight. It is bad practice to run a printer unattended, because anything can and will happen. The ribbon might jam; paper might go awry. If a process running outside of working hours unavoidably includes printing, plan to be there.

7.4 When You Develop the System

If you have followed the recommendations thus far in this book, you have developed a substantial and impressive system management plan that will serve you well when you decide to make changes to the system itself, even if only to adjust the existing configuration. The range of changes you will consider is great: from upgrades to expansion to new capability. Changes are sparked from at least three quarters:

1. The system itself might ask for a change. For instance, suppose you have several PC's with two full-height floppy disk drives. One of the drives fails, prompting you to upgrade the PC by replacing the floppy drive with a hard disk.

2. The people who use the system will ask for change. For example, a manager might contact you to discuss the possibility of adding software to assist him with decision-making.

3. Finally, you, the system's manager, will initiate system changes. Suppose your RAM worksheets (see Section 5.4) reveal that the accountant's PC, loaded with 640K, uses up to 620K whenever she updates spreadsheets. That leaves little breathing room, so you decide to expand her PC's RAM by adding a 2 megabyte Above Board.

However the idea arises, someday you will consider a change. Always manage it—however minor—with care. System change is particularly delicate when it means that people who use the system will have to adjust the way they do so. In addition, there is always the chance that you will throw a wrench into a perfectly good system.

To help you ensure successful system development, this section highlights what is important to address, both before and after making changes. And, because impromptu change is not the only type you will make, use the information at the end of this section to prepare a system development plan.

Prepare Procedures for System Development

The purpose of system development—and of system management in general—is to benefit your firm: its goals, its balance sheet, and its employees. To do so successfully, you need procedures for each of the three stages of the system development process: proposition, investigation, and implementation. The following information should help you to develop procedures that work for you and your firm.

Proposition

Many changes for your system might be proposed: some will die as soon as they are uttered, others you will want to explore. Facilitate the proposal process and clarify how you will decide which proposals are worth consideration.

1. First, how is development proposed? Every firm should provide its staff members with a channel to request new equipment or software. Through what mechanism should people in your firm recommend system enhancements? Should you use a system users' group partly for this purpose? If not, should people feel free to raise system development matters at regular staff meetings? Should you have a suggestion box? Will you accept *ad hoc* requests?

2. When a proposal is made, who should make the decision to proceed? Should it be made by departmental supervisors, individual work groups, a company-wide users' group, you, upper management, or a combination, depending upon the nature of the change proposed?

Investigation

Once a proposed change makes it past first base, you have to investigate further before deciding to implement it, if at all.

3. What criteria should you establish for product selection? There are several common ones, such as reliability; ease of use; quality and quantity of vendor support and vendor training; well-organized, well-written, well-indexed, and thorough manuals; and potential for compatibility with future system developments.

    Should you restrict products to those specified as company-wide standards? For example, should you stick with one brand of printer, one brand of terminal, and one brand of PC? Should everyone use the same word processing package, the same spreadsheet program, and the same software for communications?

4. How should products be evaluated? There are at least three stances from which to evaluate a product:

    First, is it a good product? Is it ready for market? Does it do what you need it to do? How will you decide? Will you rely on published reviews? Will you attend product demonstrations? When might it be worthwhile to seek the opinion of others who have purchased the product? Will you run pre-purchase tests? If so, where? In the vendor's showroom or in your office? What tests will you run to judge the product?

Tip
About Standardization

There is much to be said for standardization. With standard products you gain the following advantages: training is easier; installation is easier; vendor support comes more easily; people know what to expect of the system; you can move equipment around with minimal hassle; the constellation of supplies and accessories you need is both easier to keep in inventory and cheaper because you can buy in larger quantities; and, finally, you are not driven wild trying to keep track of everything.

Second, is the product compatible with your system? Compatibility can be a charged issue. How do you evaluate it? It is clearly a case of incompatibility when your computer cannot drive that nifty laser printer, but how do you evaluate manufacturers' claims of compatibility when the lines are less clear? (As far as I am concerned, "compatible" means 100 percent compatible. Anything less than 100 percent spells both incompatibility and trouble.)

Third, will the product run peacefully with your existing system? Whether a product runs peacefully on your system is sometimes more than simply a matter of compatibility. Sometimes you have to consider other issues, such as how a new program might interact with your other programs in RAM. If you are considering a specialty program, find out whether there is a possibility of collisions in RAM, given the constellation of programs you have (see Section 5.3).

5. Can your system accommodate the proposed change? Does your existing system have the hardware required to make use of a proposed software program? For example, a daisy wheel printer cannot print the graphs you might design with the program you are considering, no matter how much you plead. Or, is there an empty expansion slot in each PC that you'd like to add memory to? (Your system boards maps

will tell you). Is there enough RAM to run the on-line the-saurus that you want? (Find out by consulting your RAM worksheets, presented in Section 5.4.)

6. In addition to the proposed item, must you buy other prod-ucts in order to implement the change? Possibilities include cabling, additional equipment, add-on boards, furniture, ac-cessories, and supplies. Whatever you are planning to buy, describe your system to your vendor and ask if there is any-thing more that you will need beyond the equipment or software under consideration.

   However, you must explore possible needs on your own because you cannot rely on the vendor always to bring needed extras to your attention. A vendor might innocently overlook your need for an item or might not elicit from you all of the information necessary to determine how to meet your particular system's requirements. For example, maybe you need an expansion chassis to accommodate the new board you want to add to a fully occupied PC. Or you might have to add a translator unit to your IBM PC-Network before you can add even one more workstation. And, suppose you are adding two new PC's to your system. How could the vendor anticipate that your firm's printing needs will require you to add another printer?

7. Is site preparation involved? Use the checklist in Table 7.6 to be sure that you fully understand what is needed to prepare your site for the proposed change. The architect's blueprints of your facilities can be most helpful here if they are avail-able. They will provide important information such as where bearing walls are located and where power outlets exist.

8. What will be the impact on people? Some changes take place and they are hardly noticed. But, most system changes re-quire people to make adjustments, some of them significant. An example is when you move people from a single user world into one of networks or multi-user systems.

   Procedural changes or alterations in working conditions are not bad in and of themselves and people will accept some changes without too much difficulty. For instance, employ-ees might welcome an unknown printer that they under-stand to be far superior to the current one, even if the change

---

Table 7.6

SITE PREPARATION AND SPACE PLANNING CHECKLIST

• Overall Space
  —Identify the space required.
  —Calculate to see that the space will accommodate your change.
  —Identify and specify required remodeling or construction, if any.
  —Prepare a tentative room layout that shows where equipment and furniture will be located.
  —Secure necessary approvals to commit the space.

• Power
  —Verify that existing lines provide sufficient power.
  —Do you need new power lines?
  —Are dedicated lines required?
  —Do you need additional power outlets?

• Other
  —Do you need more telephone lines?
  —Is the lighting appropriate?
  —Must additional cable be laid?
  —Is special air conditioning required?

---

means that they have to learn all over again how to insert paper, change ribbons, and set the top of the form.

9. What will the change cost? Get figures for everything, including the items you identified in items 6 and 7. If the change involves reconstruction, get estimates. Remember to include the most often overlooked item: staff training.

10. What type of training will people need and is it available? The importance of proper training cannot be overly stressed. Lack of training breeds resistance, and nothing undermines the system more than resistance. Further, nothing ensures

success more than the support and commitment that people put behind a project.

Be sure people are adequately trained to handle system developments. Sometimes all that they need is a twenty-minute instruction session. Other times they need extensive schooling that extends beyond the period of formal training into informal on-site support provided by in-house people. Refer to the training tips.

Training Tips

Tip #1: Training options. You have several training options to choose among:

- Vendor-provided training.

- External training programs
  - a. Training centers
  - b. Colleges and universities
  - c. Consultants

- On-line tutorials or cassette tape training
- Formal in-house programs
  - a. Designated staff members
  - b. In-house users' group

Tip #2: Choosing the best option. To choose the best of the options available to you, consider the following ideas.

- No single option is the best in all cases. Sometimes, you will be better off bringing in a consultant, and other times you will be wise to send a staff member to a university extension class.

- Inexpensive training can be expensive. While there sometimes is little correlation between the price and the effectiveness of training, mediocre training is the most costly in the long run. Pennies saved on training bills can cost your firm dearly. Your goal is to bring everyone up to speed quickly. The sooner people are able to use the system's tools, the sooner they can be productive.

- Match the training program to the people who will take it. Some people prefer small group instruction; some work best one-to-one with a tutor; others thrive working on their own if a resource person is available to answer questions. Involve people in the training method selection process. Ask *them what methods they personally prefer.*

- Put people in the driver's seat. In nearly every case, hands-on, personal training is infinitely superior to theoretical coursework. The more practically oriented a program, invariably the more effective it is.

- The more specific the training program is to what your firm actually needs and does, the better. It is most desirable to have each item on a class agenda be of particular import. The ideal program is one held on your site, taught with your firm's system, and specially designed to produce or make use of the actual data in your firm. Such tailor-made classes are expensive, but sometimes worth it.

- When you need extensive training, evaluate carefully each program that you are considering. Get references from former students. Ask the trainer about teaching methods. Perhaps send only one or two of your staff members to see whether it would be worthwhile to send others.

- When you opt for in-house training, formalize it or it will not work as effectively as it otherwise might. Give trainers recognition. Add the training function to each trainer's job description. Set aside special times for training sessions.

11. Every proposed change has its costs and its benefits to weigh as you decide whether or not to implement the change. Be sure the gains are worth it before you disrupt people. You might learn that a change that is in nearly every way desirable is simply not worth the cost in the grief it would cause to people using the system today. For instance, suppose you are considering adding the sales department to your network. The department is undergoing rapid growth, with several incoming employees. The new sales manager has uncovered serious personnel problems. At this time, being added to the network is a distraction that they do not need in the department, so you and the sales manager decide to postpone it.

For extensive changes, you might have to prepare formal justification. Under what conditions is this required? Most firms formally analyze costs and benefits only when a change entails expenditures over a certain dollar amount.

Implementation

If the proposed change will bring gains that are worth their expense, now is the time to consider implementation. This stage will be easier if you have included others throughout the previous stages of the decision-making process.

12. Inform people immediately. As soon as you know that a change will be implemented, tell everyone affected as soon as possible. The extent of the information you impart will vary according to the extent of the change. Convey the benefits to the firm and, if you can, convey the benefits each employee might enjoy personally. Tell people how they will be affected otherwise. Describe the change in their terms, from their perspective. Describe the training that they will receive and what you have planned to help them during the period of adjustment. Tell them about in-house and on-site support that will continue beyond the initial training period.

13. Schedule and make arrangements for necessary site preparation and for equipment installation. Identify who is responsible for each step in preparing the workplace for system change. For example, if you expand your local area network, who will order new cable, new equipment, and new furniture? Who will see that the premises are prepared for its installation?

14. Schedule and make arrangements for staff training. Be sure people receive their training shortly before they must put it to use in their jobs. You want to avoid the problem of having people spend a lot of time being trained only to forget what they learned because the particular product they learned to use was not on site until a month after the training program concluded.

15. Test the new addition. No matter how well you tested the product before it arrived on the premises, test it now that it is connected to your firm's system. You want to be as sure as possible that there are no glitches.

Run vigorous tests (or have your well-trained backup person do this). Put new software through its paces. For example, load the maximum number of programs possible with your new windowing program. With equipment, run its self tests (see Section 8.1) and then proceed to tests using your firm's actual software and data. For example, print one of your data files that calls for all of the special effects that your new printer is advertised to produce: boldfacing, superscripts, proportional spacing, and so on.

Tip	*If you are upgrading your operating system, be absolutely sure that you have a copy of the old version at your side in case you run into trouble with the new version.*

16. Revise documents and procedures in your system library. When you add a new piece of equipment, review and update your hardware documents. If you buy a new application package, revise your software documents. Ask yourself if any procedures need revision. For example, with a new application package, you should review your records management and security procedures. Distribute to everyone the revised documents and procedures that they need.

17. What if it is a bomb? There is no such thing as a bug-free anything. Whenever you add something to your system, there are always a few wrinkles that you will have to iron out. But, sometimes, new hardware or software will not work out. The first thing to do is be sure. Read the documentation and contact your vendor for help if necessary.

    If you determine that there is no way that the new addition can coexist with your system or the people using it, remove it immediately and return the system to its former state. Then negotiate with the vendor about returning the item.

    There might be times when the lines are not so clear. One system manager loaded a multi-user system with its advertised maximum number of terminals, printers, and other peripherals, only to find people complaining that the system's level of performance was intolerably slow. Other people, with different needs or tolerance, who use an identical system might have no objection to the same level of system performance.

Plan for Change

Whatever the size of your firm, you will benefit from using a written system development plan as a road map to keep the bumps and wrong turns to a minimum. Enlist others to help you, including key personnel from every level of your organization if you can.

The development plan has three parts: it describes your system today, where you intend it to go tomorrow, and what you plan to do to take it there.

Begin your system development plan with a brief description of your system today. Draw upon documents in your system library, such as the system devices map and your software inventory. Specify who uses the system and for what purposes. For instance, maybe your system is used throughout the firm strictly for word processing. Include in your written development plan all pertinent system library documents and your firm's organization chart.

Identify and rank problems. What shortcomings does your system have as you and others see it? What are the complaints you get from other staff members? Is there enough equipment to go around? Are people adequately trained? Does one brand of equipment continually break down?

Next, describe where you would like to see the system within a specified period, say six to eight months or maybe a year from now. Establish both specific and general goals. For example, suppose only your accounting department is automated. Will you expand the system into the marketing department within six months? For which activities? Within the accounting department, should you convert additional activities from manual to automated methods?

Identify solutions to the problems you listed in Part I. Be as specific as possible. For instance, if people frequently complain that the printer is unavailable when they need it, you might plan to add a new printer next month.

You will want to subject the planned changes to the same rigorous examination that you apply to changes proposed on an *ad hoc* basis. Refer to the procedures you established with the help of the previous section.

Schedule a periodic review and update your plan with the help of the others.

7.5 The Annual Review: A Checklist for Overall System Management

In this final section on avoiding trouble, we will look at a catch-all mechanism every system manager needs, the annual review. Occasionally, you have to put off a particular task, either out of choice or circumstance. For instance, in Chapter Three we saw that you might decide to postpone adding replacement pages to your operating system manual. Or maybe your firm asks a departing employee to come in as a consultant one day a week until a particular project is completed. In that case, circumstance would prevent you from deleting the person's logon id on his or her last day as an employee.

Although you will delay some activities, you do not want them to remain undone indefinitely. Even the little tasks pile up and can cause minor explosions. The page replacement task is an example. One system manager let it go for almost two years without trouble. Then, one afternoon he encountered his first problem with data integrity. He knew to get everyone off the system while he repaired the damage, but, because data integrity repair commands were part of what had been upgraded, it took more time than it should have for him to check and repair the damaged file system. Finding the needed information involved the clumsy task of hunting through the various packets of replacement pages. Needless to say, neither he nor anyone else was happy about it.

The annual review will help you to avoid minor problems like that one, as well as major problems such as security breaches by former employees. Do not use the annual review as a schedule. Here's why. Refer for a moment to the series of tasks on the following checklist. Notice that the range of tasks is broad. Some should be performed daily, such as making a partial system backup; some quarterly, such as conducting disk housekeeping; some annually, such as conducting a system evaluation; and others intermittently, such as updating the system library. The purpose of the annual review is to see that these tasks *are* being done.

When you conduct yours, you will identify anything that slipped through the cracks during the previous twelve months. Some system managers prefer to conduct such a review every six months. You be the judge. However often you use it, this review will be your added safety-net for problem-avoidance.

A Checklist for Overall System Management

Review this checklist (annually or semiannually) to ensure that you have completed important system management functions. The tasks are listed in their order of appearance in this book, with chapter references to direct you to where you will find information.

Check if Completed	Function	Chapter References
_____	Conduct evaluations of the system and of your system management plan	1
_____	Review all system library documents to ensure that they reflect the current system	2–3 and 4–7
_____	Review your records management plan	4
_____	Check that your records retention and disposition schedule is followed	4
_____	Conduct disk houskeeping	4
_____	Evaluate how efficiently RAM is being used on your system	5
_____	Evaluate and audit your security system	6
_____	Change all system passwords	6
_____	Check that former employees are no longer able to use the system	6
_____	Perform equipment maintenance tasks	7
	Conduct an equipment inventory	7
_____	Check file integrity	7
_____	Make partial and complete file backups	7
_____	Review your system development plan	7

Conclusion

In this chapter and in the preceding ones, we looked at many strategies and ongoing procedures to help you manage your system successfully. Each procedure is designed to help you promote top system performance, to avoid trouble, or both. With these procedures, you will screen out most of the problems that plague computer systems. But, because we cannot always avert problems, it is time we turned to steps you can take when you encounter the unavoidable ones.

8

Establish Troubleshooting Techniques and Procedures

Introduction

Even when you take every precaution described in earlier chapters to keep your system in prime condition, your system still will run into trouble from time to time. The best you can do is plan for that inevitable day when something goes wrong.

The system's credibility and yours depend most on how you handle problems. During my first two weeks managing a system, I was trigger happy. If a terminal went down or a printer froze, I reset the system every time. The others were as green as I was. But, no one was very happy with these repeated system resets. Luckily, I soon found less disruptive ways to solve problems.

Other managers might call the vendor at the first sign of trouble. While vendor assistance often is needed, even in the most extreme circumstances you have to provide a "front line" defense. Your quick action during a crisis can mean the difference between data that is lost or data that is salvaged. In addition, there are many instances in which a system manager's intervention eliminates unnecessary service calls and enables people to return to work quickly.

So, while this chapter will not replace vendor assistance, it describes troubleshooting techniques that will prepare you to handle most of the serious situations you will encounter before they become disasters. It will prepare you to steer safely through quagmires the system drags you into when you least expect it. You also will find sample procedures to handle both common problems and occasional crises.

Each procedure is designed to stand alone. That way, you can turn to it for help when you are immersed in chaos. For example, when you unexpectedly run out of disk space or when system performance abruptly drops, you will find the steps you need to lead you out of trouble all in one place. (Such convenience is at the cost of a bit of repetition.)

8.1 A Quick Guide to Troubleshooting

Troubleshooting in an office environment is inevitably complex. This quick guide is an overview of how you can cope with unexpected problems. Once you use it, you will find yourself able to minimize and even avert trouble later.

Take Advantage of Simple Tests

To begin this chapter devoted to trouble, let's consider the good news: more often than you might expect, pinpointing the cause of a problem is simple. You can run a few quick tests that are easy to conduct and that also produce reliable results because they test at the most basic level of operation, involving no complicated data exchanges. Add each one of the following quick tests to your repertory of troubleshooting skills:

Test #1: Power on self-test. The first is the simplest test. In fact, it is so simple that you usually are unaware that you are running it. The computer automatically conducts a "power on self-test" each time you activate the system. That test immediately alerts you to trouble with many parts of the system, including the CPU, RAM chips, and even the communication links in a network. Whenever the system detects a problem during this test, it notifies you right away.

Test #2: Device self-test. Another easy test to perform is the self-test available with most peripheral equipment. Terminals, printers, and modems have them. Typically, you run these tests with the equipment in question operating independently of the computer, in what is called "off-line" mode. Become familiar with these tests before you encounter trouble. Check your manuals for instructions.

Test #3: Tests run via equipment or operating system commands. Your equipment or operating system probably allows you to check for trouble with data files, disk drives, printers, or software. For instance, with the IBM PC family, we already have seen that you can check the integrity of data files using the DOS CHKDSK program or the XENIX **fsck** command (see Section 7.2). In addition, the keyboard's PrtSc (print screen) key allows you to test a printer by printing the contents of the terminal display directly, instead of through an application software program. Tests like these can isolate the cause of problems, simplifying diagnosis. Your system probably has comparable tests. Check your documentation.

Test #4 Observation. The last easy test is one people frequently forget: visual observation. Many apparent problems turn out to be false alarms. When you run into trouble, check the basics. Examine the indicator lights on equipment.Maybe the modem is in test mode or the printer is off-line and that is why equipment refuses to respond. Also check that the power is on, that cables are connected, and other obvious matters are in order, such as whether the printer has a supply of paper.

Master these four quick tests to make your troubleshooting job infinitely easier. Run them before you use more complicated means to diagnose a problem.

If you are unable to identify the source of the problem with a quick test, you will have to resort to other tests, such as running diagnostic software that your vendor may have provided with your system. Advanced diagnostics are available for those who want to go deeper into troubleshooting. Then again, you might prefer simply to call your vendor.

Six Rules for the Successful Troubleshooter

Whenever you run into trouble, no matter how bleak and distracting the situation is, you will troubleshoot successfully and stay sane if you follow these six rules:

Rule #1: Stay cool. Stay cool, even when it's hot. Do not take the wrath and frustration of others personally. Troubleshooting situations are inherently stressful. They frequently bring out features of people that we would rather not see (including our own).

Rule #2: Be safe. Follow the safety precautions that your documentation recommends. Vendors are not kidding when they ask you to turn the power off before you work inside of a device or to keep your hands away from a CRT tube even if the power is off.

Rule #3: Persist. Be persistent. Track down every problem. Tempting as it may be, never let a problem go by without understanding why it occurred and, if possible, without identifying what you can do to prevent it from happening again. Call the vendor if you are unable to sort out the problem on your own.

Rule #4: Protect software. If possible, never use an original software diskette in the course of troubleshooting. You may destroy it. Use one of the backups you made when you purchased the software. (Obviously, this is a problem with software with a copy-protection scheme that prevents you from making backups.)

Rule #5: Choose minimal impact. Follow the rule of minimal impact: all else being equal, troubleshooting measures should affect (1) as few users as possible and (2) tasks in order of least importance first.

Rule #6: Keep people informed. Whether you have good news, bad news, or no news, keep people informed. Open and honest communication is worth more than just about anything else.

Table 8.1

TROUBLESHOOTER'S RULES

#1: Stay cool.
#2: Be safe.
#3: Persist.
#4: Protect software.
#5: Choose minimal impact.
#6: Keep people informed.

A Framework for Troubleshooting

In most troubleshooting situations, you will perform a series of steps that fall into a set pattern because the goals are always the same: to solve problems quickly, without rancor and with as little disruption as possible. Critical common-sense steps are compiled in the framework for troubleshooting procedures that follows. Use it as a blueprint to plan how you will handle specific problems with minimal disruption to people and minimal damage to data and equipment. Later in this chapter, you will see examples of how the framework can be applied. Depending on the nature of a problem, you might add steps, omit steps, or order those listed below in a different sequence.

The framework shows how important other people are to your success in resolving trouble. Impress on people how important their role can be and carefully train them to do their part (steps A and B). From time to time, reinforce the idea that you need them for everyone's sake. People will be cooperative if you convey how important their role is in making the system available for themselves and for the others.

Step A: Document the trouble. Ideally, whoever discovers a problem should (1) write down the sequence of commands issued just prior to the onset of trouble, (2) write down all messages displayed on the screen, and (3) note exactly where data entry or processing left off. This information will help you to track the source of the trouble as well as help the person to resume work after the problem is solved.

Step B: Notify the system manager. Whoever discovers the problem should inform you immediately, so you can take Steps C through K.

Step C: Alert others. If the problem might affect others, alert people so that they can take necessary precautions to protect their work. Though people greet system problems with distaste, they appreciate advance warning.

Step D: Determine the scope of the trouble. If you are to solve a problem quickly, you have to know what it involves. Identify the equipment, software, and data files associated with it.

Step E: Diagnose the problem. List all possible causes of the problem. Plod through the list, beginning with the most likely source. Question people, run necessary tests, and decipher computer-generated messages.

Step F: Resolve the problem. Take appropriate action. If necessary, call your vendor.

Step G: Be sure the problem is solved. You do not want people to resume working with a system that continues to have a problem. Replicate the situation that preceded it. If you can, use the information gathered in step A to repeat the exact series of commands that led up to the start of trouble. Use the same workstation, the same software, and the same data file. You want to be sure the trouble is solved before you send out the all-clear signal.

Step H: Fix damaged files. Check the condition of files on the disk (see Section 7.2). Repair any damaged files. After you are sure all data files are intact, erase any garbage files that the problem created.

Step I: Inform people. Let people know when you have solved the problem. Explain what the trouble was and how you eliminated it. Now is a good time to thank those who helped you.

Step J: Document the problem. As fully as you can, document the problem and its solution.

Step K: Recap. Mentally review the episode. If possible, take steps to avoid a recurrence.

Table 8.2

SUMMARY FRAMEWORK FOR TROUBLESHOOTING

A. Document the trouble.
B. Notify the system manager.
C. Alert others.
D. Determine the scope of the trouble.
E. Diagnose the problem.
F. Resolve the problem.
G. Be sure the problem is solved.
H. Fix damaged files.
I. Inform people.
J. Document the problem.
K. Recap.

8.2 Troubleshooter's Guide to Everyday Problems

We have looked at the overall structure for troubleshooting, its basic rules, tests, and procedural components. This section guides you more specifically in handling some of the common problems you will encounter. Although the information here cannot replace your documentation, it will save you time by filling in the gaps.

Learn to Investigate a Frozen Device

Eventually, you will have to contend with a frozen device, that is, a device that is locked, refusing to respond to commands. Printers, modems, and terminals are the most notorious for freezing. Except in cases of system failure, freezing nearly always is traced to a faulty cable or to a software problem. You have to be particularly careful with devices that freeze as a result of software trouble because they rarely freeze alone.

Consider these cases. Two devices can freeze simultaneously. For example, when a printer is frozen, frequently a terminal locks up, too. Similarly, sometimes a device freezes with a software package, such as when a modem freezes with its communications software. Freezing also can be contagious. One device freezes and minutes later the ice spreads. For example, terminals frequently freeze by themselves before the lockup infects other parts of the system.

Don't Be Fooled

Before we look at a procedure to handle frozen devices, we need to consider that equipment sometimes only appears to be frozen when it is not. An obvious case is equipment that is set to operate in local mode, but there are two other common examples:

First, a person inadvertently enters commands that lock the keyboard. Until someone unlocks the keyboard, the workstation or terminal behaves as if it were frozen.

Second, imagine the following scene. Staff member A shares a printer with staff member B. Staff member A is printing a file, page by page, having instructed the printer to pause between the pages. When A is called to the telephone in the next room, the printer continues printing until the end of the page and then waits for a command to proceed. Meanwhile, staff member B, unaware that A has engaged the printer, issues a command to print a file. The result: the printer will not respond and staff member B assumes that the printer is frozen. But this "frozen" printer is simply pausing until it receives the command to continue printing A's file.

Procedure to Handle a Frozen Device

Regardless of the type of system you manage, the steps to handle a frozen device are essentially the same. The following procedure is designed for a system serving multiple users; if yours does not, eliminate steps two and five and follow the other steps in sequence.

Step One. The person operating the device when it freezes should (1) note exactly the sequence of commands preceding the problem; (2) write down any messages displayed on the screen;

(3) note where data entry or processing left off; and (4) contact you immediately so that you can take the following steps.

Step Two. Inform everybody. Identify the frozen device and warn each person to stop using the system if you have reason to believe that further work is in jeopardy.

Step Three. Examine the problem device so that you are sure that it is not a paused device masquerading as a frozen device. Perhaps all you need to do to free the frozen device is enter a command or respond to a prompt.

For example, with frozen terminals or monitors, issue the "unlock" command. Check the screen prompt. Or, if a printer is frozen, check the terminal or personal computer last known to have issued a command to print a file. Next, see if the printer is in local mode. If not, ask others if they have the printer engaged so that you can check their terminals or PC's accordingly.

Step Four. Refer to the charts in this section showing common trouble and solutions for terminals and printers. These charts might help you resolve the problem. In particular, check that the switch settings are properly set on the frozen device.

Step Five. If the frozen device is engaged to a process, such as a software program or a printing process, free the device from the process. UNIX systems use the **kill** command. With DOS systems, holding down the CTRL and Break keys simultaneously should disengage the process.

If you are unsure if the device is engaged to a process, find out by issuing an operating system command that tells you which process each device on the system is running. UNIX systems use the **ps -a** command, XENIX the **ps-e** command.

Step Six. If the command to disengage does not free the device, turn off the power on the problem device and count to ten before you turn it back on.

Step Seven. If step six does not work, test whether the problem is with the cable, the device, or the port. (See the section "Cable, Device, or Port?" below.)

Step Eight. If freezing persists, reboot the system. Carefully follow your procedure to reboot during a work period (see Section 8.3).

Step Nine. Fully test the system and the problem device after you reboot. Even if things are working, you must be sure that they will not lock up again. Run through a number of tasks, such as creating, saving, and editing a file. Run the device's self test. If possible, recreate the circumstances that immediately preceded the freeze. Run your diagnostic software to further verify that all is well.

Step Ten. If the device fails its tests, you have a hardware problem and it needs repair. If the system fails its tests, you probably have a software problem. Both cases bring you to the very *last* resort: call the vendor.

Step Eleven. If a hard disk is involved in the freeze, it is possible that files stored on it were damaged. Check the integrity of all files and make necessary repairs. Include system files as well as data files (refer to Section 7.2 for details). Afterwards, erase any garbage files that appeared on the system as a result of the freeze.

Step Twelve. As soon as the problem is resolved, contact the person who originally told you about it. Tell this person everything you know about the problem: why it happened and what had to be done about it. If in the process you have discovered something to help other people avoid similar trouble, contact them too. It always helps to educate them about their system.

Step Thirteen. Mentally review the episode. If possible, take action to avoid a recurrence.

Step Fourteen. Document the problem and its resolution.

Cable, Device, or Port?

When you run into trouble with the system, the problem is not necessarily with the software or with a device. In fact, the problem frequently is with a cable, sometimes with a port. When you inspect a cable, look for the obvious. You might find loose wires or a tear. Entire systems can go down because of a minute rip in the cable that connects the hard disk controller board. So, even if you do not see anything wrong after you examine a cable, do not rule out the cable as the possible cause of the trouble. The following tests will help you isolate whether trouble with a device actually is caused by a problem with its cable, the device itself, or its port.

Because you are dealing with three variables (a cable, a device, and a port), you will isolate the source of the problem by keeping two variables constant. The order of these tests is not sacred. But, to conduct them you have to know which cable connects the problem device to which port. Depending on how many devices your system has, this can be an exceedingly complicated task. However, with your system devices map (see Section 2.2), you will identify immediately which cable/device/port relationships apply.

Test #1: New cable/same device/same port. Use a new cable, identical to the suspect cable, to connect the suspect device to its original port. If the suspect device now works, the trouble is with the original cable.

Test #2: New device/same cable/same port. Leave the original cable attached to the original port, but switch the device end of the cable to a new device. The new device must be of the same kind as the suspect device. For example, if the original problem is with a terminal, the new device must be the same type of terminal. If the new device works, the problem probably is with the suspect device.

Test #3: New port/same cable/same device. Leave the original cable attached to the suspect device, but switch the port end of the cable to another port on the system. This new port must serve the same kind of device as the suspect device. If the suspect device now works, the problem probably is with the original port.

These three tests often will come in handy, especially when you use the procedures immediately following to handle problem printers and terminals.

How to Handle a Printer Problem

If you have ever tried to print a file you spent hours developing and found the printer not working, you probably will agree that it is near the top of frustrating computer experiences.

Printers have a reputation for being difficult, starting the day they arrive because just getting one installed properly can be troublesome. Then, once they are working, most are noisy and every one of them demands attention. Some people find just keeping a printer supplied with paper and ribbon an annoyance in itself. Furthermore, because printers have moving parts, they are subject to problems that plague you, ranging from paper jamming to ribbons twisting to covers being left ajar. Check these elements first whenever you have a printer problem. Appreciate a printer's indicator lights because they notify you about what state the printer is in. Many "broken" printers are "repaired" quickly because of these lights. For example, you often will discover that a non-responsive printer's on-line light is off. Depress this light to re-establish communication between the printer and the computer.

A surprisingly common source of printer trouble occurs when someone accidentally changes the on/off positions on the printer's switches. Why this problem is so common remains a mystery, particularly because these switches usually are located inside of the printer. With its switches improperly set, a printer usually prints garbage. Settings vary depending on the printer and the computer, so it can be a challenge to decipher what the patterns mean. You will have no trouble correcting the settings if you followed Chapter Two's steps to create the system switch settings map (see Section 2.4).

You will encounter other sources of printer trouble. Table 8.3 charts six common problems with printers and the likely causes. Your system library should be helpful to you in some situations, so under the comments column are the names of specific library documents to consult. Notice the repeated troublemakers: cables, paper, and ribbons.

Before You Call the Vendor

One bit of advice needs stressing. Before you call the vendor when you run into printer trouble (or trouble with any equipment, for that matter), remember that not every printer problem is due to trouble with the printer itself. The real cause might be something associated with the software. The source of trouble could be the data file being printed, improperly installed software, or a bug in the program used to print the file. That is to say that you should not jump to conclusions. One of the first questions vendors usually ask is, "Did you run the self-test?" When you suspect hardware failure, run your printer's self-test. If it checks out, the printer is OK and you have to look elsewhere for the source of trouble.

If you suspect the software, try printing a different file using the same program. That test will establish whether the problem is caused by garbage in the particular data file being printed when trouble began. If the original data file contains no garbage, it is possible that the software is improperly installed. So, try printing files created with another program. Run each of these tests and check the common printer trouble chart before calling your vendor.

Table 8.3

COMMON PRINTER TROUBLE CHART

Trouble	Cause	Comment
Completely dead	Power supply lost	
	Fuse blown	
	Hardware failure	Call the vendor.
Power on, no response	Paper or ribbon out	
	Cable disconnected	
	Paper caught	
	Cover open	
	Off-line	Check indicator lights.
	May not be released by a process	Detach the printer from the process.
	If your system has two printers, your print command may have asked the other printer to perform, instead of the one you intended.	Send your print command to the right printer. Check the **peripheral devices map** (for PC's) or the **multi-user system devices map**.
	Printer isn't shared or requested for use. (LAN's only)	Your **software defaults maps** may be of help.
	Hardware failure	Call the vendor.
Prints intermittently	Loose cable connection	
Prints garbage	Disrupted cable connection	
	Ribbon twisted or not installed properly	
	Switch settings wrong	Check the **switch settings map**.
	Data file trouble	
	Software improperly installed	For a quick reinstallation, use the **paper copy of the installation**. Watch for the source of trouble.
Paper jams	Blockage in paper path	Remove debris, such as gummed labels.
Poor-quality printout	Jammed or exhausted ribbon	
	Exhausted print head	

> | Warning |

> *Print head mechanisms move with speed and force. Avoid injury. Always turn off the power before putting your hands inside of the printer.*

How to Troubleshoot Terminal Trouble

Terminals are a bright spot in troubleshooting. They are one of the most reliable devices on a system. Like printers, terminals work hard, but they are much less likely to cause you grief, mainly because terminals have so few moving parts. (Keyboards, of course, have moving parts just like printers, and they suffer a lot of use, but they rarely fail unless mucked up with food and other debris.) However, occasionally terminals do have trouble.

Terminal switch settings mysteriously are changed as often as those on printers. The results are similar: garbage on the screen or no contact with the computer. Use your switch settings map (see Section 2.4) to check the correct settings.

Another problem is telephone lines, which can play havoc with remote terminals. Often, when someone dials on a nearby telephone, random characters dance about on the screen. That disruption may not destroy any work, but it is a real nuisance. An easy remedy is to lower the rate that data is transmitted over the cable—the baud rate. (Be sure to update affected system library documents!) But, there is an unfortunate trade-off with this remedy. Although a person can work without distraction when using the terminal, the lower baud rate slows things down.

> | Tip |

> *Generally, if only one terminal behaves strangely, rule out a software problem for the time being.*

Run the terminal's self-test if you suspect hardware failure. As with problem printers, running this test in advance saves time if you ultimately call your vendor.

Table 8.4 charts five terminal problems you might encounter and their causes. Notice the ubiquitous cable as a common source of

Table 8.4

COMMON TERMINAL TROUBLE CHART

Trouble	Cause	Comment
Screen goes blank	Power supply lost	Check for damaged files.
	Power surge	Reset or reboot the system. Check for damage.
	Cable loose or disconnected	
	Overheating	Clear air vents. Make adjustments to reduce the temperature.
	Fuse blown	
	Hardware failure	Call the vendor.
Blurred characters on the screen	Overheating	Clear air vents. Make adjustments to reduce the temperature.
Garbage on the screen	Power line trouble	Reset or reboot the system. Check for damage.
	Cable transmission interference or excessively long cable	If possible, use a shorter cable. Otherwise, lower the baud rate. Check and update the **switch settings map**.
	Telephone line interference	Lower the baud rate. Check and update the **switch settings map**.
	Switch settings wrong	Check the **switch settings map**.
	Port trouble	Call the vendor.
	Hardware failure	Call the vendor.
Terminal works but can't establish contact with the system	System not running	
	Cable loose or disconnected	
	Port trouble	Call the vendor.
	Switch settings wrong	Check the **switch settings map**.
Keyboard locked	Lock command inadvertently issued	

trouble. Again, system library documents appear in boldface under the comments column so that you can refer to them easily.

Three Warnings

1. Unless the test you are running mandates that the power be on, *always* turn the power off before you work on a terminal.
2. Even with the power off, the cathode-ray tube in a terminal, called a CRT, retains an electrical charge that can cause serious injury. That charge must be discharged before you touch the insides of a terminal. Residual charges are so potent you should *never* work inside a CRT housing without someone close by to provide aid. In fact, the interior of a terminal is so dangerous to inexperienced hands that I discourage you from putting yours on the line unless you are well-trained for it.
3. CRT's usually are coated with poisonous material. If you run into a broken tube, do not touch it with your bare hands. Use a tool or wear heavy rubber gloves to protect yourself.

What to Do When System Performance Abruptly Deteriorates

Aside from trouble with a specific piece of equipment, you also might encounter generalized system trouble. For instance, occasionally, system performance sharply degrades without warning. When a system grinds to a crawl, people feel as they do when they step off a moving sidewalk. Forward movement is intolerably slow; the cursor slugs across the screen; and fingers move across the keyboard in turbo-time, but it seems as if the display echo will never catch up. You are certain you could get the job done more quickly with an abacus.

Sudden degradation is extremely disruptive. You will hear about it instantly if you are away from the system when it happens. People tend to want this problem solved now.

Usually, the problem occurs because of some type of system overload. Use Table 8.5 to handle a sudden slowdown in performance. Systematically check the possible causes. The list begins with the most likely cause and ends with the expected last resort solution.

Table 8.5

CAUSES AND PRESCRIPTIONS: ABRUPT DETERIORATION IN SYSTEM PERFORMANCE

Possible Cause	Prescription
A piece of equipment is not turned on, creating an endless communication route from the computer to the device. This situation drains the system and slows its performance. (This is not the case for every system.)	Make sure every device is turned on, regardless of whether each one will be used during the day.
A system cable has an unstable connection, creating an endless route such as that described above.	Solidly connect *all* cables or disengage them from the system.
Too many staff members simultaneously are running processes that drag the system. At its most severe, this problem is one cause of a system lock-up.	Check which processes all staff members currently are running. Identify processes that can be rescheduled for another time or redirected to another system.
	If this overload develops into a chronic problem, you might solve it if you add memory to the system or reassign processes to another system.
The system is running its maximum number of processes.	If possible, check the processes others currently are running to identify those that can be discontinued or redirected.
	If the system will not allow you to check the current processes, you will have to ask people to save files in progress and log off of the system.
	If you find this problem to be chronic, you may be able to increase the maximum number of allowed simultaneous processes. Some operating systems, such as UNIX, allow this increase if you reinstall the system. Check your operating system manuals.

Table 8.5

CAUSES AND PRESCRIPTIONS: ABRUPT DETERIORATION IN SYSTEM PERFORMANCE

(continued)

Possible Cause	Prescription
You just added a new piece of equipment to the system, pushing it over the brink of system capacity. It is not unusual for a system to slow to an intolerable crawl after connection of a new piece of equipment, even if the total number of devices is within the number that the manufacturer claims is the system's capacity.	Before you do anything, discuss the problem with your vendor. A solution may be as simple as adding a new power supply or as complex and expensive as buying another system.
A sharp increase in data stored on disk reduces free space below the tolerable amount. When this increase happens suddenly, it usually is the result of a mistake by an inexperienced person using the system. For example, consider how easy it would be for someone inadvertenty to duplicate an entire directory and its files on disk, gobbling up a huge amount of space in a moment and bringing the system to its knees quickly.	Check available space on disk. To get disk storage down to size, refer to Sections 4.1, 4.2, and 8.3.

Last Resort

If you cannot solve the problem yourself, follow the usual last resort: call your vendor.

Tip

Some systems with multi-processors are designed to slow down instead of crash when one of its processors fails. In this case, you need your vendor.

8.3 Indispensable Troubleshooting Techniques

Whenever trouble strikes your system, it is a tremendous help if you have planned precisely what action you will take. Being prepared can make the difference between success and failure (and whether or not you keep your peace of mind), whether you are dealing with relatively non-threatening problems like broken terminals and printers or trouble that puts data files or the system in general in jeopardy.

This section will help you develop indispensable custom-made procedures for your system, using the framework for troubleshooting from Section 8.1 as a pattern. We will begin with suggestions to develop a temporary equipment replacement procedure. After that you will find two ready-made procedures, also based on the framework, to handle trouble of a more serious nature.

Prepare for Inevitable Equipment Failure

Equipment inevitably breaks down. Since you and other staff members rely on the system to do your work, you have to plan for the day when equipment fails. You can manage without some equipment some of the time. For example, you might get by without a modem for a few days. But what about a printer?

It is your job to be sure that the system is available to people. Warranty agreements rarely provide the security you need. If you do not want to be victimized, you have to take additional steps.

You have several options. Negotiating with your vendor is the obvious first step. For example, your vendor might be willing to provide loaner equipment while yours is being repaired. Your vendor also might agree to a favorable turnaround time for equipment repairs. Agreements with vendors can be helpful, but typically they do not go far enough, and you do not always get the agreements you prefer.

Be shrewd. Take internal precautions beyond those that you have taken in contracts or agreements with outside vendors. When it comes to trouble, you need a fall-back position. The best fall-back position is one over which you have complete control: set up a temporary equipment replacement procedure.

As you do so, think about more than your terminals, personal computers, printers, and modems. Remember that circuit boards and disk drives fail, too. Find out what your company is willing to buy spares of (modems? terminals?) and what it needs to replace via your replacement procedure (PC-AT's?). Weigh the cost of buying backup equipment against the potential cost of lost productivity. Buying backup equipment might be cost-justified if its cost is outweighed by the cost of idle personnel.

Consider these three options for an equipment replacement plan:

Option #1. Before you have trouble, establish a priority for using equipment. Assign the temporary replacement function to particular pieces of equipment in selected departments.

For example, a consulting firm commits one terminal of three in its training department to be available should one of those in the accounting department be sent for repairs. This way, people know in advance that they will have to relinquish one of their terminals whenever one in the accounting department fails.

Option # 2. Hopefully, your company has adequate resources to allow you to buy some backup equipment. A law firm has an unattached terminal on hand designated primarily for equipment replacement. But, it never goes unused. When it is not needed as a replacement, the terminal serves as an extra for temporary personnel. Still, everybody understands that the terminal's primary purpose is to replace any suddenly faulty terminal. This route is relatively inexpensive and extremely effective.

Option # 3. A third option is to use scheduling. An educational institution offers people flexible schedules between 7 a.m. and 6 p.m. whenever a given number of terminals are out for repair. If your company is small, you might use scheduling techniques based on processes instead of time of day. For example, a court reporting firm has eight people who share three workstations in a network.

During breakdown periods, the owners suspend accounts receivable processing and assign available equipment to highest priority client jobs.

| Tip |

In all cases, whenever and however equipment is loaned or transferred from its original spot, you must be notified, no matter how informal the arrangement. Be sure to update the system library as needed.

What to Do When You Run Out of Disk Space

One day, your system will refuse to obey a command to save data. It simply will not accept another word or number, including updates to an existing file. Most of the time you can avoid disk overload by following procedures to keep disk population down to manageable size (see Section 4.2). But, no matter what precautions you take, some day you might face a full disk. Running out of disk space can be a much more serious problem than a disabled piece of equipment when you have an equipment replacement procedure.

When a disk indicates it cannot take any more, you actually have two problems: (1) you have the immediate problem of one or more people needing to save work in progress; and (2) you have the less immediate problem of figuring out why the disk is full so that you can take steps to avoid a recurrence.

We will look at solutions to both problems, beginning with a series of steps to handle the immediate crisis. These steps are designed for a shared hard disk, but you can adapt them for a hard disk on a stand-alone PC.

Handle the Immediate Situation

Before trouble occurs, advise people not to panic if they ever see a DISK FULL message. Make them familiar with the procedures in this section.

As soon as you know that a disk is full, you have to be extremely careful to save everyone's work in progress. If it is possible to do so at all, you will accomplish it by following these steps.

Step One. The *last thing* the person discovering the problem should do is touch the keyboard. Everything should stop until you plan what to do next.

Step Two. The first thing that the person should do is notify you.

Step Three. Halt all work on the system immediately. Inform people that they should do *no* further work and make *no* requests to save files. They should not even log out because the steps you are following might release enough free space for them to save their files successfully. The situation calls for decisions to coordinate everyone's activities.

People should take the precaution of noting at what point their unsaved work begins and leaves off so that they will know the extent of work lost in case they ultimately are unable to save it.

Step Four. Assign priorities if you have to. Meeting a payroll deadline probably is infinitely more important than the hour's updates to a mailing list. Whatever priority is assigned, steps five through seven will help you to salvage what you can.

Step Five. Some people might be using a software package that allows them to specify a disk drive when they save a file. Find out who they are and instruct them to save their files, using a disk drive specifier other than the one complaining that it is full. Depending on your system, they might be able to save on another hard disk or on a floppy diskette.

Step Six. To help people who cannot save files in step five, make room on the "full" disk. If you can, move files from the full disk to another disk drive, first copying them to the new drive and then removing them from the full disk. Continue until you have enough available space for people to save their work.

Step Seven. If you are stuck, a last resort to save work in progress is to print the contents of the screen. Although the work will have to be re-entered, this step enables people to salvage at least one screen of information that they created.

Resolve the Problem

As soon as the urgency of potentially lost work is past, resolve the problem that started the trouble to begin with. As mentioned in Chapter Four, if you are using a UNIX-based operating system, such as the IBM PC-AT's XENIX, you know that you should keep between 15 to 20 percent of disk space free, depending on fluctuation in the size of your file systems and directories. Whatever free space your system requires, you must re-establish it now.

Step One. It is possible that the disk is not full, but that its directory is. A full directory is a different problem from a full disk. Even if the system says otherwise, a disk can have plenty of storage space available and still consider itself "full" because each disk has only so many possible directory entry slots. If the number of files stored on disk exceeds the number of allowed directory entries, the system will prohibit you from adding another file to the disk, regardless of how much file storage space might be left. When this happens, the system responds with a message that tells you the disk is full.

How can you distinguish a full disk from a full directory? You have two ways to figure it out:

The first way is to compare the amount of space that the files occupy with the total size of the disk. (Operating system utilities will help by showing available disk space.) If you find plenty of disk space, the number of allowable directory entries probably is exhausted.

The second way to check whether the problem is a full directory instead of a full disk is to refer to your system documentation. Find out the maximum number of directory entries that your system allows. Compare the allowable number of directory entries with the number of files on the disk. Do not be thrown off if the number of files is fewer than the number of directory entries. Operating systems typically have files that are called *hidden files* because they do not appear in directory listings. Hidden files take up directory entries just like other files do. Also, some software programs use extra directory entries for files that exceed specified limits. For instance, one of your programs might assign a new directory entry for each 64k of space in a given file.

When the problem is a full directory, you do not necessarily have to erase or redirect files. If your operating system allows tree-structured directories, you have the option to reorganize the directory on the "full" disk. Because the number of directory entries is at the maximum, first transfer files to subdirectories that already exist on the full disk. Such transfers will reduce the pressure on the main directory. With the pressure off, you can create new subdirectories and reorganize the files.

Step Two. If the problem is not a full directory, the disk is truly full. One obvious solution is to conduct a disk spring-cleaning session, deleting unnecessary files. If you have not done this recently, it is clearly time for it (see Section 4.2). But, if you and others have been careful to avoid storing unnecessary files on the disk, housekeeping might not solve the problem.

Step Three. Your disk might have free space that is unusable. Remember from Chapter Four how data is stored on disks in sectors and tracks. Some operating systems do not use disk space as efficiently as others. Sometimes available space is in chunks that are too small to use, so space sits empty. If that is the problem, follow the procedure in Chapter Four to rearrange files on contiguous space to eliminate wasted disk space.

Step Four. To alleviate the problem, you might have to redirect some data files to another disk or system. Because this process is disruptive for the people whose work is affected, before you take this action people have to agree to it. Depending on the number of people and the amount of work involved, you might have a huge coordination job on your hands.

Clearly, this route is not one to pick hastily. Be sure redirection is the best choice before you propose it. Obviously, this solution is impossible if your system has only one hard disk. In that case, you will have to resort to the last option.

Step Five. If all other solutions fall short of your needs, a last resort is to add another hard disk to your system, sometimes an unavoidable alternative.

Develop a Procedure to Reboot During a Work Period

At the beginning of this chapter, I described how during my first weeks managing a system I reset it whenever I encountered "inexplicable" trouble. During those early days, I inconvenienced a number of people a number of times. Of course, it was the wrong course of action. POWER, RESET and CTR-ALT-DEL are not panic buttons to push each time the system misbehaves. Rebooting is a valid course of action only when you have entirely lost control of the system.

The rebooting process usually is a significant inconvenience, particularly with a network or multi-user system because everyone's work comes to a halt until the system is re-established. Typically, the procedure takes the system down for twenty or more minutes while you reboot and perform whatever housekeeping tasks are required before you can release the system again.

Consequently, rebooting during a work period is not trivial. But, when you must do it, use the following procedure. Follow only steps four and five for your system's stand-alone personal computers.

Procedure to Reboot During a Work Period

Step One. Contact everyone using the system. Advise each person to log out, after they save currently open files if they can so that no one loses work. Do not rely on a mail utility or a write utility to carry this important message since people sometimes step away from their terminals. A verbal message is the only reliable way to get this message out.

Step Two. Ask people to stay off the system until you tell them they can use it again. (This step is particularly important if your system displays a prompt on each workstation *before* you complete your post-reboot tasks.)

Step Three. If possible, tell people how long you think that the system will be down. If you expect you will have to do some troubleshooting after you reboot, your system probably will be down longer than the typical twenty minutes.

Step Four. Remember to save the files *you* have open. Also, save *all* data files stored on RAM disk(s) before you move to step five. Frequently, files stored temporarily on a RAM disk (see Section 5.2) are lost when a system reboot is required simply because they are forgotten in the turmoil of the moment.

Step Five. If you can, backup to tape or floppy diskette all files created or modified since the last time you made backups. (In other words, do a partial backup, described in Section 7.2.)

Step Six. Follow the directions in your manuals to shut the system down in an orderly manner. Then, proceed with your system's reboot process.

WARNING

Do not reboot if a disk drive indicator light is lit or you might jeopardize data. Wait for the light to go out.

Step Seven. Perform whatever routine tasks are needed to make the system available to others. Before turning the system over to them, make sure that it is operating as it should. Test whatever it was that went so wrong that you had to reboot in the first place. If you can, recreate the problem to see if it recurs.

Step Eight. Only when you are satisfied that the system is functioning properly should you turn it over. Let people know that it is again safe to log on.

8.4 Learn to Cope with System Failure

In this section we will consider what is probably your worst on-the-job nightmare: system failure. System failure is the greatest fear of most system managers and probably the most extreme problem you might encounter.

System failure, or crash, means the system has dissolved in its own black hole. The range is broad: your system can lock up or it can go entirely dead. In every case, work that was in progress is lost. Luckily a system crash is rare. You even can avoid some of them if you take a few precautions. And, with a little planning, you can minimize the impact of the unavoidable ones. This section will help you do both.

Guard Against the Common Causes

Of the five common causes of system failure, you can take steps to lessen the possibility of a crash caused by four of them. (With the fifth, a software bug, you are probably helpless.)

1. Operator error. With new systems, operator error is the most likely cause of a crash. For example, suppose you are installing two new terminals on an IBM PC-AT with the XENIX operating system. You could crash the system if you did not know that a full minute has to elapse between issuing the **enable** command the first and second time.

Even seasoned systems are not immune to crashes caused by operator error. You can combat the problem with good training, for yourself and for everyone else. The more familiar everyone is with the system, the fewer crashes of this type that you will have.

2. Power trouble. We talked about the power threat in Chapter Seven. If the power supply goes awry, the black hole beckons. And, you know that power line trouble threatens not only work in progress, but the very electronics themselves. Even continuous low voltage alone can cause serious damage to your system.

It is easy to guard against power line trouble, but it can be expensive. If the section about power line trouble in Chapter Seven did not prompt you to take this measure, consider again adding an uninterruptible power supply (expensive). *Definitely* install surge protection (relatively inexpensive) to guard against power line fluctuations. My $75 surge protector saved my system the night a squirrel lost its life on a power line above my office.

3. Hardware malfunction. Hardware failure is a common cause of a system crash. All systems are susceptible to it. Sometimes it is unavoidable because processors do fail. But, remember the system mentioned in Chapter Seven that suffocated and crashed because of dust balls. If you keep your system well-maintained, you should never suffer that embarrassment.

4. System overload. When you put too many demands on a system, it freezes. We already have seen several examples, including a system with no free space (see Section 4.2), a system that overly commits RAM (see Section 5.4), and a system with too many intensive processes being run simultaneously (see Section 7.3). In each of these cases, it comes down to pushing a system beyond its limit. Do not ask your system to do more than it is capable of doing.

5. Software bug. Lurking in your system there might be a software bug that one day will bring the system to its knees. It might be a bug in the operating system or in applications software. Wherever it is, there is little you can do to prevent it once you own the program. You can, however, communicate your trouble to the software developer. Maybe a refund is in order (do not count on it), or maybe a "bug-free" revision of the program has been released.

Minimize the Impact

Do what you can to avoid system crashes. But, expect it to happen some day. There is no such thing as 100 percent insurance against a system crash. If you cannot entirely avoid it, can you control its impact? Absolutely.

Often, only work in progress is lost, but not always. If a disk is damaged in the course of a crash, you stand to lose a lot. You can

Table 8.6

COMMON CAUSES OF SYSTEM FAILURE AND HOW TO AVOID THEM

Cause	Solution
Operator error	Provide thorough training Establish careful procedures
Power problems	Install power line protection
Hardware malfunction	Maintain equipment
System overload	Maintain enough free space on disk Do not push RAM to its limit Coordinate system-intensive processes
Software bug	Be watchful

cut your losses dramatically just by systematically backing up data files (see Section 7.2). If you do a daily backup, even a damaged hard disk means just a day's work lost. Losing a day's work is painful, but not so devastating as losing a disk full of files.

Tips to Handle a System Crash

You particularly want to be prepared to handle a system crash, mainly because it is so extreme and happens so rarely, usually without warning. It is easy to panic in response to a crash, even with one on a stand-alone computer. The tips in this section will help you to combat the crisis and safely restore things to normal after the storm has passed.

Tip #1 is for managers of multi-user systems or local area networks. All of the other tips will be useful for *any* system that fails, i.e. stand-alone computers, multi-user systems, or LANS.

Combatting the Crisis

Tip #1: For managers of multi-user systems and LANS. In the unlikely case that you have warning that your system is about to crash, alert others on the system immediately. Otherwise, notify them as soon as you learn about the trouble. Ask them to note where they began working and where they left off since the last time they saved files in progress. Tell them to stay off the system until you contact them.

Tip #2: For managers of all systems. With a system crash, error messages are like gold. Note, document, and decipher any that the system sends. Consult your manuals to determine how you might correct the problem.

Tip #3: For managers of all systems. Reboot with the reset button, CTRL-ALT-DEL, or the power switch, depending on the type of system you have. If the system refuses to boot, the problem might be with the operating system.

It is simple to determine if that is the case. Most systems check for boot instructions in drive A before looking elsewhere. With hard disk systems, if drive A is empty, the second place checked is the hard disk itself. So, if your system has a hard disk, insert in drive A the diskette with the current version of your operating system. If the system still fails to boot or if the system has no hard disk, try booting with a backup diskette copy of the operating system in drive A. Do not use original operating system diskettes. If that step fails, insert an earlier version of the operating system, if you have one. You should have one in your system library (see Section 3.1).

An out-of-date version is better than no version at all, and if it works, you might choose to re-install the successful version of the operating system on the hard disk. That will both allow people to work again and give you time to investigate and solve the problem without the added strain of thinking about the lost productivity the firm suffers every minute the system is not functioning.

Tip #4: For managers of all systems. If the system resists booting from both the current and previous versions of the operating system, the problem probably is hardware-related. Keep in mind, however, that a hardware-related system crash does not always mean that the system must be sent away for repair. Sometimes the problem can be resolved on site, and on occasion, with surprising ease. For example, sometimes you can solve the problem by reformatting your hard disk. (Be sure it is backed up before you encounter system failure!)

Tip #5: For managers of all systems. When you suspect the system failed because of hardware trouble, one of the first things to do is examine the system's cables. Even a small tear, strategically placed, will bring a system down. One of the common cable culprits is the one that connects a hard disk.

Tip #6: For managers of all systems. When you determine that the cables are intact, bring out your vendor-provided diagnostic software. Using it might isolate the trouble and identify a solution. If the system refuses to respond to diagnostics, you probably should call your vendor. Some system managers will prefer to follow the advice under Tip #7 before calling the vendor.

Tip #7: For managers of all systems. When you are at the end of the line in trying to diagnose the cause of a failed system, you have two other alternatives to try, but only if you are adventurous and also trained to remove circuit boards and to install disk drives. Before you follow this tip, be absolutely sure that you are not jeopardizing your warranty agreement or service contract:

First, *turn off the electricity*. Then, open the enclosure to remove and check each controller board for gummy pollution at the contact points. If you find goo, use a cotton swab and alcohol to remove it.

Second, if all boot attempts from a floppy diskette fail and your system has more than one diskette drive, physically replace drive A with another of your diskette drives. Your system manuals should lead you through this process step by step. With a new drive installed as drive A, power on and try booting once again.

Tip #8: For managers of all systems. When the system appears to be running again, do not assume that everything is all right. First, check the integrity of the system's files (see Section 7.2). Restore files that you find damaged as a result of the crash. Restore system files first, application software programs next, and data files last. If you have a substantial number of files to restore or if the entire hard disk must be restored, first restore only what you need to conduct the test described in Tip #9. Lengthy restoration would be fruitless if the system is about to crash again.

Tip #9: For managers of all systems. Run various tests to determine if the system is out of trouble. If you can, recreate the situation that preceded the system crash. Software-related problems can be tracked-down that way. A program that usually works just fine might lock up the system only under circumstances like those that preceded the crash.

Conduct the following test. Invoke the software programs that staff members were using. If you can, re-enter data up to the second-to-last point prior to the crash. Before you continue, save the work so that it will not be lost again. If the system locks at the same point as before, do not despair. You have learned two valuable lessons: first, the trouble is not yet solved, and second, the software program in use is a likely suspect.

Tip #10: For managers of all systems. When you believe the trouble is behind you, erase trashed files and temporary files resulting from the system crash. Only when you are sure the system is back on its feet, should you notify people affected that they can use the system again.

Tip #11: For managers of all systems. Reflect on what has happened. Document the problem and how you resolved it. If necessary, update system library documents such as the system devices map (see Section 2.2) and software installation documentation (see Section 3.2). Those documents would need updating, for example, if you replace a piece of equipment or make an adjustment to how a particular piece of software is installed. Do what you can to avoid a recurrence of the problem. Finally, congratulate yourself for getting through this crisis successfully.

Develop a Procedure to Move the System

A system crash sometimes precipitates a trip to the vendor. Regardless of the reason you might have to move your system, it always is a significant event. Even when you move yours down the hall, it is traumatic for you, for your information and for the system. It is even more jarring when it has to go across town or across the state!

When you are moving a system, there is a lot to protect: programs, data, and the equipment itself. (Remember that equipment includes what is outside of view: disk drives, circuit boards, and so on.) The following procedure will help you protect it all during every phase of the moving process and after the system is back home again.

Procedure to Move the System

1. Preparation

Step One. Back up data and program files on each hard disk to tape or diskettes. (Even a move down the hall can destroy data on a disk.)

Step Two. If the hard disk does not have to travel, remove it. There is no need to expose it to potential damage in transit or, worse, from being erased or overwritten in the process of system repair. Keep it safely in the office.

Step Three. If the hard disk must travel, immobilize the heads to protect the disk. Your system probably has software that allows you to "park" hard disk drive heads. If you have an IBM PC-AT, this software is on your diagnostics diskette. For other systems, it might be an isolated file on the operating system's diskette or a program provided with the hard disk when it was purchased. Check your documentation.

Step Four. To protect the floppy disk drives, put a cardboard insert or a blank floppy diskette inside of each drive. Tape the drive doors shut.

2. Packing

Step Five. Power off each element in the system. Disconnect all exterior cables. Coil and fasten them. If possible, tape each one to its device.

Step Six. Inventory *every* piece of the system that is travelling. (I failed to do this inventory once and one of my cables was left behind at the vendor's. It is difficult to say which was more frazzling: facing a 40 mile round trip in the rain a second time or convincing the vendor's people that my cable was somewhere in their domain.)

Step Seven. Hopefully, you still have the original packing material and boxes for each item in your system. If so, use it. If not, pack each device separately and in such a way as to immobilize it.

Step Eight. If you use carriers, such as Federal Express, UPS, or the U.S. Postal Service, consider using those special labels that change color when handling exceeds a specified "G" force. This label will alert the people handling your packages that the contents are sensitive.

3. Back Home Again

Step Nine. As soon as the system is back home, first make sure you have received back *everything* you sent. Check your inventory. If something is missing, call the vendor immediately.

Step Ten. Systematically set up the system according to the vendor's instructions. Your system library will help you set the system up as it was before it left. Reseat all add-on boards, including those not touched by service personnel. If the process of travelling unseated them, the system might not run.

Step Eleven. Test everything. Run diagnostics. Run programs. Be sure the system is functioning properly, even if the vendor assures you it was okay when it left the repair shop. Something might have been damaged in transit to your office.

8.5 Troubleshooter's Communication Tips

The first four sections in this chapter emphasize key troubleshooting procedures and techniques. There is another aspect to troubleshooting which we have mentioned in passing, one that spans practically every troubleshooting situation. This section is devoted entirely to the subject of troubleshooting and communication.

Communication is fundamental to successful troubleshooting. System managers communicate with other staff members, with vendors, and, so to speak, with the system itself via the messages it sometimes sends. You are at the center of this constellation. These communications take on a special dimension when a system is in trouble. The tips in this section will help you to deal with all three, in reverse order: the system, the vendor, and other staff members.

Manage Those Cryptic Messages

You and others probably are far too familiar with messages that suddenly appear on the screen. They are often cryptic and they always interrupt you when you are trying to get something accomplished. At best, these messages generally provide relatively bland information. You probably have seen the "WAIT" message so many programs send to tell you to sit tight until the computer handles a task out of view, such as performing a calculation on a spreadsheet or moving the distance of ten pages in a text document.

However, these messages rarely bring *good* news. Do you recall how you felt the first time you saw a DISK FULL message?

No matter how annoyed we are to see these messages, we must remember why they appear: they are our best warning system. They tell us things we need to know about a process we are running or about the condition of the system. They notify us when we are in trouble and sometimes warn us of snarls ahead. We may not like to see them, but we should appreciate them.

Ideally, a message should be in plain language, such as DISK FULL. But, too often, computers communicate in gobbledegook that must be deciphered. Even if you feel completely confident to handle common messages, this section will help you to respond more effectively to them. You also will learn to be more in control of situations when you see a message you do not recognize. We will see where messages originate and what categories they come in before we examine tips for message management.

Most messages you get probably come from the operating system and your applications programs. If you use a programming language like BASIC, you will get messages from it, too. If you are able to recognize the difference, you will spare yourself the futility of looking in the operating system manual for a message sent by a program. Cutting research time like that can be a big help in a crisis.

General Categories of Serious Messages

Our systems talk to us all the time. They tell us that they are calculating, they ask us to wait, and they let us know when they are in the process of saving a file. In other words, they are telling us that they are doing exactly what we asked of them. We are not concerned with these friendly messages. Here, we are looking only at messages designed to tell us that something is wrong. Serious messages come in three categories:

1. Internal error messages. Internal error messages alert you when something is seriously wrong with the program itself that you are running. (WordStar's message INTERNAL ERROR: ADDRESS IN THE HOLE is an example of a particularly cryptic one.) Whatever the problem is, it does not always cripple the system. Often, the message appears, you exit the program, get back in, and move along with your work—until the message unexpectedly reappears. But, rarely does the problem go away.

Invariably, internal error messages mean big trouble. When one appears, beware of imminent or unpredictable program failure. If you manage a local area network or multi-user system, warn everyone using the program to save open files immediately. People can continue using the program at their own risk, but doing so endangers their unsaved work.

Internal error messages usually necessitate a call to your dealer. Corrective measures typically range from reinstallation of the program to downright replacement of the original program diskettes. Sometimes, in the case of an unresolved bug buried deep in the program, you will have to find a way to work around it until the vendor releases a version free of that bug.

2. Device-related messages. The computer sends device messages when it is reading from or sending information to a device. (Devices include printers, disk drives, and even RAM disks.) In most, but not all cases, these messages warn you about much less threatening conditions than do the internal error messages.

There are three common reasons that a system sends device-related messages:

First, there can be a serious problem with the device itself. DISK FULL is an example. Another example is CAN'T COPY PROGRAM FILE, which appears if you are trying to copy a program from a damaged diskette. Typically, you have to take immediate action when you see this type of message.

Second, the system can be responding to an unacceptable command. With inexperienced people, this usually is a matter of training. With experienced people, most unacceptable commands are typographical errors. For example, if you accidentally enter "dur" instead of "dir" to run a directory from the DOS operating system prompt, you will see the message BAD COMMAND OR FILE NAME.

Third, the system can be telling you that it is set up improperly. DEVICE NOT READY is an example. Most set up problems happen because someone forgot to do something. Check the device that you are asking the system to address. Make sure that the printer is on. Plug in the plotter. Insert a diskette in the floppy disk drive.

3. Programming messages. If you write your own programs, you might get programming messages. One example is the FILE NOT FOUND message that BASIC will send if you reference a file that does not exist on the specified disk. These messages are last in the list of serious messages because they are the least likely to appear in most business environments.

One exception is when you write programs to customize the system. Expect to see these messages if you write script files with UNIX or XENIX or batch files with DOS.

Tips for Managing Messages

I have yet to meet someone completely in control of every possible message-related situation, but you can put yourself more in charge of *your* system's messages by following these recommendations:

Tip #1. Before you run into trouble, become familiar with the possible messages you might receive from your operating system(s) and your applications programs. Review your manuals carefully to give yourself a sense of what to expect. You will learn the scope of possible trouble, the kinds of messages, and the steps to take to solve a problem. If a few catch your eye, test yourself. See how well you can unravel them.

Accept the fact that you may not be able to find information about a particular message in your manual. Too often, messages are discussed in places where you are unlikely to find them. Also, some messages might not be discussed at all anywhere. Some vendors are trying to improve their documentation, and documentation today is much better than it was a year or two ago, but that effort is little consolation when you are dealing with an emergency and cannot find the information that you need.

Tip #2. Write down messages that you do not fully grasp or that you do not recognize. Contact the vendor in a calm moment to get an explanation. With some vendors, you have to be persistent because they are hard to reach after you buy their product. I once was frantic to track down an elusive message, but each time I telephoned, all I got was a recording. So much for support. I had to *write a letter* to get the problem resolved. When you obtain answers, write down what these messages mean and what to do about them.

Tip #3. No matter how frantic and urgent the situation, track down every error message that appears, including those that appear harmless. Do not let one go by, or it might return as a problem later.

Tip #4. Recognizing a message when it appears is a skill that each staff member should acquire. Coach everyone to learn it. Inexperienced people often do not know a message when they see one. Because they are more likely than an experienced person to cause operator-generated trouble with the system, teach this skill to new staff members early.

Tip #5. Ask people to tell you when they see messages warning of danger or messages they do not understand. Train people to recognize signs of impending system failure so that they can alert you and others the moment these signs appear.

At one firm a young man working after hours saw SEEK ERROR on the screen. A SEEK ERROR is a precursor of a hard disk crash. Unfortunately, the next day he forgot to notify the system manager. Shortly afterwards, the hard disk failed. Data was lost that could have been saved.

Message training is particularly important when you have a multi-user system or a local area network. With both types of systems others will suffer if people do not know how to handle messages.

Tip #6. Give people a list of common or important messages that explains the meaning of each one and the action each requires. Emphasize how important it is for them to contact you immediately whenever a threatening message appears. If possible, post copies where people will see them because it is common for people to file informational material like this out of sight (and out of mind).

Troubleshooting and Vendor Relations

The effort you exert to understand messages your system sends will help you immensely, not only when you are troubleshooting by yourself, but also when you have to contact your vendor. In this section we will look at the importance of vendor relations.

Your work will be infinitely smoother if you stay on good terms with each of your vendors. Sometimes that is difficult, such as when one fails to return your calls, or when one is impatient with you. However, never forget that after the sale, you probably need the vendor more than the vendor needs you. Because the vendor's control over your system translates into a measure of control over your company, the situation calls for diplomacy while you assert your rights.

After the system is installed successfully, most of your subsequent contact with the vendor will be in the context of trouble, and thus every call for help sets up a potentially explosive situation. You are likely to feel frantic in the face of an untimely crisis. Conversely, from the vendor's end, imagine how tedious and repetitious telephone troubleshooting probably is for their service personnel.

Seven Rules for Successful Vendor Relations

You can calm people and foster good feeling by following these seven rules:

Rule #1. Be as knowledgeable as possible. Continually educate yourself about the system. Technical support personnel frequently complain that many people could solve their own problems if they would simply check a page or two in a manual.

If your vendor publishes a newsletter, read it to stay abreast of updates.

Rule #2. If you can, convey to the vendor that you are knowledgeable about the system and its documentation. This knowledge goes far to establish your credibility with service personnel and technical support.

Rule #3. Diagnose and handle problems yourself whenever possible. Do not telephone the vendor as soon as you run into difficulties. Be known as one who calls only when absolutely necessary, after you have exhausted your own means.

Rule #4. Establish yourself as the one and only person in your firm who contacts the vendor. (Only when you are indisposed should your backup have to do it.) Other people should go through you instead of directly to the vendor. This rule is essential for two reasons:

First, if everyone feels free to telephone the vendor and does, you will soon have an unhappy vendor. Most vendors prefer to work with a single individual. Remember, it harms relations when the vendor has to "educate" more than one person at your end.

Second, multiple contacts, especially when the system crashes, means multiple calls and unnecessary chaos. Imagine the confusion, duplicated effort, and flared tempers when two people from your end are trying to resolve the same crisis with two people at the vendor's end.

Rule #5. Although you must limit the number of people at your end who can call the vendor, you need as many key contacts as you can make at the vendor's end. This means technical support staff, salespeople, development staff, and management.

Trade shows and perhaps conferences for your industry can provide easy access to the vendor's people at all levels of the organization. Take advantage of their presence when you attend these shows.

Rule #6. Do your best to stay dispassionate when blood pressures rise. If it is your own, take a deep breath before you utter a sentence. If not your own, take two deep breaths and offer an understanding word or two.

Rule #7. Be sure the vendor lives up to agreements and that you are satisfied with how problems are resolved. Always express appreciation for a job well done. This courtesy helps immensely the next time you need help.

Prepare Before You Place a Service Call

Sometimes you have no choice but to place a service call. Be prepared before you do it.

1. Before trouble. Know your legal rights and responsibilities. In advance of trouble know the terms of your purchase agreements and warranties. Know what is expected of you and what is expected of the vendor.

For example, is on-site service supposed to be provided within four working hours? What services will the vendor conduct on your premises? Does the vendor provide loaner equipment in the event part of your system must be taken away for repairs?

2. In trouble. When you make a call, be ready to provide pertinent information about the problem at hand. Get to the point immediately. The vendor probably will want you to describe the symptoms you observed, tests you conducted, and results you found. Relay *exactly* any error messages.

Provide as much information as possible to help the person on the other end to help you. If you have at hand system library documents such as your system devices map, system boards maps, software inventory, and RAM worksheets, you will be able to provide specific details about your system, such as the boards and their slot numbers, serial numbers for software and equipment, the amount of memory on the computer, and the constellation of programs being run.

The better you inform the vendor, the more likely it is the problem will be resolved with dispatch. If an on-site service call is required, it is also more likely you will receive a person who understands the problem and has needed tools and parts on hand.

The Importance of Communicating with Staff Members

When you are in the middle of a troubleshooting situation, you have no choice but to pay attention to error messages and sometimes to deal with your vendor. In these moments, it is easy to forget about the people most important and most interested in what is happening: the people who use the system.

Whether you have good news, bad news, or no news at all, follow rule #6 for the successful troubleshooter and keep people informed. People need to know if electronic mail is not working, if a printer is down, and if you fear a hard disk crash is imminent. They also need to know if you have nothing new to tell them about a problem that has been pending for, say, an hour.

As long as people are kept informed, they can accept just about anything and can work with the confidence that you will notify them at the first sign of trouble and keep them posted about your progress.

Getting the Word Out

When there is trouble with the system, get the information out quickly. You have several ways to communicate.

Face to face is the most reliable, but is not always possible. For example, you might have people at workstations located downstairs or across the street. Typical computer systems allow three means of sending one message simultaneously to everyone.

1. Message of the day. You probably are able to send a "message of the day." Typically, this message is displayed only when a person logs on to the system. It is best suited to sending non-critical notices and it is quite useless for notifying people about urgent matters.

2. Electronic mail. Electronic mail is one of the enormous benefits computers offer. Take advantage of it, but recognize that it is not the most reliable means to make timely contact.

You should know how your system informs you that you have mail. XENIX uses the status line to alert you that you have mail waiting whenever you are in the visual shell, the system's interface between you and the operating system. Other systems inform you about new mail only when prompted. For instance, you will know about it only when you log on or ask if you have any. With the prompt method, it is possible for you to send mail at 8.01 a.m. to someone who will not know that it is there until the next morning at an 8:00 a.m. logon.

3. Instant bulletins. Maybe your system allows you to send immediate bulletins to people on screen. (XENIX uses the **wall** command.) This capability is handy. But, people are not always attending to their terminals or workstations even when they are logged on. An absent staff member is unable to save a file in progress, so if you are about to reboot, the file will be lost. Therefore, do not rely on this method when you have an imminent emergency system reboot. Use method #4 instead.

4. Telephone. The first three methods have shortcomings. When the system is down, you cannot communicate at all using any of them. You also can never be sure when people receive an electronic message unless they acknowledge it. Too often a system manager mistakenly believes people have been warned of an unavoidable mid-day reboot.

When you must be sure the others get your message and they are out of earshot, be safe: use the telephone. If the recipients of your call are out, find someone who can handle the situation for them. In emergency situations, voice-to-voice communication is the only reliable way to be sure another person gets your message.

8.6 Establish Your Troubleshooter's Survival Kit

Thus far in this chapter, we have seen how you might respond to specific troubleshooting situations. Most system troubles occur with little or no warning, so that means that you need immediate access to whatever tool might help you to get the system running properly. Take a minute to consider three premises implied in that statement.

"Immediate access" means that the needed item is part of your troubleshooting kit. You do not have to rely on borrowing the item. When you have to switch cables, counting on using someone else's screwdriver translates into avoidable, unacceptable, and extended delay.

"Whatever tool" means that you will use any possible tool, even cotton swabs or a dentist's mirror, if it will help you get the system functioning again.

"Get the system running properly" means *no* temporary solutions unless you have absolutely no other choice *and* you must get the system running *now*. For example, your modem fails in the process of transmitting information immediately required at its destination. You know that the spare modem has been unreliable since it was dropped last week, but for the moment you have no choice except to hook up the modem and hope you will be able to transmit successfully. (In such a case, if you are prudent, you will make arrangements right away to have both modems repaired.)

Whenever you are forced to resort to a temporary solution like this, as soon as the critical moment has passed, get moving to find a permanent remedy. Remove temporary solutions the moment you can or the source of the problem will plague you sooner or later.

With these three definitions in mind, use this section to start your troubleshooter's survival kit. You will find a fairly comprehensive list of necessities, some of which you will use for troubleshooting and for problem avoidance. Anything principally used to avoid trouble is marked with a star.

Fill Your Troubleshooter's Tool Chest

Your troubleshooter's tool chest should include anything you think might be helpful. It includes hand-held tools, security blankets, diagnostics, and miscellaneous essentials.

Your most effective troubleshooting tool is yourself. You know the system. Your mind can analyze and resolve problems. Your intelligence, knowledge, and your ability to remain calm will serve you each time you run into a problem or a mystery to solve.

Hand-Held Tools

Be sure your inventory of hand tools is complete.

Telephone	Telephone access is a must. With a multi-user system you cannot do without it at the system console. Without one, troubleshooting on site is an in-

credible hassle and in fact impossible when it comes to troubleshooting with the vendor.

A telephone should be near each workstation. This way, you often can help another staff member without having to travel from your office.

★Screwdrivers   You can get inside of just about any device with a set of screwdrivers. Removing a disk drive for repair is virtually impossible if you do not have the proper one. Have a variety of sizes, standard, Phillips, and torx.

Dentist's mirror   Add a dentist's mirror to your tool chest. (These are expensive, so ask your dentist to give you an old one.) This mirror will allow you to see what otherwise would be outside of your view, such as a piece of paper trapped in the underside of a printer tractor.

Miniature flashlight   A miniature flashlight will enable you to peer into those small, dark places you occasionally must see into so that you can take care of trouble. I have used one mainly to locate snips of trapped paper that "freeze" printers.

Tweezers   Tweezers come in handy when you want to extract a small particle from an inaccessible location. In tandem with the miniature flashlight, tweezers help you remove scraps of paper from the innards of your printers.

Battery-operated mini-vacuum cleaner   With a mini-vacuum cleaner you can remove dust particles and small items that are harmful to the system from hard-to-reach areas. I know of at least two cases where a frozen system was brought back to life after vacuuming away dust balls accumulated in the enclosure housing the hard disk.

*Paint brush

Use a paint brush to sweep dust from keyboard crevices and those spots inside system enclosures that you cannot clean with a mini-vacuum cleaner

Compressed air

Also known as "dust particle remover," compressed air will dislodge debris that will not budge unless you blow it away.

*Cotton or foam swabs

Use swabs to clean and lubricate parts of the system. Follow instructions in your documentation.

*Toothpicks

Toothpicks come in handy when you want to lubricate out-of-the-way places. Follow the instructions in your documentation.

*Device lubricant

Keep tubes of the lubricants that the manufacturers of your equipment recommend.

*Disk drive head cleaning kit

These kits clean floppy disk drive heads. There is much debate over whether they do more harm than good. Many of them use an abrasive that wears down drive heads.

Use these kits sparingly. I believe in waiting until you have a problem with the drive, for instance a read/write error. Then, clean the heads to see if that solves the problem.

Hand Tools for the Advanced Troubleshooter

If you are adventurous and if you want to dig deeper inside of the machine, you might need the tools listed below. First be sure that using them will not involve performing tasks that will violate your warranties or service agreements.

Chip extractor

With this tool, you can extract removable integrated circuit chips from system boards. Use it when you have to replace a faulty RAM

	chip. (Always turn the power off first!)
Alcohol	Over time, cigarette smoke and other air pollutants find their way to the inner recesses of your system. If they badly gum up the gold contact points on the removable circuit boards, they interfere with how the system operates. Alcohol applied with cotton swabs is excellent for cleaning gook from these contact points.
Cable gender changers & cable assembly kit	Most likely, you do not need these because you will not want to bother. But, in an emergency, some system managers are willing to make custom cables. If you are one of these people, you can do the job with cable gender changers and assembly kits. Like electrical plugs and their outlets, cables have male and female genders. With the gender changer or assembly kit, you can change the gender of an existing cable or assemble a cable from scratch.

Spares

Spares for the system are like spare tires or spare fan belts for your car. Keep a supply of spares that you might need at a moment's notice.

*Formatted diskettes	Keep a supply of formatted diskettes on hand. Think of how handy they will be if you find yourself with an insufficient number while in the middle of a backup procedure.
Print wheel or head	No matter how many characters your print wheel or head should print before it fails, eventually you will have

to replace it. Without it, the printer will not print. Having a spare can save more than just time.

Cable

Spare cables are useful when you discover or suspect a faulty cable. Spare cables are a must if you manage a local area network. Within minutes, a device can be serving you again if you keep spare cables on hand. One spare cable for each ten devices is good insurance.

Fuses

Sometimes the very part you need to get a device working again is a $.25 fuse. Keep spare fuses for your printers, monitors, terminals, and for every other piece of equipment that uses them. (See VOM under Diagnostics below.)

Spares Service Personnel Might Not Bring

Service personnel providing on-site repairs cannot or do not always carry everything they may need. That sometimes delays getting the system back on its feet. Keep the following three items on hand as insurance.

Disk drive motor belt

Keep on hand spare disk drive motor belts in case of emergency.

RAM chips

Some day you may have a faulty RAM chip. These chips have become so cheap that it makes sense to keep spares.

Floppy disk drive

Floppy disk drives also are inexpensive enough for you to keep at least one extra one on hand.

Diagnostics

You will find diagnostics useful to the extent that you want to be involved in troubleshooting. Several aids are available.

Advanced
diagnostics

Advanced diagnostic software is available for some systems. You will

Disk drive analyzer

not usually receive them as a matter of course. Ask your vendor about them.

You can buy software that will analyze the status of a disk drive. Generally, these programs test alignment, speed, clamping, and read/write ability. Unless you intend to do advanced troubleshooting, you do not need this software.

You certainly do not need it to isolate a problem disk drive. Test how a suspect drive runs with various floppy diskettes. Once you establish that the problem is with the drive itself, more likely than not it needs a trip to the repair shop.

See if it is more cost effective to keep a spare drive on hand than to repair defective drives.

Port extender

A port extender is a box that allows more than one device to share a port. Its primary purpose is to increase system efficiency by expanding the number of devices that can use a port, but the port extender is extremely useful for diagnosing problems.

Consider the ease with which you can run the tests to isolate whether a problem is with a device, its cable, or its port (see Section 8.2).

Power line monitor

This device warns you of problems with a power line by keeping track of voltage level, frequency, and power failures. Depending on your system, this can be a cost effective way to help you manage it. Check with your vendor and double check with an experienced electrician.

Cable tester

You have seen that cables are a frequent source of trouble. A cable tester

	helps to identify problem cables and cable connections. Managers of local area networks will find this product particularly useful.
Volt ohm meter (VOM)	Blown fuses do not always appear to be blown. If you have a VOM, you can check suspect fuses to see if they are indeed blown.

Contacts

A troubleshooter's tool chest is not complete without a list of contacts.

Vendors	Keep handy the names and telephone numbers of service personnel for each device and software package on the system.
Managers of systems like yours	Vendors are extremely useful, but sometimes your peers are more so. Get the names of people who manage systems like yours. Users' groups or personal referral are good ways to find them. You will share special secrets and tips that only system managers discover.

8.7 Vendor Services

To whatever extent you choose to troubleshoot, there will be times when you have to call upon a professional technician to service the system's equipment or software. That brings us to the question of service and preventive maintenance agreements. After the warranty period, these agreements are for your system what health insurance policies are for people. What are the chances you will need vendor service? Computer repair companies might tell you that the average PC with a printer has 2.1 breakdowns per year which require vendor service and that the first breakdown might be a printer problem, the second a failed hard disk. Such information is useful for discussion, but may not necessarily apply to your experience. Whatever figures you are given, your microcomputer system may encounter no breakdowns in a single year because there is a high variance in breakdown rates. For example, two law firms housed in the same building purchased their microcomputer systems from the same vendor within two months of one another. The first firm has been trouble-free for four years. The second firm has been unlucky, with multiple breakdowns that began during the second year the system was in place.

Do You Need Contracts?

Although you may have encountered no difficulty as yet, there will come a time when you will need vendor service. So the question is whether you want a service agreement or whether you prefer to seek service when it is needed and pay on a time and materials basis. As with all other computer-related questions, the answer depends on your particular situation.

Here are elements to consider. The number of microcomputers on site is relevant. Generally, if you have only one or two machines you risk bringing your business to a halt if even one PC goes down. But, if you have, say, twenty-five PC's, you have many to call on in the event of trouble with one, even with three.

How you use your micros is equally relevant. An import business that has only one PC to take sales orders could lose thousands of dollars a day if the PC fails. Compare that loss with the situation of a writer who uses one PC to collect information for a book. System downtime for the writer is an inconvenience instead of the cause of serious financial loss. The same reasoning holds true for firms with fifty or one hundred PC's.

Another element to consider is your firm's tolerance for risk. Tolerance is sometimes quite unrelated to the firm's objective dependence on the computer. For some people, the cost of a service agreement pales when compared with sleepless nights.

Finally, ask whether the funds spent on service agreements might be better spent elsewhere in the firm.

Find The Best Service for Your Firm

You should be able to contract for quality on-site service for around 10 to 12 percent of the list price of a complete system. (Expect volume discounts. They can range from 20 to 35 percent if you cover as many as fifty machines.) The cost of service provided on a time and materials basis varies widely. Whether or not you opt for a

---

Table 8.7

ANSWER THESE QUESTIONS TO SEE IF YOU NEED SERVICE CONTRACTS

---

1. How many computers do you manage?
2. For what purposes does your firm use its computers?
3. What is the firm's risk tolerance?
4. How does the vendor's service differ between its contract and its time and materials clients?
5. Might the cost of a contract be better spent elsewhere in the business?

---

contract, these considerations will help you find the most favorable arrangement:

1. Do you want on-site, carry-in or pick up and deliver service? If you can afford it, on-site coverage provides the least disruption and the most security. For situations that require the system to be taken away for repair, see that your agreement provides for pick up and delivery. For most businesses, it is not worth it to disconnect a suspect PC, load it into a vehicle, drive it across town, pick it up when it is repaired, bring it back to your firm, and reconnect everything.

2. Can the company service all of your system's possible needs? What is the range of products you want covered? Some service providers are restricted in the products they are competent to repair. Pick one capable of repairing every product you decide to cover.

3. How dependable is the company? Ask them how long they have been in business. Get references and check as best you can the provider's record. Dependability is sometimes unrelated to the company's stature in the industry. At this writing, a governmental agency is considering bringing a lawsuit against a computer manufacturer that has provided inferior service ever since the company made an unsuccessful bid for more of the agency's business.

4. Ask the company's representative to recommend the service option most likely to serve your firm's needs. Honest companies do their best to advise you even when it means you will buy a less expensive policy than you might without their advice.

5. It is unwise to contract with the first firm you contact. Compare options available from several firms. Cost and quality of service vary. For each vendor, ask these questions:
   What is their response time?
   Do they provide loaners?
   What is the average turnaround time for repairs?
   What preventive maintenance do they provide?
   Is telephone consultation included?
   Is travel time charged?
   Do they provide contract clients with different service or turnaround time than clients they serve on a time and materials basis?

6. If you negotiate a contract, get it in writing.

Conclusion

The recommendations in this chapter will help you to act quickly and responsibly to the common and not-so-common troubles that you and your system will encounter. You can be sure that you can rely upon the skills and strategies you have gained even if you find yourself in a situation that we have not specifically covered. Your troubleshooter's training should help you to avert repercussions from trouble and to poke all of your system-related problems quickly into the past. Good luck!

A Glossary
for Microcomputer Managers

Access permission: Defines what a person can do with a file or a directory. For example, read permission permits a person to look at the contents of a file or a directory and write permission permits a person to change the contents of a file or directory.

Adapter, adapter board, adapter card: See **circuit board**

Annual review: A system manager's procedural safety net, for periodic verification that ongoing tasks are being performed. The review is not necessarily conducted annually.

Application program: Software that allows a person to perform specific tasks. Examples include word processing programs, spreadsheet programs, and database management programs.

Archives: The store of historical information you wish to retain, but not on a hard disk. Archival files typically are stored on floppy diskettes or tape in a system library.

Automatic processing file: A file that lists a series of **operating system** commands to perform a sequence of operations, without requiring a person to attend the process. These files are called **batch files** under **DOS operating systems** and **script files** under **UNIX operating systems**.

Back up, backup: (verb) To make a duplicate copy of information stored electronically on a hard disk or floppy diskette. (noun) A duplicate copy of data or programs. It is your best insurance against system or hard disk failure.

Note: Boldfaced words in the definitions are defined elsewhere in the glossary.

Backup, Full: A complete backup of everything residing on the disk or diskette being backed up.

Backup, Partial: A backup of files altered since the last **full backup** made for the disk or diskette being backed up.

Bad sector: An unusable area on a disk.

Batch file: See **automatic processing files**.

Baud rate: The speed with which data is transmitted; expressed in **bits** per second.

Bit: The basic unit of information that a computer uses, either 0 or 1. See **byte**.

Board: See **circuit board**.

Boot: To start the system.

Buffer: Memory that the computer uses to temporarily store data on its way from one part of the system to another. Buffers are present throughout the system. For example, the buffer in a printer holds information on its way to be printed and a keyboard buffer stores keystrokes.

Bug: A problem in a software program.

Byte: Usually eight **bits**. Used to measure computer storage.

Card: See **circuit board**.

Central processing unit: The part of the computer that performs program instructions. Also called **CPU**.

Chip: A wafer that contains integrated circuits.

Circuit board: A thin piece of plastic or fiberglass containing the basis for electrical pathways that allow the various components of a computer to function. Also called **adapter card**, **adapter board**, **adapter**, **card**, and **board**.

Code: The series of instructions that make up a computer program.

Command: Instructions that a person issues to a computer.

Compatibility: Peaceful co-existence. We speak of **software** and **hardware** being compatible with other software or hardware. And, with computers, compatibility means 100 percent peace. Anything less can translate into incompatibility and trouble.

Concurrent Processing: The concurrent handling of more than one task by a single **CPU**.

Configure: The process of setting up **software** or **hardware** to meet your particular needs.

Controller card: The **circuit board** that allows a particular **device** or devices to communicate with the computer. For example, a disk controller card allows a disk drive to function with a computer system.

Conventional memory: Random access memory that **DOS** can recognize and use. 640K is the limit for DOS versions up to DOS 3.2.

Copy protection: A method by which **software** developers try to prevent the unauthorized copying of their products.

CPU: See **central processing unit**.

Crash: A system failure. When either **software** or **hardware** fails.

Critical node: A PC in a **local area network** that can bring down the network if the PC malfunctions.

CRT: The cathode-ray tube in a video display. Also refers to the display itself.

Cylinder: A logical way of dividing hard disk space. A cylinder is equal to a single **track** on more than one surface of a disk.

Data: Information. This includes information that makes up a **software** program and information you create using **software** programs.

Data integrity: A condition in which a person can trust that the data is not corrupted by the inner workings of the computer system or by human hands. Can be said of files.

Debug: Identifying, locating, and correcting problems with **software**.

Debugging program or tools: Software designed to help with the debugging process. See **debug**.

Dedicated: Part of the system, usually a piece of equipment, reserved for one and only one purpose. For example, a cable and its printer can be dedicated to one personal computer. Or a hard disk on a **local area network** can be dedicated to provide files to PC's on the network.

Default: A definition or value that comes into play in lieu of another definition or value being specified. For example, a word processor might have a default right margin of column 65 which will be operable unless someone changes the default value.

Default, operative: The **default** value that a person specifies when **installing** a **software** program.

Default, original: The original **default** set by the product manufacturer.

Device: A piece of equipment on a computer system.

Diagnostics: A piece of equipment or a program that allows a person to test whether the various parts of the system are functioning properly.

Documentation: Written descriptions of how a system is **configured** and instructions for its use.

DOS, MS-DOS, PC-DOS: An **operating system** used on personal computers.

Downtime: A term to describe the periods when a system is unavailable because it is not functioning.

Electronic circuit board: See **circuit board**.

Enclosure: A cabinet that houses computer system **circuit boards**.

Encryption: The process of making programs or data unreadable by scrambling the contents of their files. Used for security purposes.

Equipment maintenance schedule: A schedule of tasks you must perform regularly to take care of the system's equipment.

Expanded memory: Random access memory for a personal computer that allows it to use more than the 640K of **conventional memory**.

File integrity: See **data integrity**.

File server: See **network server**.

Free space: Unoccupied space on a hard disk that is available for your file system.

Hard copy: A paper copy of information stored electronically.

Hard disk partitions map: Documentation that represents how a hard disk is allocated to **operating systems** or file systems.

Hardware: Equipment that makes up a computer system.

In-house users' group: A collection of individuals who regularly meet to share information and to assess and plan the development of a computer system.

Incompatibility: See **compatibility**.

Install: The steps involved in setting up **software** to work with the specific **hardware** on a system and to work according to the preferences of the people using the software.

K byte, Kilobyte: 1024 bytes. Used as a unit of measure for computer storage. See **byte**.

LAN: See **Local area network**.

Library inventory: An inventory of the **system library** holdings.

Load: To copy a **software** program or a data file from disk storage to **random access memory**.

Local area network: A communication system that links computers and their **devices** for resource sharing, file sharing and information exchange. Also called a **LAN**.

M byte, Megabyte: A unit of measure for computer storage that equals 1024 **kilobytes** or slightly over one million **bytes**.

Memory: The part of a computer system that stores information.

Memory board: A **circuit board** containing **random access memory** chips. Also called a memory expansion board.

Memory requirement: A necessarily imprecise figure that **software** developers must use to specify the minimum amount of **RAM** a system needs in order to run a particular program.

Memory resident program: A program kept in **random access memory** after it terminates. Unless you issue a command to remove it (not possible with all programs), it remains there from the moment it is invoked to the moment the system is powered down or **rebooted**.

Message, computer: Messages that the computer displays on the monitor's screen. Sometimes these report on a task that the computer is performing and sometimes they report on problems or error conditions.

Minimum memory requirement: See **memory requirement**.

Modem: A **device** that allows a computer to receive and send information over a telephone line.

Motherboard: The main **circuit board** of a computer. Other **circuit boards** can be inserted into **slots** on the motherboard to allow various parts of the system to function or to expand the system's capabilities.

Mount: To make a UNIX or XENIX **operating system** aware of a file system. Its opposite is umount, to dismount the file system.

Multi-user system: A system in which multiple users share a single central processor (**CPU**).

Network server: In a **local area network**, a computer that shares devices and data with other computers on the network. A computer that shares data files is called a file **server**. A network may have more than one **server**.

Office of Record: Within an organization, the department or unit of people with official responsibility for a document or documents.

Off-line: Not connected to the system.

On-line: Connected to the system.

Operating system: The **software** program that controls the operation of the computer, allowing all of the **devices** to function as a system.

Page: A single screen's worth of data held in part of the video display **buffer**.

Partition: (verb) To isolate portions of a hard disk for specific purposes, such as for an **operating system** and its files. (noun) An isolated portion of a hard disk. A hard disk would be partitioned so that it can be used to run more than one operating system.

Password: A security measure to control system access. Used to screen unauthorized people from using the system and to define the privileges of authorized people.

Patch: To alter original **software** instructions.

Peripheral: A **device** connected to a computer that allows people to put information in or take information out. Monitors, disk drives, and printers are peripherals. In this book, the term is used to specify equipment that is external to the basic computer itself: modems and printers for example, but not video displays.

Permission: See **access permission**.

Piracy: Software theft.

Platter: A circular surface on a hard disk that stores information. A hard disk can have more than one platter.

Port: The point of connecton on a computer where a **device** is attached by its cable.

Productivity program: See **specialty program**.

RAM. See **random access memory**.

RAM disk: A portion of **random access memory** isolated (via a **software** program) to function like a disk drive.

Random access memory: Memory inside of the computer that the **central processing unit** can address directly. Also called **RAM**.

Reboot: Re-start the system. See **boot**.

Reserved drive name schedule: A record of the names each PC on a **local area network** assigns to the disk drives it uses.

Retention and disposition schedule: A record of how long records must be kept on the system and archived in the system library, and of their fate when the records are no longer needed. See **archives**.

Resident: See **memory resident**.

Root directory: The central directory on a disk. The root directory can contain **software** programs, data files, and other directories, called **subdirectories**. The root directory is so named because subdirectories branch off from it like branches on a tree. See **tree-structured directory**.

Script file: See **automatic processing file**.

Sector: A logical way of dividing **tracks** on a disk into equal segments.

Server: See **network server**.

Site license: Permission to use a **software** program on any number of computers at a specified site, usually an entire company.

Slot: The plug-in point on a **motherboard** that accepts **circuit boards**.

Software: Instructions that tell a computer what to do.

Software defaults map: A record of how the **default** values are set for each **software** package used on the system.

Software inventory: A record of all **software** packages your firm owns for its system.

Specialty program: For purposes of this book, **software** designed either to add features to your **operating system** or standard programs or to improve their performance or ease of use.

Spooler: A **specialty program** that takes data being sent to a **peripheral**, for example a printer, and stores it in **memory** until the peripheral can accept the information.

Stand-alone personal computer: A personal computer that is not connected to a **local area network** or to a **multi-user system**.

Subdirectory: A directory contained within another directory, beginning with the first level held in the **root directory**. Subdirectories can themselves hold other subdirectories. See **tree-structured directory**.

Switch block: A unit of switches on **circuit boards** and on **devices** that must be set to on or off positions according to how a system is arranged. For instance, the switches on the blocks on the **motherboard** of a PC are set to reflect the **RAM**, floppy drives, and other options on the system.

Switch settings map: A record of the on/off position for each switch on each **switch block** on the system.

System boards map: A record of the type and location of expansion **circuit boards** on the system and the location of empty **slots**.

System devices map: A record of all the system equipment.

System files: **Operating system** files that are devoted to managing the system itself, as distinguished from data files or other **software** program files.

System sketch: An optional picture you prepare of the entire system.

System library: The collection of documents and data the system manager needs to manage the system, including but not limited to those that describe every part of the system and those that **back up** information stored on the computer.

Track: A way of dividing disk space. A logical circle on a disk along which information can be stored. See **sector**.

Tree-structured directory: A directory system organized like a tree, with a **root directory** corresponding to the tree trunk and **subdirectories** corresponding to the branches.

UNIX, XENIX: An **operating system** originally developed at Bell Laboratories. Typically used on **multi-user systems**.

Index

About the Author

Judith M. Frank owns Frank Communications, a consulting firm in the San Francisco Bay Area which helps individuals and businesses to manage their microcomputers. When she conceived of this book, Frank was a pioneer microcomputer system manager. She holds a Master of Arts degree in English from the University of Wisconsin, serves on the Board of Directors for the Computer Press Association, and currently is writing her second book.

© *1987 Andrée Abecassis Photography*

Fasten your seat belt!

For the serious computer user who wants to soup up his PC—make it faster, more powerful, more fun—the experts at PC WORLD have a fascinating new book and software program that can make your personal computer truly personal.

Called *The Fully Powered PC* with *PC World Utilities Disk*, it takes you under the hood of your PC. It shows you how to construct your own system, how to combine many single-purpose systems, and how to call up a dozen or more applications with little more than a keystroke.

It puts you on the fast track by showing you how to put applications programs into active memory so they run faster, design menus to

guide you through systems you've created, even customize your computer to find and dial telephone numbers. It even includes public-domain software that add still more powerful features to your PC.

In other words, *The Fully Powered PC* helps you create a system that performs exactly the way *you* want it to. And isn't that why you bought a PC in the first place?

For the IBM PC, XT, AT or compatible. $39.95 at all computer stores. To order direct, call TOLL FREE: 1-800-624-0023, (in N.J. 1-800-624-0024), or use the coupon below.

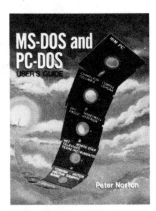

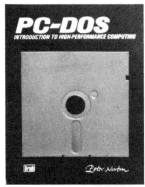